David Gascoyne was born in 1916 in Harrow. His first book of poetry *Roman Balcony* was published when the author was only sixteen and his novel *Opening Day* followed a year later. *A Short Survey of Surrealism* appeared in 1935 and *Poems 1937-42* collected the work from one of his most creative periods. Other works include *A Vagrant* (1951), *Night Thoughts* (1956) commissioned by the B.B.C., *Collected Poems* (1965) and *The Sun at Midnight* (1970). David Gascoy⸺   ⸺ly.

DAVID GASCOYNE

COLLECTED JOURNALS

1936-42

With an introduction
by
Kathleen Raine

SKOOB BOOKS PUBLISHING
LONDON

Part I originally appeared as *Journal 1936-7*
from Enitharmon Press, 1980.

Part II originally appeared as *Paris Journal 1937-9*
from Enitharmon Press, 1978

The drawing by Lucian Freud 'Portrait of David Gascoyne'
1943 (black and white chalks on buff paper) appears by kind
permission of James Kirkman Ltd.

Published by SKOOB BOOKS PUBLISHING LTD
11a-15 Sicilian Avenue
off Southampton Row
Holborn
London WC1A 2QH

ISBN 1 871438 50 0 Paper

Typeset by Moss Database in ITC Garamond
Printed in Singapore by Des Meyer Press

My thanks are due to the Ingram-Merrill Foundation for their
support during the preparation of this work.

David Gascoyne

FOREWORD

There is a mysterious process constantly at work in history which consigns to oblivion whatever belongs only to the passage of events, while at the same time gathering into 'the artifice of eternity' whatever in the process of time Imagination has experienced and transmuted. In David Gascoyne's three journals, written by the poet between his twentieth and twenty-sixth year, we see the living imagination itself at work in its task of transmuting the temporal into the eternal. That a young poet, in outward and contingent things so powerless, should have borne witness to the inner realities of the tragic years leading up to the Second World War is an awe-inspiring instance of the power of those values David Gascoyne knew he must serve, at whatever cost. His record will take its place, in his poetry and in these journals also, within the annals of that enduring history.

Everything was against him from the standpoint of this world: without money, or a University education (fortunately for his genius!), or powerful family connections, denied, by his homosexual tendencies, the security of any enduring personal relationship, he yet suffered his circumstances and his destiny totally and uncomplainingly. Nevertheless he always knew that on another level great power lay within him; as a poet he felt his task to be 'to achieve spiritual greatness'. Far from this being a personal ambition, he was aware that in his subjective experience he was recording and participating in the shared inner experience of his world. On August 16th 1939 — a few weeks before the outbreak of war — he wrote:

1

I believe ever more positively that my own inner struggles represent only an unusually acute consciousness of an experience almost exactly similar to that which an ever-increasing number of people all over the world are becoming vaguely, inarticulately, conscious of going through. This experience has to be given a coherent expression, objectivized, universalized. It provides a fundamental significance to this otherwise meaninglessly incoherent moment of human history.

This experience he saw, indeed, increasingly, as the end of 'history' and the time of 'the open tomb' in which the divine in humankind awaits its spiritual resurrection.

These journals are to be read in the context of David Gascoyne's poems, great poems, which give prophetic words to realities of the *mundus imaginalis* whose agent he knew himself to be. The angels who keep the inner worlds of the individual soul and of civilizations are never 'ineffectual', and it is their truth these journals reflect and transmit. Without a trace of worldliness, David Gascoyne resembled (so I long ago saw him) that angel who in a story by Tolstoi was sent down to earth, naked and defenceless, but still possessing the angelic wisdom that always does, and will, represent the judgment of the eternal on the temporal order. Without moral judgment or worldly calculation David met the people and situations of each day with a kind of grave willingness to love. He did not judge or reject, but met everyone at the level of their true being. His impatience was reserved for the pretentiousness of whatever did not belong to that inner reality, and his anger was absolute against all that violated it. He was a subjective, but never a personal poet, being at all times 'engaged' in the events of his time. His brief membership of the Communist party, his engagement in the

Republican cause in the Spanish Civil War (he broadcast bulletins from Barcelona for a time), his participation in the Surrealist Movement as representing an affirmation of the Imagination against Cartesian rationalism, and his gradual realization of the meaning of the figure of Christ, form a consistent growth towards that spiritual understanding to which he aspired and to which his poetry bears witness.

His mother was related to Cyril Maud and Winifred Emery, and would herself have liked to be an actress, a career her family discouraged. David, when only fourteen, was taken by a school-friend of his mother's, Rebbie Freuer Wright, to the Poetry Bookshop, where Harold and Alida Monro used to organize poetry-readings. David remembers T. S. Eliot giving a reading of poems by Christina Rossetti. Through the Monros, and David Archer of the (communist) Parton Street Bookshop David soon made his way into London's poetry-circles of the early 'thirties. Soon he was being published by Geoffrey Grigson in *New Verse*; by Tambimuttu in *Poetry London*. Antonia White introduced him to her friends Emily Holmes Coleman and Peggy Guggenheim and George Barker. He became associated with the Mass Observation group, and especially Humphrey Jennings; with Herbert Read, Roland Penrose, Julian Trevelyan and the English Surrealists; and with Peter Watson and Cyril Connolly's *Horizon* circle. For David the touchstone in all things was the Imagination, and where this was absent (as with William Empson and the Oxford political poets, Auden, Spender, and Day Lewis, and the novelist Christopher Isherwood) there was a corresponding distance of relationship, yet without personal hostility: David was no man's enemy and never condemned.

But he already knew himself to belong to the larger imaginative whole of Europe's poetic and philosophic tradition, finding his way to Paris when he was only seventeen; and from that time Paris — the intellectual centre of Europe, and at that time hospitable to expatriate artists — was to remain his spiritual home. Lawrence Durrell, Henry Miller and the painter Soutine, members of the circle contributing to *The Booster*, were early friends. Pierre Jean Jouve and his wife Blanche (one of the earliest Freudian analysts), who held a weekly *salon* in their house in the rue Tournon, introduced him to French writers and philosophers: Gabriel Marcel, the painter Balthus, Fondane, Jean Wahl and others of the Existentialist philosophers contributing at that time to the revue *Ducalion*. He became actively associated with the Surrealist Movement, the poet Eluard, André Breton, E. L. T. Mesens the Belgian, and the rest. He met everyone from Gertrude Stein and Anais Nin to Picasso, and disliked Stravinski's music. He was, by nature, one of the number of the dedicated artists of his time. Nothing could be more different than the simplicity with which David Gascoyne entered that world from the social ambition of those not of their number to 'meet' people with famous names. In compensation for 'a complete incapacity for dealing with the practical, an inadaptibility to society' David confessed to:

a not very valuable conviction that one belongs to a kind of spiritual aristocracy; the 'desolate clarity' of one's vision of one's life and *la condition humaine*; a (sometimes) rather exhilarating sense of pioneering on the limits . . . the possibility of being able to write poetry, or whatever it may be, that will have at any rate the value of being the product of a real contact with spiritual truth, — its intensity, its depths, its exaltation, its naked certitude.

4

He was deeply read in the works of European imaginative literature and philosophy—the Existentialists Kierkegaard and Chestov (whom he rates infinitely above the publicist Sartre) besides the German philosophers, mystics (especially Boehme) and the whole canon of European poetry. He absorbed paintings, old and new; films, Russian and otherwise; and music (he had been a chorister in Salisbury Cathedral until his voice broke at the age of fourteen). All that was comprised in the imaginative culture of his world David absorbed and his own poems resonate within that great octave. If he has been hitherto undervalued in England it is because that music is out of the range of a culture for which the Imagination is deemed to be imaginary. All the more is David's poetry needed in a country so spiritually undernourished by the dominant cultural values of our time:

> Poetry is not verse, it is not rhetoric, it is not an epigrammatic way of saying something that can be stated in prose, nor is it argument or reportage. In England, the whole question needs to be cleared up and restated. What I call poetry is not understood in England, but I believe it to be something of far greater value than what is at present understood there. The tradition of modern English poetry is really something quite different from the tradition of Hölderlin, Rimbaud, Rilke, Lorca, Jouve. — I belong to Europe before I belong to England. The values I believe in are European values and not English ones.

From the standpoint of this world the young David Gascoyne might be criticized for his passivity in practical affairs, for those long lonely days not occupied in industrious writing, but in doing, outwardly, absolutely nothing but to suffer his solitude and helplessness, or else to seek the company of others, often for the mere sake of distraction from that solitude. So has Coleridge been criticized for his lack of industry; the comparison is apt, for David, like Coleridge, was for ever making plans and resolutions, lists of essays and books to be written, which to our loss never were. But like Coleridge also (though David's output is far less) on another level, no other English poet has been so incessantly and strenuously engaged in the profound exploration of the thought and feelings and spiritual aspirations of the greatest minds and the creative development of his own. And somehow (again like Coleridge) all *has* been said in his work, none of which is trivial or of the second order, none repetitive. Rather than criticize the young poet for his failures to engage in life, to form satisfactory personal relationships and the rest we should be humbly grateful for his presence in our dark time, as one carrying, for that time, the burden of those inner worlds of which he was so deeply aware, and of whose redemption he never lost hope.

David never sought to evade active participation in the Second World War. He was fully prepared to be called up, but fortunately for us he was rejected for active service, and served in his own way as an actor on tour with a repertory company for ENSA, entertaining the troops. As a war-record that must seem slight enough, but the war to which David was committed was the everlasting battle 'against principalities, against powers, against spiritual wickedness in high places'. In this Great Battle no poet of his generation has played a part more inwardly heroic.

The judgments of love are hard to bear: it is a reproach to the rest of us that for all his hopes and new beginnings and moments of sudden joy, nothing improved for David in the years that followed: on the contrary the too great burden he carried led to breakdown, not once only but on a number of occasions, before he emerged, as from a dark cloud, into the

6

serene years of his late marriage, and the grave dignity of England's last great poet.

Although these diaries are in a sense supplementary to the poems, many of whose experiences, and images, are reflected in their pages, they are themselves, in their degree, works of pure imagination. While political poets put their politics into verse, David Gascoyne brought 'the politics of eternity' to bear on 'the politics of time'. The purity of the light he sheds will be valued by poets of a less spiritually benighted age than our own has been; and if the spiritual resurrection for which he hoped is beginning to come about he himself has played a noble part in making that resurrection possible.

Kathleen Raine

I

This is the limbo circus of the man
George Barker

22.IX.36

It is useless to keep a journal, said M., a young man of my acquaintance: the important things endure in the memory and are always there when one wants them; the rest doesn't matter. But how do we know what matters, that the memory is infallible? It is not, alas! I shall never cease to regret that I was too lazy to keep a journal in Paris, 1933, and would give anything to be able to remember, in their entirety, a few days of my life at that time. Is this absurd?

The whole question of journals is absurd. The way one's first entry, for instance, consists always of a dissertation of this kind. The way they stop. In order to be able to continue writing this one I have to have some imaginary audience in view. You are reading this? But I had to pretend that no one would ever read it! What could be more ridiculous than to wish to achieve a cross between Pascal and Jean Cocteau? Yet that seems to have been rather the idea that had formed in the back of my mind . . .

I have mentioned laziness: no vice is more particularly mine than sloth, as we shall no doubt see before we have reached the end of many blank pages. I am not writing this, however, in an attempt to overcome this weakness, but rather as an exercise in individuality. In order to find out who I am? Yes and no. To stretch the muscles of my ego, rather; to overcome a certain timidity where my own personality is concerned and in doing so, to resolve certain intimate problems which cannot be mine alone. All this embarrasses you? That was partly my intention.

Where am I now? *For Future Reference,* then: There is no longer any doubt that a new period in my development is just about to begin. There is nothing unusual in that; one's life always undergoes a change at this time of the year(?) The salient facts are these:

1. I joined the C.P. yesterday. The recent Zinoviev-Trotsky affair, which for a few days I thought had shaken my convictions considerably, has had exactly the opposite effect. There is no longer any honest alternative for me than direct action in the direction of Communism. What I had been told before is true: to understand Marxism means inevitably to work for the Party. Nothing has helped me to grasp the whole thing more than T. A. Jackson's *Dialectics,* which, in spite of its execrable style, etc.

(A certain smugness in the use of the words: C.P., honest alternative, direct action, the Party, etc., which has always irritated me in Communists of my acquaintance, particularly Roger Roughton. I suppose I am still a little selfconscious about Communism? Does 'joining the Party' have this effect on one? But I am making much of little; and I had determined to be quite casual about it all.)

2. I have undergone a difficult crisis during the last month, from which I come out chastened. I have had to admit that *nothing* I have written so far is of the least value, and very

nearly came to the conclusion, once and for all, that writing is 'no use' anyway, though I don't think that would have prevented me from going on doing it, as I have nothing else to do, and have not, to my chagrin, the strength of mind of a Rimbaud or a Duchamp, who both came to this conclusion — and acted on it.

3. New mental contacts: D.M.[*], though I don't yet know whether this is going to be of much importance. To exchange ideas of any level of intelligence is remarkable enough in a place like this, but I must admit that certain things about him irritate me: his pedantry, for instance, and his particular kind of unsophistication; chiefly, perhaps, because he doesn't appear to 'grasp' my own qualities. His hermit aspect, his complete lack of ambition and spiritual self-absorption interest me, though. Emily Holmes Coleman[§], whom I met last summer, offers prospects of a kind of intimacy from which I should be likely to benefit because it is so rare. Her complete lack of reserve is perhaps only apparent, but her warmth and enthusiastic interest in other people's characters make her an ideal *confidante,* which I have never had before; or at least not one of such highly developed sympathy and intelligence. Our 12-hour conversation last week, at her Oakley Street (Chelsea) flat, has exhilarated me to an unusual extent, and started several new trains of thought for me, particularly a renewed interest in the past and a desire to read a number of things which never much interested me

---

[*] A municipal librarian at Richmond, Surrey.

[§] American writer, friend of Eliot, Djuna Barnes and Peggy Guggenheim. Known for her novel about a stay in an asylum: *The Shutter of Snow*, (published USA 1930, republished by Virago 1981). Died 1974 in America.

before. All this, too, has forced upon me a fresh realization of my relative immaturity, with which I now feel more at home . . .   Humphrey Jennings, who was at Emily's last Wednesday, seems to be going to have an increased influence on my ideas: there is no one like him, and I would sacrifice half-a-dozen acquaintances for his, though the feeling I have for him is entirely intellectual. Antonia White, Emily's friend, whom I met for the first time last week, and from whom I received an invitation this morning, also interests me very much: an extraordinarily lively intelligence and at the same time completely feminine: I look forward to knowing her better, but have a feeling that we shall not meet very often(!)[*] She must consider one very young. I imagine though she is too *sensible* to make one feel so at the time.

One of the strangest results of last Wednesday's discussion (Emily Coleman, Antonia White, Humphrey Jennings, another man, extremely intelligent, whose name I forget — Peter?[§] — and myself are all meeting again this week, when we shall see whether we really do form a rare and happy mixture, or whether it was simply an accident) has been a sudden deep interest in Tennyson, of all people. *In Memoriam* has given me greater pleasure than any other poem I have read for months.

25.IX.36
Never to know what is waiting for one round the corner — it is too much! How could I have guessed that what happened on Wednesday was going to happen? It is true that I knew I

---

[*] This exclamation mark no doubt inserted later.

[§] Almost certainly Peter (later Sir Samuel) Hoare, another Oakley Street resident and close friend of Emily's.

was going to have to change, but not at the cost of so much stress, of so grotesque an occurrence as that which has just taken place . . .

How little I know myself, and how completely *hermetic* I am! How afraid of the self-indulgence of showing myself as I am to anyone else at all, even to myself ! Yet I have had to make this effort.

It is so absurd that I can hardly bring myself to set it down on paper: a woman of 37 — a woman who has had three husbands and two children, has been in an asylum, is being psycho-analysed and, having been living alone for about a year, is starving not so much for sex as for simple affection, or rather an object of affection — has fallen in love with *me*. We sat up talking about it until six o'clock in the morning. She wants to explore, not so much my body, as my soul! (And she had only met me once before.)

My reactions to all this were chaotic and I am hardly proud of them. Terror, pity, self-mistrust, mistrust of her, etc. I simply did not know how to adapt myself to the situation. There is not the least possibility of my ever loving her, I am far too conscious of her age and she has no physical attraction for me. All she asks for though, as far as I understand her, is a close spiritual intimacy — or at least, that first — and I do not know whether I can really give her even that, although there is no reason why I should not, even if I do not 'love' her. But why, O why, has all this come upon me? the egoist asks. Why should my precious inner solitude be disturbed into a deliberate consciousness of itself ? (I am still holding back, evidently.) Why should the poor thing have chosen me? If I am afraid, then nothing but misery can ensue for both of us; if I am not, then I might be able to give her

13

some slight happiness, which she needs so badly — and why should I not do that? (The philanthropist speaks?)

However, I think I know now what I should have done, what I shall have to do. When I left her, after we had been together for 24 hours, I realised that I should take her by the hand and lead her back into a state of wide-eyed virginal and stainless candour — we should be the Babes in the Wood, I would hold her in my arms, the darkness would be lowering all around, and the birds would come and bury us with dead leaves. Two orphan children wandering hand-in-hand through the strange streets, faintly smiling, a little bewildered. Everything wistful and pathetic, as in *Nadja* (which is hardly wistful in the Barrie sense, but which describes almost exactly the kind of relationship I mean — though Antonia is hardly a Nadja). I know I am quite good at this sort of thing, having accomplished it very successfully with a strange Russian woman in Paris last year. (She told me her life-story just as Antonia did, and it was much the same, and she was much the same kind of unhappy neurotic — I curse myself that I cannot for the moment recall her name, which was odd.)[*] We spent the day together, once, without any money, wandering hand-in-hand through the Luxembourg gardens, gazing with wonder into windows of shops around the quarter — designs made of human hair under glass horrified her in the rue Bonaparte — and sat, a little tired, on a seat in the garden-square just off the Place de Belfort, eating the buns which I had bought at a nearby patisserie with my last sous, while children played all round us.

---

[*] Manya Gorochowska

14

28.IX.36

The Yew

More berries than one could count upon the yew — scarlet
against green foliage so dark and glossy that the sky behind
it seems even more luminous and remote than it should be
for the time of year, though the first of October draws nigh.
We set the radiators going today, for the first time this
autumn.

This morning a letter from Antonia:

> I want nothing but that you should feel free with me and that I
> should feel free with you.
>
> An infinite number of relationships are possible between us and
> the only one that has any value (if by a happy chance we find it) is
> the one which gives us the most increase of life and freedom. You
> have already given me some increase of life — I hope I may have
> something for you but we cannot tell yet.
>
> We have found that we can communicate in some ways; that is
> enough for now. But if you feel strained, worried, and anxious, that
> is already a sign that it is too difficult for you.
>
> We have met at a time when we are both in a transitional stage —
> the next year is probably a critical one for both of us.
>
> The qualities I value in you I would value in a person of any age.
> I have known enough people to recognise that they are rare. Almost
> all young people of talent and intelligence are attractive, but I believe
> that your particular quality is not a mere accident of youth . . . etc.

No, I am no longer worried or strained. But I would like
to stand up in a room full of cynics and declare that it is far
more alarming than gratifying to discover that one is attractive
to women — (I do not mean just 'womankind' — a particular
kind of woman.) I have read more than once that nothing
makes a woman of her age happier than a very young lover.
But I am not doing this out of kindness: I do not care enough

15

for the rôle. I want 'experience', though it is true that I have had experiences of this kind before. When am I going to have an affair with a girl *younger* than I am? That would be far more difficult.

I suppose one is 'incomplete' until one's heart has functioned in at least a dozen different ways?

If it is difficult to love, it is far more difficult to be loved. To have one's egotism forced upon one, the wretchedness of one's feeling of gratification! Humility is not a virtue I admire, but oh!, I need it now. It is no accident that as I was about to leave her flat, I carelessly picked Barbellion's Journal from the shelf and asked to borrow it, simply, as I thought, out of mild curiosity. Now I feel as he felt when he read the Journal of Marie Bashkirtseff (I alter the sex in paraphrase): 'He feels as I feel. We have the same self-absorption, the same vanity and corroding ambition. He is impressionable, volatile, passionate — ill!' (not that, thank Heaven!) 'So am I. His journal is my journal' — but that's absurd, because I've hardly written more than 20 pages of journal in my life, though I intend to continue now, and to try and strip myself as Barbellion did in his.

A Wall of Trees

Un grand silence régnait sur les berges prochaines. Le bateau filait avec un bruit calme de machine et d'eau. On eût pu se croire au coeur de l'été. On allait aborder, semblait-il, dans le beau jardin de quelque maison de campagne. La jeune fille s'y promenerait sous une ombrelle blanche. Jusqu'au soir on entendrait les tourterelles gémir . . . Mais soudain une rafale glacée venait rappeler décembre aux invités de cette étrange fête.

On aborda devant un bois de sapins. *Sur le debarcardère, les passagers durent attendre un instant, serrés les uns contre les*

*autres, qu'un des bateliers eût ouvert les cadénas de la bar-
rière . . .'*   Alain-Fournier: *Le Grand Meaulnes*

When I came to the sentence underlined above, there rose
before my eyes an image so strangely vivid that I knew it must
have a particularly personal significance: a smooth stretch of
grass, and then, like a wall, the edge of a forest of firs or
pine-trees rising up, closely planted and with branches high,
the trunks growing uniformly from a smooth and mossy floor
devoid of undergrowth . . . I have never visited such a spot.
There is no particular reason why it should haunt me, I
thought, until suddenly I remembered Roland Cailleux, and
a scene in a hotel bedroom about eight months ago. In the
morning he showed me a collection of colour-photos that he
had taken near his home in France. They were transparent
and had to be held up to the light, which gave them a
strangely glittering yet remote effect. One of the pictures was
of the edge of a forest, just as I have described, and it seemed
to me then like a scene from a dream. Although taken in the
middle of summer, there was a certain *frostiness* about its
brilliant colour, which accounts for the way I was reminded
of it by the phrase from *Le Grand Meaulnes*, — *'une rafale
glacée venait rappeler décembre . . .'*

I have not seen or heard from Cailleux since then. We only
knew each other for twenty-four hours, yet I remember him
clearly and not without tenderness. I was warned against him
afterwards by someone who knew him, and can well imagine
there to be something peculiarly 'evil' in his passionate, bitter
and anarchic French soul, — yet cannot feel the less affection
for him. I know that he must be entirely unscrupulous and

17

untrustworthy, yet believe that, somehow, with me he would be different, were I ever to meet him again.

1.X.36
Went last night to the Queen's Hall with D.M. — a Bach programme. Anodyne music which I can no longer enjoy except with a detached part of myself. It was with only a detached part of myself, I suppose, that I spent the whole evening.

Met D.M. as we had arranged, at the Langham Hotel. There he sat, a small figure drinking black coffee in a corner of the vast and brilliantly illuminated lounge, while the hotel orchestra scraped away at *Chanson d'Amour* and women in evening dress glided in and out of the restaurant. He was wearing his best dark suit, with a stiff collar, and on the chair beside him were the books he had been buying at Bumpus's during the afternoon. *Les Plus Belles Pages de Paul Verlaine* in an expensive binding, a University lecture on John Clare, a copy of *Struwwelpeter*, a German book of coloured pictures of plants, a manual of typography and a collection of German Students' Songs.

We hurried across Portland Place — it was about a quarter to eight. He was ahead of me and, pushing my way after him through the crowd, I found him offering Gallery tickets to the commissionaire at the entrance to the Circle, who corrected him brusquely. We made our way out again, and up the iron staircase to the Gallery, where only a few seats were left. When we were at last seated, near the middle of the back row, where I had some difficulty in finding room to deposit my ridiculous legs, he darted off again, first to enquire whether it was possible to obtain a transfer to the Circle, (unavailingly, as it happened, for all the seats were booked), and then to get a copy of the programme. At intervals throughout the concert he supplied me with interesting information regarding the works played, their origins, the way they should be rendered, etc. Or alternatively, as during the interval, when we fought for cake and coffee in the bar, he remembered apposite extracts from the novels of Aldous Huxley.

At Waterloo, on the way home, he requested me to give him the return-half of my ticket, saying: 'Allow me to indulge a little fad of mine.' His purpose was to transfer the tickets in order that we should travel home first-class. 'After listening to music, one hardly feels like facing a carriagefull of one's fellow men', he explained when we were seated and the train was moving out of the platform. I glanced through his copy of Verlaine's poems; and, when he deplored the gaudy pink and gold bindings, hazarded that it was more or less in keeping with the contents. I showed him one of the few Verlaine poems I can bear — the fragile little grey and black *Colloque Sentimentale,* and he shuddered, on reading it, and remarked: 'This might have been written by a schoolmistress'. I argued that the sentimental banality of the dead lovers' conversation was no doubt intentional, and that the effect contrived at was the pathos of faded rhetoric. He pondered this for a moment, and then said: 'Rather like Flaubert's *Bouvard et Pécuchet*?'

Presently he showed me a poem he had been writing in the Langham Hotel before my arrival. It was unfinished and, according to M., bore too close a resemblance to Yeats' 'Metaphysical Songs' . . . By way of exchange I produced my 'Elegaic Stanzas for Alban Berg'. The first section reminded him of something he had read of Victor Hugo's; after reading the second, he looked up furtively and remarked, with

19

conscientious honesty: 'This is not very good?' On the rest he did not venture any comment except to point out the defects of individual lines and to enquire the meaning of the word '*câline*'. I should have liked to say: It may be the worst poem that I ever wrote or that you ever read, but I wouldn't accept your stunted judgement of it, however balanced and well-weighed your words . . .

No, I do not think I shall ever communicate very much to M.; but I cannot help being mildly interested in him as a specimen of something or other. I should be ashamed to feel like this about most of the people I know, but think I am justified here.

My one desire is to be as intensely alive as possible in the present. I am either a man of feeling or I am a log, and I am not a log. What does M. know of violence and nostalgia? Yet they are all that makes life something more than mediocrity and boredom, they are the deepest current of our time, and as far as I am concerned, to be unaware of them is to be dead. 'Something great and obscure is striving to express itself through me.' One day, perhaps, I shall genuinely explode. A perpetual explosion would be my ideal mode of life: I must be very repressed, after all.

9.X.36

Last Sunday to the Anti-Mosley demonstration with Emily Coleman, who insisted on coming with typical ardency, and yet sat trembling with suppressed agitation all the way there in the tube. H. had told her she was liable to be deported as an alien if she were to get arrested and, despite her terror of having to go back to America, this seemed only to add to her zest for the occasion. At Aldgate we looked around for signs of the Twickenham branch, but the crowd was already too

thick and they must have been moved on somewhere else. We
moved slowly along the thronged pavement towards the
corner of Leman Street. Half the road was taken up with
Underground railway excavations (?) and the intention of the
crowd — who kept shouting 'They shall not pass!' — seemed to
be to obstruct the remaining half by simply swarming across
it. But the police kept shoving us back on to the pavement,
supposedly in order to let the traffic pass. The nearer we got
to the corner, the thicker and more chaotic the crowd, which
by now was singing fragments of the 'Internationale' and the
'Red Flag', and shouting 'Red United Fighting Front!' The
kerb of the pavement and stray pieces of wood kept getting
mixed up with our feet; the crowd swayed erratically from
side to side; we were jammed tighter and tighter together,
and Emily began to pant something about Margaret Clitheroe
and to look very white. At last the police, who had now
formed a long chain beside us, decided to clear the pavement
altogether. Random charges and sorties were made; and they
began to shove us, one by one, with a great deal of struggle
and resistance, into a gangway leading back to beyond the
road-up boards.

The next thing was to get inside the enclosure round the
excavations. Some way down the opposite pavement we
found a hole in the boards and wriggled through, to find a
great hole about 30 ft. deep almost under our noses on the
other side. We managed to clamber across this, and took up
our position at the foot of a pile of bricks covered with
tarpaulin, just beyond which was another pit. (If the police
had charged us we should have been stampeded into one or
other of them.) We were now almost exactly opposite the
spot we had reached on the other side of the road. Just to
our left was a junction of five streets: I had a fine view. A man

climbed up a nearby lamppost and draped it with the red flag, to the great enthusiasm of the crowd. Mounted police kept appearing. Everyone was waiting in a state of intense excitement for the procession to appear. Nothing happened, except occasional outbursts among the masses packed along all pavements, followed by rushes of policemen. One of these charges resulted in the smashing of the front window of the tailor's shop on the corner opposite, and the injury, so I read afterwards, of six people. Ambulances kept passing; and whenever a detachment of mounted police went by, the crowd hissed, booed and jeered. One felt an almost revolutionary tension. Emily was in a great state by this time, and had to keep making the most naive and inapposite remarks, to which I did not feel capable of replying . . .

Rumour and speculation passed from mouth to mouth. A man standing on top of the pile of bricks behind us declared that he had seen John Simon and the Chief of Police go by in a closed car. 'They've changed the route of the March', said others, 'and the police are keeping us here while they get away with it.' But soon there were distant cheers, and we saw large bands of mounted and unmounted police dispersing in the direction from which they had come. Like wildfire the news spread that the March had been finally banned. Midst cheering and shouts of victory, the enormous crowd broke up and went their ways, while an airplane circled low above the streets. We did not see the worst of the afternoon, but it had been exciting enough.

Back to Emily's Chelsea flat for tea and supper. M., a quiet, dark creature with high cheekbones and hurt eyes, came in later. She also had been to the demonstration: we were all tired and I found it difficult to talk to her. Her job is to answer queries for one of the big dailies; and like all Emily's women friends, she is deeply unhappy about something. 'You are all eating your hearts out,' I told E. 'Yes, a queer nest you've fallen into,' she said.

Antonia came in the evening. I felt that she felt I was frightened of her eye; she was horribly nervous and made me feel the same. Presently she offered to put me up for the night, as it would be difficult to get back. I wanted to refuse but, fearing she would interpret this wrongly, said I should be very glad. When Humphrey came up and started a purposely trivial conversation about film stars, she said she was tired and that we must go home. We went back to her flat in a taxi.

A long and difficult conversation in front of a gas-fire. Entrails, entrails . . . At four in the morning she lay on the divan in my arms and could not bring herself to go to bed. She put her hand over my heart: 'I can't feel a thing,' she said.

Next morning I was awakened by her husband, Tom Hopkinson. He comes to the flat every morning to take the children to school. He put his head, his red face, round the edge of the door and smiled in mild surprise. I very much wanted to laugh.

A difficult and tiresome day ensued. We went to the trade-show of a revolting Austrian film about choirboys in the morning; half way through she had to leave in order to go to her analyst . . . At lunch, in one of those depressing little tea-roomish restaurants where women from West-End dress-shops have their mid-day meal, we began to quarrel. My clumsiness at fault; the incident somewhat involved. It took her half the afternoon, wandering about in a bitter wind down Bond Street way, to get over it. We ended up by going to the National Gallery where, I must admit, we enjoyed ourselves very much. Our greatest thrill was one of the latest acquisitions: a *Fête à Rambouillet* by Fragonard. I have never before seen a Fragonard that I liked at all; this one is perfectly amazing — full of the most intense poetry, both strange and rare. To the right, a mauve-canopied gondola full of vague figures is approaching a steep bank scattered with mauve, dream-distant flowers — amaranth? — behind which there loom great dark-green ivy-decked grottoes full of stone steps, statues and mist-white ghosts. All this is bathed in a ray of calm late-afternoon sunlight; while the left of the picture is all in shadow, like that cast by a storm-cloud. Between steep banks of ivy tumbles a green cascade, with patches of hard white stormy light upon its foam. A mysterious avenue of great trees recedes into the distance . . . Although it is far more exaggeratedly romantic, with the gondola and the *Fête Galante* figures, I was continually reminded by it, as we gazed, of the scene from *Le Grand Meaulnes* which I quoted a few pages back. We also enjoyed very much, among other things, a *Madonna and Child* by Quentin Matssys: a very dark-toned and faded picture which the eye passes over, at first, without seeing anything. But the more one looks at it, the more one becomes aware of the artist's extraordinarily deep experience of life, — his patience, wisdom and compassion.

13.X.36

On Tuesday to lunch with Roland Penrose, who has just returned from France with his wife, Valentine: a rapt, dark, quiet woman with an occasional expression of bad-temper, preoccupied and seldom speaking unless she has something to say. A rather stuffy, frustrated afternoon, unremarkable. I never seem to be able to establish any communication in this house, with its soft carpets and lights and paintings . . . When

I left there, I went for a walk on Hampstead Heath, with a thick cold growing in my head and a sore throat coming on. Ducks on the ponds, the water flaking into silver, the October sky remote and luminous. As the afternoon bordered on dusk, I climbed to the highest point of the Heath. A fresh wind blowing. Highgate far on its hill beneath slow-tumbling clouds to the left; to the right, below, London spread out under mist and smoke, grey-blue, immense, mysterious. What a heart-shaking spectacle it will be from this height some night soon to come, when the enemy squadrons blackening the sky rain down destroying fire upon those roofs! I turned away. An old woman was coming up the hill as I went down, gathering sticks into a black bag and muttering to herself . . .

Moped about next day with a fierce cold. In the evening was seized with the desire to write a seven-page letter to Kay Hime. Wrote also to Antonia, to assure her of a 'wise tenderness' which afterwards seemed horribly insincere. When she is not there I just feel numb towards her. Not so with Kay. We are indeed a bride and groom, and shall remain so, indissolubly clamped together, in spite of all the superficial fluctuations of our feelings for one another.

D.M. came to tea on Thursday and infuriated me: we have nothing to say to each other — he finnicky and precise, I restless and insatiable and vague. Our conversations are quite naturally absurd. Directly after he had gone, I went up to dine in Hampstead. Herbert Read was there, talking with difficulty, not saying much. I tried hard to be a little animated, but it was like trying to push a wall over with one hand — the Lees, Hugh Sykes Davies and Humphrey Jennings came in afterwards, for a 'Committee meeting'. Humphrey, as usual, was boiling over with energy and excitement; he brought a lot of photos with him which he had just taken, one of which —

a horse and an electric-light bulb — he gave to me. When the 'business' was over, I listened to him having a most animated discussion with Valentine Penrose, who had evidently taken to him. *'Voilà un vrai revolté!'* she cried, turning to the room at large.

I stayed the night there: the last train had gone; and next morning, after breakfast, had a long talk with Valentine, whom I find extremely sympathetic, but still a little evasive. She appears to be steeped in a kind of Oriental subjectivism, and frequently mentions India. We talked about Rimbaud, and she grew enthusiastic. It is clear now why she cannot live with Roland for very long at a time. 'How well I understand Rimbaud', she said, 'and his hatred of perfection. That is what is the matter here', — she indicated the room with a vague gesture — 'all these pictures. I should like to take a piece of chalk and scribble on them all!' How Roland's *sens de correction* must exasperate her sometimes.

They are shortly going to Barcelona, armed with cameras and introductions from Fenner Brockway of the I.L.P., to work for the P.O.U.M., an apparently Trotskyite organization. Valentine has suggested that I should accompany them. 'You must come,' she said. 'You will feel that you are alive out there. Here, everything is so unreal.' I have thought and thought about it, and though I long to take just such a headlong plunge, still cannot make up my mind. If I do not go, it will not be because I am afraid . . .

Saturday was my birthday. I am 20, but hardly feel that it is worth mentioning. In the evening, after a street-corner meeting in Twickenham, went up to a party at Esmond Romilly's. Drink, talk, smoke, a gramophone playing. Cyril Connolly and Jean, surprisingly, were there. And Arthur

Calder-Marshall and his wife. And Sheila,[*] who immediately made great friends with Mrs. Calder-Marshall, who is so unusually beautiful that at first one refuses to believe it. 'A suburban Greta Garbo', I remember calling her just after our first meeting. But she is quite genuine. She described to me a house they have just taken, down near Tower Bridge, and I warned her how depressing they would find the proximity of the Pool after a short time. I am to go and visit them there.

I spent the night at Esmond's. Soon after I had gone to bed, when everyone had left, I was attacked by a raging toothache, the worst I have ever known. The night passed in groaning and pacing to and fro. After a short sleep, I awoke to find how sordid an after-the-party room! We went out at one, to lunch in the Tottenham Court Road Corner House. Then I left Esmond and went to Tower Hill to take part in the Anti-Fascist procession to Alexandra Park. I helped to carry the Twickenham branch's banner. We passed through streets where I had often walked on sombre evenings in 1934 . . . All was well until we approached Green Street, where the blackshirts have their headquarters. A small crowd of dupes shouted menacingly at us: 'Where's yer Union Jack?' 'Why don't you go back to Palestine?' 'Down with the dirty Yids!' In spite of interruptions and minor disorders, we entered the Park and held a great meeting there. The speakers — Johnny Campbell among them — addressed us from a cart, round which a great crowd stretched away towards the surrounding trees, dotted with red flags and banners. As dusk fell, we marched slowly away, singing the 'Internationale'. As soon as we got outside the Park, it became apparent that the Fascists have won many converts in the East End. Crowds of hysterical

---

[*] Legge: the 'surrealist phantom'.

shopgirls and raw youths yelled at us from the pavement almost all the way along the route. We were spat on. Mosley has succeeded in identifying Communism and Jews in the 'minds' of the most irresponsible section of the East-End population . . . Night fell, the sordid houses stood out against the dark red sky, the light of streetlamps fell on the faces of the marchers shouting slogans: 'Jew and Gentile Unite for Freedom against Fascism!'

21.X.36

On Friday met Kay H. who was up in town for a few days. She had her dog Zeus with her, in the middle of Piccadilly, and looked as if she had just returned from a long country walk. I took her to the habitual surrealist meeting-place in Leicester Square. Mesens was there, and seized upon me as an occasion to be very long-winded and didactic about my having joined the C.P., the Moscow Trial, the 4th International, etc. I tried to be stern, and succeeded in putting his back up considerably. Infuriating little man! He never listens to a word one says and will allow no interruptions. Meanwhile, Kay, bored by the conversation, began to grow restless, and Zeus to whine. I had no money, and could not go until I had borrowed some. At last, when most of the others had gone, I succeeded in borrowing 10/- from Roger,[*] who had just arrived with Sheila. They had been to Newmarket for the day. Presently we all went out to dinner at the Commercio. It was amusing to see Sheila and Kay together for the first time, sniffing each other suspiciously, each finally deciding that the other wasn't so bad after all.

---

[*] Roughton

We all went on to a party in Grosvenor Square, above the antique shop. A tiresome party . . . dancing, beer, uninteresting, insincere conversations. As I had been unable to be alone with Kay all the evening, she became pettish and attached herself to some unbearably self-satisfied looking creature who looked as if he must have been at school with her at Bedales. Tatiana came, and I managed to appropriate her for most of the evening, though we have absolutely nothing to say to one another. She looks unusual, that is all. As she was going, I heard Stella say: 'She came up to me and said: "Will you show me where I can powder my nose, I mean really *really* powder my nose?" '

At last Diana took me to Waterloo in her car. There was a workman's train at half-past three, but the porter would not let me through the barrier because my ticket had expired. I went to Kennington Road to sleep at Tiny's.[*] I let myself in with my special latchkey and crept guiltily up the stairs. She woke up with a terrified start when I switched on the light in her room.

On Saturday evening I had to go over to Hampstead. Mesens again was there, as annoying as ever. After dinner we had to go round to see Hugh Sykes Davies, who has an abscess in his anus and is about to be operated upon. A great moist warm wind blew up from the Heath and shook the trees in the lamplight as we left the house, while Valentine stood at the door and waved goodnight. In a moment of exaltation, I cried, as we strode down the wet pavements: *'Mais ne pensez-vous pas que c'est un moment de grand drâme, maintenant que le monde va éclater en flammes*

---

[*] Referred to elsewhere as R.F.W.

29

rouges et que tous les individus se désintègrent?' — *'Ah! mais tu es encore si jeune, cher ami,'* said Mesens, and went on where he had left off talking about some woman . . .

Early next morning, I again had to stagger up to Hampstead with a stack of surrealist bulletins which I had forgotten the night before. Roland and Valentine were just about to leave for Spain: we said goodbye. I still do not know whether I am going to accompany them; if I do, I must send on a telegram to them in Paris, where they are going to stay for the next few days, as soon as I make up my mind.

I walked across the Heath. The most perfect of English autumn mornings: calm radiance of the sun and sky, the distance clear, the trees indescribably bronze and gold. Dogs, children, nursemaids, solitary strollers with the Sunday papers under their arms. Climbing up a slope, saw Joad of Joad Hall and his family 'having fun' together, as usual. 'But Daddy, Daddy!' cried the co-educated-looking daughter, as she tugged at the philosopher's sleeve . . .

Had coffee at the Spaniards, then took the bus to Golders Green Station, and from there to West-End Lane. Memories of my childhood and my wild and much-loved godmother, whose grave is in the cemetery which the bus passed by.

22.X.36

To see Kenneth Rae at Cobden-Sanderson's on Monday afternoon. The interview resulted in a cheque for £20. I am going to Spain!

As I left the office, the wind was blowing in great gusts, the sky was dark. In Southampton Row, my hat flew from my head and had to be rescued from in front of an approaching car. In Parton Street, I met Tiny. She had just resigned from her job, being unable to stand the strain any longer. We had

30

rather disconsolate tea in Winnie's basement café. It was beginning to pour with rain when we went out. It seemed very difficult to realize that I should be leaving England within 48 hours.

Went back to supper with Tiny in Kennington and then decided to go on to the Old Vic. On the way there, called in at a post-office to send Penrose a telegram: 'Arriving Paris early Wednesday morning'.

The Country Wife was perfectly produced, the acting and décor a delight, Edith Evans' Lady Fidget quite triumphant. 'Sisters, sisters, whither will you *wander?*' The vogue for Restoration Comedy, with all its paraphernalia of cuckoldry and whoremasters, must be as symptomatic of 'the times' as the recent Ibsen season, the Tchekov revivals (the Russian bourgeoisie in decay—yearnings, doubts, disintegration), such as this year's *Seagull*, or the boom in Housman's poetry.

Said goodbye to Tiny in Waterloo Station, then went to telephone to Antonia, whom I had been trying to get hold of all day long. She sounded agitated and begged me to go round at once to her flat. I took a taxi from South Kensington Station. I was very tired, and with the prospect of an all-night journey in front of me, was not particularly keen on staying up until half-past four in the morning, but still . . .

Extraordinary news: Antonia tells me that Humphrey and Emily are wildly in love with one another. She says that Emily's behaviour is positively violent with elation, and that she threw her hat over Waterloo Bridge.

Humphrey and Emily; Antonia and I. 'One each', I said. She laughed.

Next morning, a protracted and uncomfortable parting. We were both carrying attaché cases as we left the flat. We had coffee in a place in the Fulham Road, and Antonia said it was

31

as though we were in a railway-station already. She insisted on giving me ten shillings as a parting present for 'my birthday' — to buy books with in Paris. She had a bus to catch, and just as it drove up to the edge of the pavement where we were standing, she slipped the note into the pocket of my raincoat. It fell through onto the pavement without my noticing it. She jumped onto the bus; we waved; it drove away. I walked on towards World's End. When I felt in my pocket for the note, it had gone: I walked back to the bus stop, but it had already vanished. I thought I saw an old man fingering what looked like a 10/- note, but could not bring myself to ask him whether he had just picked it up. This seems to me to present a perfect example of Freudian 'objective chance' (*The Psycho-pathology of Everyday Life*), and reveals to me the disillusioning truth about my relationship with Antonia far more clearly than any conscientious self-examination could ever have done.

Went home. Packed. Took leave of an emotional family and staggered with heavy valise to Victoria. At last in the train, settled down to quiet contemplation of the fact that I was really setting out for Spain; had an enjoyable whiskey and soda in the train bar and read a sixpenny edition of a novel by Claude Houghton.

The dark landscape rushed by unseen, a few of the passengers, strangers to one another, tried to carry on disjointed conversations in French, I began to feel sleepy . . .

Newhaven. Stood for a long time on the deck, while the crane swung to and fro above, loading the Continental mail, somnolent swans drifted about the quiet harbour, and the scattered lights of Newhaven went out one by one. How dramatic it is to watch the island coast recede, the last lights of the esplanades merge into the night, the phosphorescent track of the boat's wake trailing behind!

The sea became choppy, but I went to sleep. A drowsy landing at Dieppe. Coffee in the station waiting-room at about 2.30, then a series of protracted attempts to fall asleep in a darkened and hard-seated carriage, while the train thundered towards Paris through the early hours of the morning.

Paris at half-past five, with a drizzling rain, was hardly welcoming. Had a sort of breakfast in a café opposite St. Lazare, among the last whores and the first chars, then drove in a taxi to Roland's hotel in Montparnasse. The empty streets, the grey first morning light. Slept until ten, saw Roland, went to breakfast at the Dôme.

Roland and I then went to visit Christian Zervos at the bureau of *Cahiers d'Art*. We sat waiting a long time on the arty modern chairs, among the iron sculpture. An extremely attractive young woman with red hair came in: American, Zervos' secretary. Presently Zervos came: short, tough, *costaud* with strong, thick white hair. We went upstairs. Then Yvonne Zervos arrived; and lastly Valentine. They talked; it was chiefly about Spain; I did not follow the conversation. When we left, we took a taxi up to the rue Legendre, behind St. Lazare, to see Paul Eluard. He had grown a moustache and looked another man. Nusch was ill, recovering from the effects of an abscess in her mouth which had been operated upon the day before, and lay on the couch with her head tied in a bandage. They were having lunch. Paul did not seem very well, either. He gave us the names and addresses of many people in Barcelona, with long descriptions of them all. His mother came in, with some fruit for Nusch, who did not seem too pleased to see her and kept looking at us as though to say 'Will she never stop talking?' every time the poor woman

33

said a word. Eluard showed us a Picasso etching: *Grand Air*, for his new collection of poems, *Les Yeux Fertiles*; the poem, in manuscript, is in the centre of the page, and the design all round it, in the manner of Blake. Picasso has also etched a portrait of Nusch.

We drove away in another taxi to lunch at a brasserie behind the Opéra. I ate oysters for the first time in my life. The sky outside was grey, and it was unmistakably autumn, yet the new taste of the oysters, and the fact of being about to set out on a journey, gave the day that vibrant freshness which belongs to spring.

Roland and Valentine went away in different directions after lunch, arranging to meet later at the Catalonian Government Propaganda Bureau. I wandered towards St. Lazare, in order to recover my luggage that I had left in the *consigne*. On the way bought a white-speckled navy-blue scarf at the Printemps store. Took a taxi back to the hotel and had a bath and changed my clothes. After this, went searching for Claude Cahun's flat in the rue Nôtre-Dame-des-Champs, but could not find the right number. Took a bus to St. Germain-des-Prés and wandered down towards the river, buying books, and photographs of Rimbaud and Verlaine, on the way. It began to get dark. On the quais I took another taxi, which drove me across the river, past the Louvre, up the Avenue de l'Opéra to a small street in which the Catalonian bureau is situated. There was no one there. I waited a long time on the doorstep, then went upstairs to enquire whether they had arrived already, but they had not, and the Spaniards in the office looked as though they wondered who I was. Then Yvonne Zervos came. (It was she who had chosen the site of the bureau and arranged and furnished it) and lastly Roland and Valentine. We went in and waited to see Senor

Dalty. The rooms were smartly furnished, with grey upholstering and walls, on which hung anti-Fascist posters.

* * *

(Interpolated for publication in 1980:)

We got our visas, and then I went back to the hotel in Montparnasse where I was staying with the Penroses. I forget how we spent the evening. Next morning, we left from the Gare du Quai d'Orsay for Toulouse, which we did not reach till late in the afternoon. We spent the night in an old hotel there, which I remember had a curious shell-stuck grotto in the lounge. After dinner wandered about the deserted streets for a while: cobblestones, an ancient arcaded square. Next morning, the Penroses, the Zervos', the young painter friend of Yvonne's, Fernandez, who had also joined us, and I all drove to the Toulouse airfield and boarded the 'plane for Barcelona. It was the first time I had ever flown. We flew over Carcassonne and the Pyrenees. On our arrival we were greeted cordially by people from the Propaganda Ministry.

We stayed at a comfortable small hotel just off the top of the Ramblas, near the Plaza de Cataluna. I was to get a job at the Propaganda Ministry, translating news bulletins during the day, and broadcasting them, in English, from a studio in the Ministry of Marine, near the port, every evening at 6 o'clock. Stephen Spender, in his autobiography *World Within World,* has written of his surprise at hearing my voice coming from a loudspeaker attached to a lamp-post at a street-corner. My parents also heard the broadcasts, which were in several languages, as they were intended to be heard all over Europe.

I was very excited by the atmosphere in Barcelona in the streets on the first Sunday morning after our arrival, the universal dancing of the traditional *sardana,* the goodwill and optimism everywhere. That afternoon, we went to my first and

35

only bullfight, which was a rather depressing affair, in aid of the families of bullfighters who had gone to the Front to fight; the toreadors who were left were naturally not much good, and the spectacle seemed to me to consist of protracted, clumsy slaughter, while the shadow of the arena-terrace crept gradually across the ring, for this was late October, and surely bullfighting ought to be seen, if at all, in blazing sunlight. After it was over, we had a brief encounter with a remarkable character, whose name unfortunately escapes me now, but who was locally very famous in his time for his peculiar wit and wisdom, the quintessence of the unique spirit of Catalonia, a man who was reputed to have had a crucial influence on Picasso, and later Dali, Bunuel, Miro and many others . . . (As far as I know this important, though perhaps now forgotten, figure never wrote or published anything, but, like Socrates, influenced people purely by his conversation and ideas, which were, as I said, peculiarly Catalan in their anarchy, destructiveness and irony.)

Another occasion at this time which much impressed me was a free public poetry-reading by Rafael Alberti and his beautiful wife, also a poet, in a quite large Barcelona theatre, which was packed with a wildly enthusiastic and very largely working-class audience.

Christian Zervos was in Barcelona with us at the invitation of the Propaganda Minister, Mirravitles, to collect material for a new work on Catalan Art, based on works which had been discovered shortly after the outbreak of the War, in the houses of exiled or executed Fascists, now requisitioned by the Government, and also in churches, cathedrals etc; and one day we all went with him to look over a very old convent which had been abandoned by the nuns at a moment's notice (of their own free-will, we were told), at the beginning of the conflict, and was to be seen just as it had been left. This was a very odd experience. There was not much in the way of art to be found, but the primitive, mediaeval conditions everywhere, the dirt, dust, tawdriness, and, in the refectory, the remains of a last frugal, apparently interrupted meal, all made a deep, somewhat macabre, impression on me.

Later, we went with the Zervos' and Fernandez, to Gerona, where some wonderful old tapestries of the Apocalypse had been discovered, which had not been seen by anyone from outside for centuries. (Photos of these were later reproduced in Zervos' definitive and still respected book on Catalan Art.) We also saw there, by the way, the machine-guns which had been placed on the turrets of the cathedral by the local clergy, to protect their property from the faithful . . .

It was so cold in Gerona that I caught a bout of *grippe* there, and had to stay in bed at the hotel for a few days, during which time I was looked after most devotedly by Valentine P., who read to me some new French translations she had made from the work of Lorca, who had then only recently been murdered.

What I saw of the Anarchists in Barcelona I found on the whole very sympathetic, though this sympathy was not at all approved of by the young English girl Communist who was my colleague at the Ministry. In spite of the United Front, supposed to join together all left-wing factions against Franco, which was proclaimed at about the time we arrived there (it did not last much longer than a fortnight), I came to find that the Communists hated the Anarchists and the P.O.U.M. (Trotskyists) much more than they hated the Fascists, and I think this was the beginning of my disillusionment with Communism as a means of creating a better world. (At the time, of course, I was still a more or less 'active' member of the C.P.)

During my short stay in Spain, I came to form a rather unexpected friendship with a young Yugoslav journalist whose name was Vladimir Djedier. He later became well-known as a Resistance fighter and a friend and biographer of Tito; though subsequently he fell from favour and even possibly went to prison for a time. Just then, he had only recently returned from an assignment following Edward VIII and Mrs. Simpson in their now famous yacht trip round the Adriatic, had taken many news-photographs, and was able to give me a detailed account of the whole affair, which was the first I had heard about it, as it was all still being hushed up in England at the time. This Yugoslavian friend and I used frequently to meet and chat in cafés on the Ramblas in the evenings (there are one or two wonderful sherry bars there). And one night we set out together on a tour (as *voyeurs* rather than as clients) of all the brothels in the Barrio Chino. This was another memorable evening. Also, as one might imagine, a rather dismal one, as all the 'houses' (we visited at least a dozen of them) were monotonously similar and, with their down-floor waiting-rooms, where the semi-clad girls sat around desultorily on benches waiting for someone from among the long queue of brutish-looking working-men to choose one of them, — all walled with tiles and with the manageresses seated in raised, glass-fronted cash-desks dealing out numbered disk-tokens, and with their sanded floors, — reminded one more than a little of butcher-shops.

At the end of my Barcelona stay, my Yugoslav friend was to travel back to Paris with me.

A first encounter for me at this time was with Tristan Tzara. I had not met him in Paris while I was there collecting material for my little Introduction to Surrealism the year before (he was then already estranged from André Breton and the others) and he had taken exception to my repeating in the book an anecdote told by Breton referring to an early collection of his poems as *Twenty Elucubrations of a Police-agent;* even going so far as to threaten me and Cobden-Sanderson with prosecution if we did not remove the offending passage, and also remove the translation of part of his *L'homme approximatif* which had appeared in the appendix of translated surrealist poems at the end of the first printing. This was done and no further action was taken. Now he suddenly appeared in Barcelona, at the head of a deputation accompanying a brand-new Ambulance Unit, subscribed for by, I think, the *Front Populaire* (at any rate, largely the C.P.), and to my surprise and with a certain reluctance, I found myself being introduced to him. To my relief he turned out to be perfectly amiable, most reconciliatory, and we were later to meet again quite often in Paris.*

A feature of the city which I must mention at some place in this account is the architecture of Gaudi. This I naturally found altogether extraordinary, and at one time or another I must have seen every building of his still then existing in the Catalonian capital. One of them, with a façade resembling an undulating sea-shore after the tide has receded, with wrought-iron balconies arranged across it to look like skeins of abandoned sea-weed, I used to see every day from the top of the tram taking me to and from the Propaganda Ministry. Another well-known building, still preserved, I believe, as a

---

* As recorded in my journal for 1937-9, and also on several later occasions, up until 1964.

sort of Gaudi museum, being entirely filled with furniture and household objects of his design, I visited one evening with the Penroses and Zervos, and we had drinks there. At that time Gaudi was little-known outside Spain, though nowadays universally recognized as one of the great pioneers of modern architecture, and his buildings, particularly the Cathedral of the Holy Family, and also the fantastic rambling Parque Güell, made a great impact on my imagination.

Mention of Barcelona suburbs reminds me of a visit I made with Roland Penrose one evening to a man then (and indeed still) considered to be the finest XXth century poet writing in the Catalan language, J.V. Foix. Rather oddly, this poet made his living as a pastry-cook, owning a rather expensive patisserie in one of the richer quarters of the city. He was a charming man and generous host, and it would have been a pleasant enough evening had it not been interrupted from time to time by the sound of gunfire from close at hand. Apparently these shots were being fired by militia hunting for suspected Fascists thought to be hiding in the gardens of nearby houses. Foix himself was politically quite neutral, but the whole district he lived in was regarded as more or less hostile to the Republicans, and the poor man was naturally more than a little nervous as to the fate of himself and family, and we left him feeling more than a little disturbed . . .

Finally, I must record what was, apart from everything to do with the War, probably the most interesting event that happened to me while I was there. This was a visit our party paid to the apartment of Picasso's sister, married to a prominent Barcelona doctor, where Picasso's mother, a wonderful old lady of about 80, was then staying. I could not speak much Spanish, but her face and gestures were so expressive that I felt I could understand everything she was saying. She talked about Pablo's childhood and youth, and the great gift he had displayed so early. She told us how her husband, a Barcelona art-teacher who had first met her on a sketching holiday in another part of Spain, had one day, when Picasso (his mother's maiden name, by the way) was about 12 or 14, made up his mind to set his son a test to decide on his future, whether he was to earn his living as a whole-time painter or not. Pablo was to paint a picture, and if the result was good enough, then he was to be allowed to become a professional artist. The subject chosen was a still life, a dead pigeon. When it was finished, naturally everyone was very impressed and Picasso had passed the test more than successfully: it was of the bird lying on its back, ' . . . and you should see the fragile little claws stretching up in the air,' the old lady exclaimed, 'so wonderfully pathetic and expressive!' Whereupon she showed us the picture. Indeed, the whole apartment, which overlooked the grounds of another convent (this one, I think, reassuringly unevacuated), was full of a marvellous small collection of early Picasso drawings and paintings.[*]

Not long after this, I had to return to England, leaving the Penroses and the Zervos' behind, as I had two reasons to prevent me from staying longer. One was that I had to take back with me a collection of Spanish War posters that were needed in London for an exhibition that was soon to be held in aid of supplies (not armaments, of course, unfortunately) for the anti-fascists, presided over by Fenner Brockway. And the other was that I had a previous engagement in Oxford to talk to an undergraduate literary society about Surrealism

---

[*] Most of which are now to be seen in the more recently created Barcelona Picasso Museum.

(this seemed rather irrelevant to the Civil War, but I think when the occasion arrived, I was able to include a certain amount of attention to that subject, too).

I travelled back to England with, as far as Paris, as I have mentioned, my Yugoslav journalist friend; and armed with a letter of introduction to Picasso from Christian Zervos (who had devoted a great many of his *Cahiers d'Art* to Picasso's work). The idea was that I should take Picasso reassuring direct news about his mother's and sister's existence in Barcelona. We arrived at the Paris railway station late in the evening, and I said goodbye to Vladimir D., unfortunately for the last time. That night I slept in a room of the Zervos' suite in a big hotel-apartment building, above the old Pergola Club, just off the Blvd. St Germain. The next morning about 11, I set out for the rue de la Boëtie, where Picasso was then still living, in a flat above the Rosenberg Gallery. It was on the top floor and I went up by lift, to find Picasso waiting for me at the lift-gates outside his apartment. I spent about an hour in conversation with him. He was extremely friendly and delighted to have news of his mother and sister and nephews about whom we talked for a while. We talked about other things as well, of course, chiefly the War, but unfortunately not much about painting, as far as I can remember, which was easy to understand, as it was at this period, about eight months before *Guernica* finally put an end to the block, that Picasso was quite unable to paint anything for a while. He seemed depressed and anxious about Spain (everyone knows of his violent hatred of Franco), and I also remember him expressing worry about his son Paulo, whose political affiliations did not quite seem to please him. This was also the time when Picasso for a while took to writing poetry, of a kind peculiar to himself, (short, unpunctuated passages of

42

prose, full of colour adjectives), some examples of which I translated and which were later published in my friend Roger Roughton's magazine *Contemporary Poetry and Prose*. (Gertrude Stein made some caustic remarks about this attempt by her old friend to express himself in writing, though it was obviously done to compensate for being unable to paint.)*

I found Picasso's apartment gloomy, dusty and untidy, with most of the seemingly randomly-chosen furniture covered with newspapers or dust-sheets. Also standing about here and there against the walls were some, but not a lot, of his canvases, a few of which he somewhat perfunctorily showed to me. He also showed me, with more enthusiasm, some of the paintings belonging to his collection of other artists' work, mostly unframed and standing about the flat also as though at random, among which I particularly remember a Cézanne still-life, a Renoir and, above all, Douanier Rousseau's famous *Mariée*. Altogether this was a visit I am very glad to have made and though I never really got to know him, Picasso seemed to remember me, smiled and exchanged a few words, when I was to see him occasionally later, particularly at Chez Paul on the Ile de la Cité, where he was often to be found at lunchtime at one period.

The next evening, I took the boat-train and ferry back to England, with the posters. I was to deliver these soon after at a meeting held at the flat of Fred Warburg, and presided over as I have previously mentioned by Fenner Brockway, chiefly memorable for the presence of the famous, or I should perhaps say notorious American Anarchist leader, Emma

---

* Later on, Picasso was to write remarkable short plays such as *Desire Caught by the Tail*, performed here at the I.C.A.

Goldman, an agèd and indeed formidable figure, who dominated the gathering by sheer *force majeure*. I do not suppose the C.P., to which I still then belonged, would much have approved of these deviant associations of mine (I.L.P., anarchists etc.) but this didn't worry me very much, as the poster exhibition was, after all, to be in aid of the, I'm afraid, already somewhat mythological United Front.*

I went down to Oxford, as arranged, to deliver my Surrealist 'lecture'. This was the first time, I think, that I had ever taken part in an occasion of this sort, and being completely inexperienced in public speaking, I was pretty nervous beforehand and, when I got there, particularly so when I found that the event was to take place in a large and imposing University building (I think the Taylorian). However, it all seemed to go down quite well; Surrealism was a novelty then and people were interested and sympathetic. What I particularly remember was meeting one or two people there whom I later got to know much better, among them Audrey Beecham and Giles Romilly. I had already met and knew Esmond Romilly quite well (they were both Churchill's, or rather his wife's, nephews), as I had often encountered him at my friend David Archer's bookshop in Parton Street, to which he had run away from Wellington, to found a subversive Left-wing magazine for Public Schools, called *Out of Bounds.* (I have already referred to a party of his earlier in this journal.) Now I met his brother, a completely different character, and found him equally sympathetic, though in another way. I never got to know him as well as I should have liked, though I saw him again on more than one occasion, and my then young friend Bettina Shaw-Lawrence got to know

_____

* These were the sorts of details one had to worry about in the Thirties.

him quite well.[*] I might mention here that I happened to be incidental in helping Giles to obtain a visa for his friend Jessica Mitford to go to Spain, where she worked for, I think, the Red Cross, met Esmond and as everyone now knows, soon married him. She needed papers, as it was not easy for anyone to get into Spain at that time, so I wrote a letter of introduction for her to the Senor Dalty at the Catalonian Government Office in Paris where I had been myself not long before.

After this, nothing very noteworthy occurred before Christmas, and the next entry is for a day or two before the end of the year.

27.XII.36

I am terrified to reflect that as, when one passes through a field, it is impossible to avoid crushing beneath one's foot the countless insects and unseen small flowers hidden away among the more resilient grasses, so one passes through life, being totally unable to avoid causing far more of those about us to suffer than we ever suspect. The cause may lie in details of our character; or even merely of our appearance, of which we shall never be made aware; the sufferers may be those to whom we never give a thought, or whom we imagine never think of us. It is not a question of being cruel through not understanding: that can at least be partly remedied; this cruelty in us remains for ever unperceived by ourselves, for it

---

[*] I was to see Giles for the last time in Paris at Rodrigo and Anne Moynihan's flat, shortly before his death. He had been a P.O.W. in Norway for most of the War, as a newspaper-correspondent, and this had undermined his health, and now his marriage was 'on the rocks'. I was saddened by his end, as by his brother's earlier.

proceeds from an ignorance which we cannot consciously enlighten, and which the experience of a whole lifetime serves to lessen to only an infinitesimal degree, if senility does not serve to increase it further.

The alone, the wandering, the lost — the bitter and dark-natured — these fill me with such compassion that I call it love. Indeed, one can hardly call that sentiment which one feels for those who must also be indomitable, proud and independent, compassion, for that is hardly different from pity, which I have always held to be a feeling one should be ashamed to entertain on anyone's account. That which I experience when I think, then, of these men, is rather sympathy, the very strongest kind and in the truest sense: to suffer with. Yet it is more than this which I feel for Cailleux, who is so truly of the race I have described.

I now know how much love I have within me, and how difficult it is for it to find an outlet. It is almost as though there were a physical constriction, or a knot, about my heart — a paralysis that settles in just when it would be possible to respond, or be responded to.

'Tell me about yourself. What is it that you feel towards me?' To no question could it be more difficult to reply. Yet one manages to ease the knot, somehow, and the tongue begins, how clumsily, to repeat what the heart knows. And then the other falls asleep; one's words fall emptily into unresponding air.

13.I.37

Belief is relative; to know is absolute. But do not confuse what you believe with what you know; what you believe, suspect; belief is kindred to desire. Belief without knowledge is fanatic and destructive, and will surrender at the wrong moment to hatred.

16.III.37

(All these notes are very disjointed and give only a very fragmentary idea of my actual existence and what's happened to me — At this point, for instance, a very full and important period has been left out — Barcelona, Valentine Penrose; the most difficult stages of my relationship with Antonia — Roland Cailleux; Mass Observation and Charles Madge; a frightful month of depression following a visit to Antonia's analyst; and now, a sort of 'reawakening'. It is my intention to arrange all these notes one day, and those of previous notebooks, and to fill in the gaps with autobiographical reminiscences. I should hate anything to be lost! It's a curious thing that when anything is actually happening to me, I feel no inclination to record it until afterwards.)

17.III.37

God! Why can't I keep a journal? Why am I just incapable of writing it down every day? Life burns one up and makes a thousand exacting trivial demands which it is impossible to fulfil. One never has time. I was reading Marie Bashkirtseff[*] the other day, and noticed how she too was obsessed not so

---

[*] (Marie Bashkirtseff. I have only skipped through the first volume of her journal so far, and find particularly fascinating the descriptions of railway travel in Russia in the 19th century, compared with those to be found in Tolstoy and Dostoievski.)

much by death, but by the fear that all her living and feeling might be wasted, that all her passionate days might pass and never leave a trace behind them. I have not got her tremendous vanity — no, one would also have to be very complacent to be as vain as that — but I cannot bear the thought that the very taste of life is so evanescent: I value all experience and want so much at least to record it.

Yes, I suppose I *am* a fragmentary being, awake and whole for only a few days at a time, in between long spells of dormancy. But today I feel so alive it is like a dynamo driving inside, even though my health is feeble and I did not go to bed till six o'clock last night. During a short afternoon's sleep just now I dreamt of the power in my own eyes: it was like searchlights blazing down two great tunnels!

I must have faith in myself, enormous faith. I can do great things if only I can have the strength to hold together and drive incessantly towards one unalterable purpose. Never mind the state of the world, never mind other people, never mind obligations and responsibilities: all that matters is one's *work,* incessantly. I read an article last night in which Rachmaninoff described how he was able to write his Second Concerto. He referred to Tolstoy working from seven till midnight every day, and saying 'I'm not always satisfied with it, but it's honest work', or words to that effect. (Funny thing — both Tolstoy and Rachmaninoff are geniuses without either taste(?) or humour.)[*]

Perhaps it is idiotic to want to be great, and perhaps it is a mistake to imagine that one can become great by simple

---

* I have restrained myself from deleting this brash and immature parenthesis.

determination; but at any rate it is futile to have powers and capabilities and never do anything with them, never leave a mark, never influence people. People who are convinced that they are geniuses always make foolish spectacles. However . . .

All this, of course, is quite contrary to the ideal of anonymity and community that I have learnt from Suarès, Caillois, Jennings. But I have now come to believe that for *me,* this ideal is a refuge, an excuse for weakness. No, I do not believe in self-renunciation, I have got to be selfish, in a particular way. The objection is that I am a 'pitiful' individualist. Very well! But there are not so many people who have got the egoist force that I have got, and those who've got it ought to make use of it. It's only too easy not to.

I have also got to be alone. Intimacies with other people like oneself only undermine one's self-confidence and sap one's energies. No more Antonias. Or only for very short periods. The Marys are all very well, but give me the Marthas in the long run.

Delusions of grandeur? (I shall reread this one day, and it will probably leave me quite indifferent. But can one be self-confident and disillusioned at the same time? I think part of whatever strength I've got comes from the fact that I know *all* my weaknesses — and heaven knows they can be depressing enough at times — and no longer feel the need to make excuses for them.)

Yesterday morning I had just settled down to a day's work, when a telegram came from Geoffrey Grigson: 'Can you come to dinner tonight at 7.30?' I did not want to go, and telephoned to say so, but finally allowed myself to be persuaded into accepting. So at six o'clock, in the pouring rain, I set off on the eternal journey to Hampstead. (Florence

Mole's sister Clara has just died. In the bus from West-End Lane to Golders Green, I passed the cemetery where she is to be buried today.) In the train I was reading René Crevel's *La Mort Difficile*, which I find very moving, not only because of the pathos of the story itself, but because of the thought that the man who wrote it, whose personality is extraordinarily attractive to me, killed himself in despair. If only I had known him, and now there will never by anyone like him again! (I only saw him once: it was in June 1935. I was sitting with, I think, G. R. Reavey, at the Flore, on the Boulevard St. Germain, one warm, rainy evening, when a remarkably attractive woman entered and sat down at a nearby table, alone. I could not take my eyes off her, and we exchanged glances several times. Presently a young man with a broad face and crisp fair-brown hair came in, wearing a cyclist's raincoat and no hat. I watched him go up to the woman's table, smiling, — it was a warm, good smile, — and present her with a small bunch of anemones. He stayed talking with her for a few moments, then went over to speak to a group of young men near the door, then went away. Later, Man Ray, whom I had already met, came in with a party of other people whom the woman joined. I went over to speak to Man Ray, he introduced me to the others, and I discovered that the woman I had been watching was Nusch Eluard, and the young man who had spoken to her, Crevel. And about a fortnight later he committed suicide. No-one really knew why, and everyone had a dozen explanations.)

Arrived at Grigson's new house, which you approach by means of a sort of country lane, was taken upstairs by a curious, aggressive, Central-European maid with thick curly blonde hair which looked like a wig, and found Allott and his wife already there, but G. not yet come home. We sat waiting round the fire and talked desultorily . . .

An unsatisfactory evening really, a waste of time, the talk entirely literary. What is he to do to brighten up *New Verse*, Geoffrey enquires. God knows! *Je m'en fous!* And all those ghastly letters he has collected from his contemporaries and other people, — what a horribly fatuous world is the world of 'young poets' and critics and all the rest! I don't want to have any more to do with it. That's where the growth and influence of Madge's Mass Observation will do good, if it can help to debunk professional poets, among other things.

Kenneth Allott's wife, Kumaari (or some such name), is very good to look at. I like her delicate figure, her voice (which is like Eunice B.'s), her hair, banked in a curious Victorian way round her head. She is quiet, does not say much, sympathetic. Allott himself I like well enough but his prompt and rather emphatic speech and his readiness with critical opinions about almost anything rather jar on me.

We walked together down the hill to Golders Green station about 12 o'clock, the rain had stopped, the air was warm. Took the tube to Waterloo, and walked home from Strawberry Hill. Striding along the wet pavements at one in the morning, enjoying being alone in a sleeping world with a large sky above me full of moving, vaporous clouds with starry rents in them, feeling grand. When I got home, sat down and worked at *April* until six o'clock. When I went to bed, the sky was turning grey, the birds were beginning to sing outside as I hadn't heard them sing for months and months. Felt physically tired, but extraordinarily 'vivid' and clear-headed.

This evening, am going to hear Busoni's *Dr. Faustus* with Antonia at Queen's Hall.

18.III.37 — *3 a.m.*

Would have enjoyed *Dr. Faustus* more if it hadn't been that Antonia was feeling depressed and wan, as usual, and to begin with had made a mistake about the time we were supposed to meet. She was so 'down' that I began to feel a little of my own vitality ooze away . . .

The music has a dark, brooding quality, as though played against a background of unrelieved dark greens and blues. It is bare, restrained, here and there extremely moving: the libretto seemed somewhat confused, and struck me as a badly digested version of the legend. Particularly noticed Faust's

> Labour, thou art the healing balm:
> Cleanse me now and make me whole!

May Blyth sang the difficult part of the Duchess of Parma with her usual artistry and verve, and was notably moving in the scene where she moves across the stage, following Faust away, alone.

19.III.37

A little mad? The type of maniac who feels himself right on top of the mountains in the blazing sunlight one day, and down in the darkness of the valleys of the shadow of death the next? Perhaps . . . No, that is exaggerated; characteristically, at any rate. 'I have lived and suffered!': that's why I write these notes — but I don't seem to have recorded my dark days. The dark days are when one feels just dead, inert, a thousand leagues from all enthusiasm; or worried by innumerable trivialities, money, responsibilities, the hopeless failings of one's character, and with a continual, senseless gnawing, almost physical, in the region of one's breast. It is impossible to write anything, even to want to, on such days. The best time is when one is feeling reasonably sane, clear-headed and alert (not the alertness which consists of an exhausting tautness and exhilaration of the nerves and perception — though I think I really prefer that to anything, really, in spite of what it costs in dreary aftermaths) — such as today.

I wonder, would these notes seem shockingly self-absorbed to a reader? I don't care. I'm not going to try to appear an exemplary, well-balanced character if I'm not one. I don't even really want to keep up the illusion that I don't expect to be read one day by someone. That's what I'm writing these pages for: to make a record of what I am so that someone, perhaps only one or two people — someone with whom I may be in love in years to come — may know me as I was, may feel some sort of contact with a sensibility, a passion, an imagination, a restlessness . . . Whoever you are like myself, we understand each other, we know each other, we touch hands somewhere.

There are very few people who know what I am really like: Only Antonia, and Kay (who does not really *know*, only vaguely perceives), and Cailleux (if he bothered, which I don't believe he does in the least), and Philip perhaps. To almost everyone else I must seem gentle, mild and dim: ineffectual. Or so I imagine; though I do get excited sometimes, and express definite opinions, and allow a hardness to enter my eyes or voice. But I think other people tire me as a rule, I cannot be bothered, I become passive with them, which makes me a 'good listener', which perhaps is why I can make a lot of superficial friends very easily.

George Barker, for instance, seemed quite surprised to find that I have really got a certain amount of violence and vitality.

53

(It was about the only time I have ever been able to talk to him at all intimately — one evening last November at Antonia's.) I wish we knew one another better, could meet more often. I feel that there exists between him and me a very strong latent sympathy, which has never had a chance to develop — into whatever it might develop into. We must be very much alike in some ways. Antonia, who knows him very well, said she thought we might easily fall in love with one another . . . He told her that there was a feeling that I was going to be a failure, a disappointment; that my early work showed promise, but that I had never really followed it up with anything solid. Well, I haven't — yet. But I'm not going to be a failure. It will probably take me a long time to produce what I believe I am capable of producing; I think I must develop very slowly. But after the thorough spring-cleaning and scouring I went through last winter — (I think the period from last September until the middle of last month was one of upheaval and redetermination) — I know now what I am going to do and what I am. Approximately.

Spring

'A man's face who has made an assignation with a girl and feels himself on the brink of a love affair . . .' I even feel that urge in me. It's the spring. But it would be fatal, I know, for my work, for my present hardly-won state of comparative balance, to rush off in search of that sort of thing at the moment. Now that I've got a certain amount of energy, I must try and conserve it for more useful purposes. (Procrastinator!) But yes, my mind (not only my mind) does quicken at the thought of hair at the edge of a forehead, a gleam at the corners of the eyes, a turning note in a voice, quick gentle movements of the hands — feline, impulsive graces, female arts.

20.III.37

A glorious spring day, although the first day of spring is not until tomorrow: everything rushing into leaf and blossom — there has been much rain recently. There have been floods, the Thames is still swollen. I went down there last night and watched it flowing, rapid, heavy, turgid, beneath the bridge at Teddington lock.

Went up to the London Library and back this morning before lunch. In the entrance hall, looking over the new books on the stand, suddenly observed William Empson on the other side. I made no appearance of having seen him, since he always seems to dislike being noticed, and became more absorbed in somebody's contents-page. Later, on my way upstairs to the French shelves, came face to face with him in a doorway. 'Oh, hello Gascoyne,' he mumbled, as though caught in a guilty situation. 'Why, hello Empson! How are you?' I said, in a tone of great surprise. He had hurried away down the stairs before I could say any more. Empson's appearance is extraordinarily unprepossessing: badly dressed; small face, small tight mouth, spectacles; slightly flushed; black fingernails. Not long ago, I jumped into a crowded underground train during the rush hour and had to stand packed between a lot of other people and at the next station, just as he was getting out I suddenly realised that the man who had been standing right next to me for several minutes was Empson. Disturbing experience. Shabby and entirely insignificant, his face quite blank, I should never have looked at him twice. What is surprising is that Madge and Kathleen Raine have the greatest admiration for him and quote all his opinions. (They were both at Cambridge with him; and he was at that time, one understands, phenomenally brilliant.) But what a bore! His poems get steadily duller and more wooden; though some of his early ones, like 'Arachne' or 'The proper scale', apart from their intellectual crossword-puzzle ingenuity (or their famous ambiguity) are, in a certain way, decoratively or evocatively, quite exciting.

Brought away from the Library with me: Gide's *Nouvelles Pages de Journal;* Freda Strindberg's *Marriage with Genius* (Strindberg has been at the back of my mind for some time, though I have read only little of him, and that too early to appreciate it; it is his life and personality that interest me more, however, for are men's works — I mean men of his type — ever more than a residue of their passion? If one admires him as an artist more than as a human being, I suppose one says that his writings are a *crystallisation* of his life? I should not care to be regarded thus myself); and an English translation of *Le Grand Meaulnes,* which Philip wants to read.

I am disappointed with Gide's Journal. It is far more like a notebook or, as he says himself, '*une sorte de cimetière d'articles mort-nés*'. Many notes on Zola, Balzac; also on words and style; preoccupation with the *problème sociale* and Communism. But almost nothing about his life, no intimacies or revelations. Not that mine is the vulgar curiosity which concerns itself only with the 'private lives' of the great; but there is nothing I like to read better than notebooks or journals which give an exact, daily record of experience — feelings, self-analysis — the human being *chez lui*, naked. I think a journal should be a continual confession of an incurable passion for life. Gide is getting old; his is the kind of maturity which makes a 'passion for life' seem a little jejune.

Le Grand Meaulnes

I referred to this extraordinary novel in these pages last
autumn. Since then it has worked its way even further into my
intimate life. I induced Antonia to re-read it, and it soon
became of the same sort of importance to her as to me. I
think she must have seen herself as Yvonne de Galais, and me
as a sort of mixture of the *moi* of the story and Augustin (or
the other way round). She later had a dream which was
obviously based on *La Fête Etrange* — a large room, a whole
floor, divided by white paper screens, which one could
rearrange at will to make smaller rooms within the room to
suit one's fancy of the moment; and wide French windows
giving out onto a lawn; and moving continually in and out,
laughing and playing or making love, a party of beautiful
young men and girls, the dreamer wandering about among
them, in search of someone . . . Since Antonia told me this
dream, it has become a recurrent subject of my own reveries.
But what is far more strange is that I have since discovered
that Cailleux, whom I had already associated with the book,
and particularly with Fritz, is also haunted by it, and has even
made a ballet-scenario out of *La Fête Etrange* (which I'm
afraid I must admit seems to me rather 'the kind of thing he
would do'. I do not approve at all. The whole atmosphere
and beauty of the scene would be lost as soon as it was
formalised and made decorative). And another thing: during
my first encounter with him I was considerably *gené* by the
sounds of the windy night outside, and of nocturnal activities
going on inside the hotel; and when he asked: 'Where then
would you, ideally, like to make love?', I tried to describe to
him a room on the ground floor of a large wooden house
near the sea. In a district such as I imagine the Landes to be.
Outside the window (a great bay window without curtains —

and the floor-level of the room raised above the level of the ground, as though the house were built on piles) an unkempt, rainy garden, low shrubs, pine-trees, and beyond, stretches of sand-dunes and a melancholy grey sea. No-one in sight. When I read Alain-Fournier, more than six months later, I realised that, except for the nearness of the sea, this was the room where the scene between Augustin and Yvonne, after their wedding, takes place. (Part II, Chap. VII.) (No, it is not the same; but it seemed so to me at the time, and still seems so, and now I shall never think of the one without the other. And perhaps one day I shall find this house, this room? A log-fire is burning in the wide grate, it is raining outside and the light is just about to fade. It may be that someone is playing the piano. It is a very spacious, high-ceilinged room, with a dark oak floor covered with thin rush mats, and whitewashed walls, and very little furniture. 'And in my heart how deep unending Ache of love.' The emotion evoked by James Joyce's 'On the Beach at Fontana' comes into the picture somewhere, too.)

What sort of house, or room, do you visit repeatedly in your imagination? It would make a fascinating subject for an *enquête*. Breton has done the thing admirably in 'Il-y-aura une fois' at the beginning of *Le revolver aux cheveux blancs;* and Eluard once told me that he also had a mental habitation of this kind; I particularly remember his description of the kitchen: dusty, cobwebbed, with a besom leaning against the wall.

One could make a similar collection of descriptions of London by foreigners: Dostoievsky, Rimbaud and Verlaine, Strindberg, Alain-Fournier — they were all in London at one time or another — (and Gustave Doré, and Van Gogh) — and all have left some sort of record of their impressions, which are naturally strange, only half-recognisable, like a dream of a place one knows. I particularly like Alain-Fournier's appreciation of the suburban villas of Chiswick and Kew, and of the atmosphere of London summer Sunday afternoons at the beginning of the century, and his saying that of all towns, he would prefer London to be unhappy in.

I seem to be writing a lot in this book these days. Cultivating my own garden, and meanwhile neglecting a lot of practical things that ought to be done. However, I think this gives me more satisfaction, on the whole.

I have been giving some time to these notes as a sort of recreation between the second and third sections of the story I am at present at work on, *April*. I think it's an improvement on anything else of the kind that I've done, but I know it's only practice, as yet; an exercise in dealing with character, and dialogue, and narrative form, and keeping 'poetic' descriptions down to a minimum. I am not altogether satisfied with the end of section 2 and think I ought really to rewrite it; I'm not sure yet; but I feel that Frédéric's collapse is a bit theatrical. The difficulty about section 3, before tackling which I am making a short pause, is Frédéric. I can see his character fairly clearly (is it fair to say that he is based to a certain extent on Cailleux?) and his background (less clearly), but still don't quite know how to present him in the round. And I'm not at all certain about his illness (diabetes), though I'm sure it's *right*, as far as the story goes.

The point of the set of stories of which this is the first — the other two are working out fairly well in my mind — is semi-psychological, semi-moral. Am I clear about this? I mean to present a type of virginity which seems to me particularly English and contemporary. *A Quiet Mind*. A shrinking from life, a desire to preserve peace and quiet at the cost of all vital experience. (In the English, this often takes the form of 'humour', the kind of humour in which seeing the funny side of a thing is essentially a process by means of which whatever it is becomes unreal, and thereby the experience evaded.) The type of person who has this attitude to life is very common. It is another manifestation of the European death-impulse, to be detected, analysed, deplored. To deplore, however, involves a moral point of view, while this seems to me to be not really a moral question, but a psychological one, since the root of it all would appear to be illness, or rather fear. The castration-complex is obviously relevant. Its causes, then, are partly the existing family-sexual situation, and partly the social-economic. In both cases, the fear is one of possible catastrophe, and the fact that the first is on the whole unjustified, and in the second altogether justified, makes no difference to the existence of the fear.

If a moral point of view comes into it, then it is rather in the positive presentation of an alternative attitude to life: a fearless attitude, a free attitude (since, I believe, freedom as an abstract principle, if it has any, simple meaning, means absence of all fear, exterior or interior, rational or irrational), a desire to embrace — the word is very apposite — both pleasure and pain, to accept entirely *whatever* comes, happiness, unhappiness, success, failure, with equal 'zest', with the kind of enthusiasm which is the opposite of apathy or disinterestedness. This is not the same thing as stoicism, which ultimately reduces everything to one level, and the attitude of which to pain does not seem to me to be far removed from that of Christian Science.

The problem is: how to cure people of their apathy and their largely unconscious fears? Does simply telling them about it do any good? The only cure, or at any rate the first essential step towards it, is obviously a change of society: revolution. The morality suggested above is perhaps a partly individualist one (though I don't mean to suggest the mere ichthyosaurus wallowing in sensation of J. C. Powys); but it is at least Communist in this: that it entails partaking of life actively and sharing responsibility; it entails being completely aware of everything, interior and exterior, without excluding those things of which one does not want to be aware because they are unpleasant or humiliating; and as far as I can see, to be aware nowadays inevitably means becoming a revolutionary sooner or later; unless, of course, one really has possessive interests at stake, for unfortunately, being aware for the ruling-class simply means become Fascist. (It is understood that when I speak of being aware, I imply active, dialectical, critical thinking, not simply passive acceptance of an arbitrary absolute, either objective = mechanistic rationalism, or subjective = lunacy.)

The problem I still face is that of how to relate the type of writing of *A Quiet Mind* to the fact that I am a Communist? Apart from the fact that I simply don't believe in either the necessity or the efficacity of directly propagandist literature, nor in 'Socialist realism' (though it depends what is meant by that term), the subjects of these stories remain individual, pressingly immediate social issues of the day. As I am aware of both sides of the picture, I know that the connection and the implications are there; but it is not so much a question of how to justify what one writes to oneself, as of how to justify it to other people who have not gone through the same kind of development, have not yet reached the problem from the same angle as oneself. However, the recent swing-over of the Party towards accepting Freud, and the fact that several of the most ardent Russian exponents of unadulterated propaganda

61

and crude realism (who were also the most hostile critics of what they called 'individualist' psychology) have been discovered to be Trotskyists, may help to make one's position easier. At the same time, though I long ago realised the absurdity of a literature based only on aesthetic considerations, 'literary' literature, and though I am only too willing to admit that a certain amount of opportunism is perfectly justified by necessity in the realm of practical politics, I cannot see how opportunism can be considered either justified or necessary in the inevitably less immediate domain of the writer's art (for one can quite well be a human artist, a Communist artist — it doesn't always mean a preoccupation with aesthetics). I must say I am, for once, entirely in accord with Gide, when he says to a Communist novelist (evidently of the 'proletarian' school):

> Et vous, en tant que romancier, vous faussez tout, si vous peignez tous les bons d'un coté, et rien que des méchants de l'autre. Laissez ces peintures, stupidement édifiantes, aux journalistes qui, lorsqu'ils sont nos adversaires, ne présentent les révolutionnaires qu'avec un couteau entre les dents.
>
> Mais vous voulez écrire pour prouver. Ce faisant vous ne prouvez rien, et vous avilissez l'oeuvre d'art. Vous dîtes que la littérature doit se mettre au service de la révolution. Si elle ne sert pas d'abord la verité, c'est une mauvaise servante, et dangereuse. Craignez que ses apparents services ne se retournent un jour contre vous.

In the stories of *A Quiet Mind* I do not intend merely to entertain, although I hope to reach a larger audience, or at least a less eclectic one, than has up till now been open to me. I am setting out to present, in the form of fiction, an objective analysis of a kind of spiritual death, and indirectly to suggest how to escape it. Since spiritual death is just as typical of the present state of society as, for instance, unemployment, and since, also, it is something I know more about and am better qualified to describe, I do not see why I should be expected to offer excuses to Comrades Alick West and Philip Henderson.

21.III.37

Slept late last night and this morning felt a little grey. The weather is grey, too. Philip is coming over to see me this afternoon, so it seems no use trying to get on with the portrait of Frédéric. Perhaps I shall feel keener this evening.

Have been reading more of Gide's *Pages de Journal*. A queer thing, the artist or man of letters knowing that he has an audience even in the solitude of his private thoughts, talking to himself yet with the intention of being heard. Gide writes down many more reflections on social and political matters than I have done here; yet I think that is only because at the time of writing he was only just beginning to develop a social awareness and to make up his mind; whereas I have already long been convinced and, though not exclusively and uninterruptedly, have taken a part in various kinds of political activity. In this journal I have devoted myself almost entirely to the other side of my life. It will not be a complete picture of me, however, if I leave politics quite out of it. It is not as though the two sides were in contradiction (or they ought not to be).

22.III.37

What has happened to my strength? Where has my vitality gone? It is terrible, this heaviness and discouragement and acedia! I have not been able to write all day. This afternoon, discovered that I am 10/- overdrawn at the bank. This continual nagging worry about money will get me down in the end. I can't work or think or settle to anything when my pocket's empty. One sits at the desk, stares at the paper, writes a sentence, and crosses it out; or draws futile arabesques in the margin or on the blotting-paper; sits doing nothing, stroking one's hair; or picks up some book, reads a few pages at random, and falls into a sterile, nostalgic daydream . . . Ugh!

Why have I not got genius? Futile plaint! Or if I have got it, why does it sleep within me, why does it not possess me and carry me away with it, like an eagle? On days like this, all I feel is an awful guilt for not even wanting to make an effort, for all effort seems vain. What a ridiculous spectacle one would present if one spent one's life deceiving oneself that one had genius, and doing nothing but imagining that one could do something great 'if only' one had the right conditions — money, love, seclusion, etc., when all the time one ought really to be doing an ordinary, dull, honest job of work, like everyone else! I sometimes allow myself to think that I have pretty well the worst disadvantages to struggle with, and that consoles me a little, for a time. But how wearying it is, this everlasting struggle with every kind of weakness and petty drawback. It is easiest to give up struggling 'for the time being', to go off in search of friends, to listen to the wireless, any kind of anaesthetic; this time, however, I will *not* give in, but simply sit here, on and on, with my nose to the grindstone, not thinking of anything else, past or future — until I've done a little work.

From a letter to George Barker.

> I should like whatever I write to be propaganda for being aware: self-aware and socially aware both at once. I should like to be one of those people who always tell the Truth at embarrassing moments; though it may not always be easy to reconcile this with being a Communist, I'm afraid. If I had to make a choice (if the two things are not reconcilable) I think I should choose — like Gide, — to tell the truth (or at least I hope so).

23.III.37

Worked at the third chapter of *April* all day today. Six pages of typescript.

25.III.37

Perhaps I may become a 'social' writer, but I shall never be a 'political' one. Apart from other objections, the influence of the political writer can be only temporary, even though it may be a vital one during a short period of time. One may be born an artist and yet, for (I think mistaken) moral reasons, decide to sacrifice the more free and autonomous laws of artistic creation to those of the necessity of time and place; yet if one *is* an artist, and can have the courage to decide to *be* one, I still believe that one's work stands a greater chance of being of service to society in the long run. I am talking of the moral-psychological artist. The time limit or speed of the influence of the undisguisedly political writer is self-evidently that of historical events, or very nearly; that of the moral-psychological writer is slower, wearing consequently deeper in the end.

The Marx-Freud problem is essentially the same as that which faces the modern writer. His other problem, which is related to it, that of the middle class. For a gradual three decades or more, writers have been dealing with pessimism, cynicism, futility. 'Their works are "made" — made often out of a considerable culture by an acute intelligence, but nevertheless made, not created. And why is this? It is because there is no love and no belief in their hearts and consequently none in their works.' (W. J. Turner, *New Statesman*, 25.III.37. Elsewhere in the same issue an advertisement protests 'against camouflage and sang-froid'.) Symptom of the end of capitalist society, no doubt. But should this diagnosis affect one's decision to occupy one's self with the cause and cure of apathy, cynicism, 'camouflage and sang-froid', etc.? Theoretically, of course, the Revolution cures all that. But will there ever be a revolution unless something is also done about these things? (My argument is *not* that of people who first advocate 'a change of heart'.) The problem is dialectical.

26.III.37
The portrait of Frédéric Delauney in *April* is taking fairly satisfactory shape. He has turned out to be the '*jeune homme stendhalien*', who '*par sa disponibilité désesperée, son impuissance à se contenter des solutions platement humaines, est le type le plus pur de tous ceux que les faillites quotidiennes à jamais ont écarté de l'opportunisme et de ses solutions.*' (Crevel.) Not quite, however; that is only what he would have liked to be. There is certainly an element of opportunism in his decision to try and make a success of being a lawyer, and thus beat the world at its own game. But this corresponds, for instance, to Julien Sorel's calculated

social climbing, after all. His ideal of passion is the same as Sorel's, with an added surrealist feverishness. No doubt it is not half so splendid to die in a hospital of diabetes as to kill oneself and the woman one loves in a church. That is all the difference between the beginning of capitalist industrialism and the end of it. The modern romantic is far more likely to come to his end in a diabetic coma: of an excess of sugar.

Knowledge combined with scepticism is constructive and will surrender at the right moment to love.

4.IV.37
It is nearly eleven — but if only it were a dark, warm night, with a moon shining, and there were a long, straight road along which one could walk for hours and have absolutely no idea of where it went! If there were something, or someone at the end of the road! Am I really a religious? Am I in exile, yearning for some ridiculous, yes, some absurd assurance of a sustaining power to which I might one day return, as to an old forgotten lover's arms, still faithful after years and years of absence? What a fool! What a chaotic, feckless, insatiable fool! And vain; because I know only too well that I am priding myself on being a fool, because I know fools are — blessed? But what nonsense I am writing . . .

For the last weeks I have done nothing but work and work at my story. It is nearly finished. I have less than twenty pages to do now, but it is taking such a long time. And now I am seized with restlessness again. I want other people. To be able to work, I have to shut myself off from everyone, to think of nothing, nothing else but of incessant writing and always the end of the story getting gradually nearer, and the pages increasing, the number of words growing. I have to be self-contained, and self-assured. But now I find it difficult to go on. Worries, money, things I have left undone, loneliness . . . I am not making any plaint, only recording an indefined distress. I feel so unfinished . . .

For the last two nights I have seen the dawn arrive. On Friday I sat up all night writing, and at 6 o'clock, in the clear, fresh early light, went out and walked along the Thames to Kingston. When I came back, at breakfast-time, the post arrived with a cablegram from Johannesburg which had been sent to Cobden-Sanderson: 'Is David Gascoyne safe? Reply Goldeye.' A mystery! In the afternoon, Philip came, and stayed till five o'clock this morning, talking. I am so tired! We went out at eleven in the car, and every now and then drove into a drifting mist. We drove out into the open country and then stopped in the solitude and the night, with masses of stars burning overhead, and discovered that we loved one another. Strange . . . I still do not quite know what he means, but it has made me happy. It is not a normal homosexual relationship, but it is more than friendship. I feel unsettled about it today.

We have for a long time been discussing spending the summer together in Cornwall. We both say that we're going to do it, but it seems very remote. Too good to be true. It will mean his giving up his job, and my getting some money somehow. But how good it would be to get away from London for a time. I should get strong and healthier, do lots of work, start a new life. Oh, will it ever happen?

I am terribly worried about Antonia. She is in such a bad state of depression that it seems she might even make an end of herself. I wrote to her tonight and am going to see her tomorrow.

6.IV.37

Most of this journal seems unreadable. Pages and pages of turgid unreadable nonsense. What childish illusions I have about myself, my work, other people! How pompous I sound! Shall I *never* grow up?

What I need, of course, is to forget *myself.* I'm just a little Narcissist, that's all. Can see nothing but my own reflection everywhere, and yet am continually patting myself on the back for seeing everything so clearly. What I must try to be is *pure in heart.* No one can ever be anything, do anything, unless they can completely forget themselves, lose themselves; no one can be really human unless they can do that.

I must destroy all the illusions I may have about my work. It's lamentably bad, I've got to realise that. Whenever I write about people, it's as though they were seen through several thicknesses of smoked glass, or through the wrong end of a telescope. (That's because I can't be human, being self-engrossed.) They hardly come to life for a moment, their conversations are like those of talking dolls. What am I go do? Go on and on pretending to be a writer, and never writing anything that lives? My style, too — angular, pedantic, awkward, dull . . . It's so depressing to have to tell oneself the truth.

I seem so humourless too, and stodgy. Such a heavy-handed touch. No subtlety. No delicatesse.

Plutôt se taire que se plaindre . . .

. . . What I wrote just now is too violent. I must try to preserve my balance. I don't feel as depressed as that. To tell the truth, my feeling is the result of seeing Antonia. She always has this unsettling effect on me. It's good to be unsettled. But dangerous. In order to be able to do anything one has to be bound together: single-minded. It is hateful to have to say so, but I must remember that Antonia is a *schizophrenic*. It seems improbable that she will ever be entirely cured; her suicidal tendency is so marked that she can't take out an insurance policy on her life . . .

She is really one of the most wonderful people I have ever known, or am likely to know, and has had more influence on me than any single person I can think of. But on the whole, I think her influence on the people she comes in contact with is bad: her husband, Silas, Emily, and now Norman Cameron, — she gradually undermines everyone's self-confidence. There are very few who can stand the dazzling (but how depressing!) light of moral Truth she radiates. Exposed to their selves, her intimates begin to wilt . . . and with what ruthlessness she tears their illusions to shreds! — very often, I believe, out of revenge for (imagined?) neglects or slights.

One can hardly be surprised that, after a time, people begin to avoid her. Once bitten — sometimes I feel myself as though I were caught in a web. (That was why I had to write her that rather brutal — I'm afraid — letter in February: in order to wrench myself free.) So she is left alone — with her terrors. But it is impossible, after hearing her last night, for instance, read that appalling poem of Clare's about:

> the huge shipwreck of my own esteem
> And all that's dear. Even those I loved the best
> Are strange — nay, they are stranger than the rest

to leave her in the state that she's in now. I have to go and try to comfort her and, in return, have all my present points of reference unsettled for me.

The trouble is, that, unless I'm very much mistaken, no *adult* life is possible unless one is resigned to going through an absolutely unending displacement process of this kind. *Songe du Matin et du Soir: on ne se repose jamais.* This is the point of *A Quiet Mind*, I suppose; but it is not enough to disturb people into an awareness of themselves and of other people; that is only a preliminary. The disturbed surface, like that of a deep pool into which a stone has been flung, soon settles down to its calm level again, having assimilated the stone. The disturbance has to be constant. How exhausting! But no development is possible without this; otherwise, one simply becomes another of *les assis*.

But I think A. carries all this to its furthest extreme. There ought to be a certain moderation in one's self-criticism as in everything else. It's all very well to be frightened of complacency; but A. seems to suffer from a ceaseless compulsion to smash all the chairs in the house with a hatchet — every day.

I am convinced that her wisdom and maturity surpass that of anyone I know. But how she surprises me, at times, by the lack of understanding revealed in her remarks about Kay, for instance, or Kathleen Raine, and by her apparent inability to adopt a reasonable attitude towards politics. The result of her double vision is to see everything as either very black or very white; chiefly very black, owing to the extreme elevation of her moral standards. A nice sort of influence for an unstable and impressionable young man!

One of the finest and most beautiful things ever written in a Journal:

But warm, eager, living life — to be rooted in life — to learn, to desire, to know, to feel, to think, to act. That is what I want. And nothing less. That is what I must try for.   Katherine Mansfield

71

If ever there was anything written that one might copy out in capital letters, and hang on the wall opposite one's desk or bed, it is that.

How eternally thankful one should be for people like K.M. and Barbellion, and Tchekov, and Baudelaire. More than what they wrote, their lives and what they were help one to live.

Je parle de ce qui m'aide à vivre, de ce qui est bien. Je ne suis pas de ceux qui cherchent à s'égarer, à s'oublier, en n'aimant rien, en réduisant leurs besoins, leurs goûts, leurs désirs, en conduisant leur vie, c'est-à-dire la vie, à la répugnante conclusion de leur morts. Je ne tiens pas à me soumettre le monde par la seule puissance virtuelle de l'intelligence, je veux que tout me soit sensible, réel, utile, car ce n'est qu'à partir de là que je conçois mon existence. L'homme ne peut être que dans sa propre réalité. Il faut qu'il en ait conscience. Sinon, il n'existe pour les autres que comme un mort, comme un pierre ou comme du fumier. Eluard

Dear Eluard! It does one good to think of him, too. To have known him will always be one of the things that give me greatest pleasure and pride. Already I feel stronger, happier.

8.IV.37

I usually come back quite exhausted from spending a day in town; but tonight, though perhaps physically tired, I feel awake and stimulated (in spite of having had a slight but almost constant neuralgic headache all day long). It does one good to go out and look at the world after having spent weeks at home, brooding over a desk.

Yesterday afternoon, while dozing, was twice disturbed by the arrival of the red bicycle. The first telegram was from Hugh Sykes Davies, who is lying in Hendon Cottage Hospital after having been operated on for fistula, poor man; and the other from Audrey Beecham, whom I met at Oxford when I went up there to lecture last November, but whom I haven't seen or heard from since.

Found Hugh sitting up in bed eating a very good dinner in what is much more like a block of modern service-flats than a hospital. He had wanted to talk to me about 'business' but there was a pleasant black and green American girl there when I arrived, partaking of sherry and biscuits, and so we just chatted about, I think, dreams, and the novels of the Brontës. The 'business', when the American friend had gone, turned out to be in connection with the Surrealist group — which I have long since had no truck with and have been wondering how to get out of — a tedious and rather complicated affair which I can't be bothered to set down here; the gist of it being that Hugh has for some time been a *secret* member of the *Party,* and thinks that one ought to put up with being in the group in order to subvert 'well-known artists and intellectuals', like Read and Nash and Moore, into signing political manifestos occasionally; with which I quite agree. He wanted to tell me this because he had heard that Roger R. and Humphrey J. had announced their intention of leaving the group at the meeting that same evening, to which I was then going on, and to advise me not to follow suit, as I might very well have done.

In the tube, on the way from Hendon to Hampstead, was amused to find myself sitting opposite a tall young man — a Jew, I should think, slightly tatty, black Eden hat, long ill-kept hands, nervous cigarette, long thin nose a little red across the bridge, small aggressive eyes, nice forehead — who was engrossed in studying a brown-papercovered copy of Read's recent *Art and Society*. In my childish way, I wanted to lean over to him and say: 'I shall be seeing the author of said work in ten minutes' time!'

The surrealist meeting, at which all the boys were present except Moore and Hugh, was gloriously funny. Roughton and Jennings suggested that for various reasons the group should disband itself, which the group, presided over by a surprisingly astringent Read, indignantly refused to do. Abuse flew from corner to corner of Roland's polite, sumptously decorated drawing room. 'I'm sorry, but all that you've been saying is *absolute balls!*' Presently Humphrey, a very recent convert to the Party line ('And do you belong to the Party, then?' he is asked. 'No', he replies, 'I am not worthy!'), announced in tones of furious, long-tried patience: 'Well, now I'd like to read you a few lines from *Lenin* on the subject', and read a long passage from Lenin on dreams, implying that the dreams of those present were of the kind that fly off at a tangent and are of no service to the 'toiling masses of humanity', — a phrase which he continued to use every few minutes for the rest of the evening. Whereupon Nash, who had been being most consistently futile ever since he arrived, completely losing the point, remarked that he entirely agreed with Lenin, and that he thought the passage quoted most applicable to the group; and then relapsed into an absorption with his little pocket asthma-apparatus. In the end, R. and J. resigned (much to everyone's relief), and we all went downstairs to drink beer and whiskey. We have, however, succeeded in obtaining the requisite 'influential' signatures to the Intervention manifesto which is to appear in the group's name on the occasion of the Artists' International Congress. I took the MS to the printers this morning.

I stayed the night at Roland's and, when everyone had gone, stayed up talking with him for some time about

Breton's *L'amour fou,* and listening to his account of a recent visit to Paris and of going with Eluard, Nusch, Cécile and Picasso jr., to see Picasso's château out at Boisgeloup. Picasso jr., who was once a *Croix-de-feu* man and is now an ardent Communist, was very worried because the purple stripe was beginning to wear off the Spanish Government flag on the car's radiator. Roland has brought back a small new Picasso picture with him: very attractive, in blues and yellow, greys and white. Rosenberg had refused to show it in his gallery, because, he said, it was indecent; and when one looks at it closely one sees that part of the picture appears to be an underneath view of a woman with her legs stretched wide apart, with a sort of sun forming her head . . .

Had lunch today with Audrey Beecham, who is charming, fresh, with a broad felt hat and a scarf — at the Shanghai in Greek Street. Enid Starkie, who is up in London reading Rimbaud in the B.M., and a young man from Hamish Hamilton, were also there. Heard from A.B. that: (1) Auden has just been awarded the King's Medal for Poetry (I can't believe this), and that when he heard the news he waved his arms in the air with pleasure; (2) Spender is very upset and will probably *resign from the Party,* because Tony H. has been put in a concentration camp in Spain for having deserted from the International column to Valencia because he had shell-shock and wanted to be sent home on leave, which the Communists, who apparently boss everything in the column, refused to allow (I'm doubtful about this, too). Am meeting A.B. for tea tomorrow afternoon.

Wandered about during the rest of the afternoon looking for a copy of Chekhov's letters, which it was impossible to find. Bought *Candide,* which I have never read. Went to the London Gallery to see Herbert Bayer's exhibition; very slick and finished, but talented too. Some nice clean shapes. Herbert Bayer, who was present at the surrealist affair last night and walked out half-way through (I don't blame him), and who also appeared at the Shanghai during lunch-time, came into the gallery just as I was leaving. He works in a Berlin advertising firm, but is Austrian by nationality; anti-fascist; paints in secret and, if discovered, risks being sent to a concentration camp. Is handsome, sunburnt, with white teeth, dark eyes, dark lank hair. Went on to Rosenberg's new gallery in Bruton Street to see the Picasso show. It was surprising to find so many canvases that were moving, — rich, violent and profound. Many works which I had not liked the look of in reproduction have a mysterious magnificent life in their original colour (the birds have just begun to sing outside as I write this). Was particularly excited by a large picture of a young dreaming girl's head, distorted, pale, crowned with a strange green wreath, leaning forward across a table painted as though seen from the floor, looking upwards at its height, and with a blurred, stretched-out table-lamp standing just beyond reach of her jagged hands. (The birds are singing hard.)

As I walked back Piccadilly-circuswards, had a gradual acute feeling of it being six o'clock in the evening and still not dark. The gentle sky pearl-grey and blue. Faces and walls and windows were suddenly interesting, full of indefinite life. As I stood on the pavement in a close restless throng of people waiting to cross Shaftesbury Avenue, a woman's fur brushed across my cheek . . Had an idea for a story with a slight theme, to be called *Frühlingserwachen:* about a young man walking bored through the streets on a warm spring afternoon, with creaking shoes, and suddenly noticing something in a shop-window, perhaps a shiny bunch of asparagus tied with a green ribbon, which reminds him of a dream he had the night before, the memory of which turns his mood from boredom into a sort of restless nostalgia. Then he reaches the office where he works . . . 'His shoes creaked; it was a warm afternoon.' —

Having a quarter of an hour to wait before meeting Philip, I then went into one of those peculiar café places which call themselves 'Honeydew' and, in a setting of white alabaster tiles adorned with large bees alighting on umbrella-like clover-heads, drank a beverage consisting apparently of orange juice and honey. Round the walls, in wicker basket chairs, young men sat reading, tarts sat looking bored. To my right, one Jew said to another: 'I like you, but I can't do business with you!' I smoked a cigarette and left.

Philip arrived on the steps of St. Martin's at just the same moment as I. We went to the Chandos bar nearby and decided to go and see *Anna Christie* at the Westminster. To reach the theatre we walked through St. James' Park. It was getting dark by now, the garden gates were shut, the men working on the Coronation stands were going home. We walked on and on, talking, past groups of Australian soldiers, past indistinct figures on benches, into Buckingham Palace Road.

We were very impressed by the play. Flora Robson, as Anna, superlative, superb. Her extraordinary taut vibrancy, the impression she manages to convey of holding back an immense perpetual flow of nervous energy. When at last she does let herself go, there is a quite terrifying power in the harsh voice, the hard swift movements. Then she sinks back into a depressed exhaustion, but which is never really inert: the electricity is always smouldering. At the end of the play, when the curtain is about to fall on the curious happy ending which almost reaches the happy banality of real life, Anna and her father and her Irish sailorman, their glasses raised, suddenly hear the ominous note of a siren drifting through the fog outside the barge, and look up to the window, startled. — Curtain.

9.IV.37

At about half-past five this morning, went down to the island leading to the weir at Teddington lock, and experienced the most wonderful peace. The grey slowly moving sky, the moving water, grey-green and white, the seagulls swooping and plovers calling across the fields on the Surrey side of the river, the cold clean gardens on the other bank and not a living soul stirring within sound or sight except one old man tending a bonfire in the grounds of the Teddington film-studios which stretch down to the river on the Middlesex side — a confusion of pillars and planks and screens and rubbish. The sun glowed a rich butter-gold through the thin slow grey ridge of the clouds and then was covered up again. There was a strong smell of gum from the poplars on the island. It seemed incredible that London was so near.

10.IV.37

> J'ai cessé depuis longtemps de croire à la vertu des conseils autres que ceux que l'on peut se donner soi-même. Celui-ci pourtant, que vous saurez faire jaillir de la phrase de Mme. de Sevigné que je cite volontiers aux trop nombreaux jeunes gens . . . qui me demandent mon avis sur leurs érits: Quand je n'écoute que moi, je fais des merveilles.   André Gide, in a letter to a literary aspirant

I am often appalled to think how far I've got to go before I shall be anything like what I want to become. I've got so much to learn, and I learn so slowly and with such difficulty. 'If the novelist has any function in our age, it is to delineate the relationship of an individual to his class, on the basis of scientific materialism,' writes Charles Madge, in the latest number of the *Left Review*. 'While his function remains in abeyance, the novel will be no more than a plaything or a drug. It demands the most clear-cut and direct approach which can be found . . . The true and difficult art of the novelist and playwright is to leave no gap between symbolism and realism, and this art was mastered by Gogol, Tolstoy and Chekov in Russia; perhaps also by Ibsen, and in a provincial way by Hardy.' One might add at least Stendhal and Flaubert in France; and one might also add several other things of which the true and difficult art consists. But on the whole, though I should certainly have expressed it differently, I feel what Madge says to be extremely true; and in a clumsy way I have been trying to formulate for myself very much the same conclusion. Yet what long miles away I am from even beginning to be able to do this sort of thing. Before anything else, before tackling 'the unsolved problem of integrating fiction and history', the novelist has got to be able to:

(a) convince the reader of the independent existence of his characters *without describing* them at length, simply by means of a few living details, dropped in as though at random;

(b) present dialogue that does not sound like a series of monologues but conveys the impression of people speaking *to one another*, without knowing they are being overheard;

(c) avoid much use of descriptions of décor or atmosphere;

(d) avoid *explanations* of his characters' psychological difficulties, their relationships with one another or their position in society;

(e) deal efficiently with Time (he must not change from tempo to tempo in one chapter; one page must not deal with five minutes' action, when the next deals with the happenings of a year, etc. etc.);

(f) have a clear, fixed attitude both to his story and to his audience: detached, but not indifferent; etc.

He must be so practiced in doing these things that he does them instinctively, without conscious deliberation. (Everyone who writes *knows* all this, of course; I am writing it down simply to remind myself, so as to have it in front of me.)

The writer need not bother about his purpose until he has mastered his technique (I hate both words). I have plenty of purpose, but practically no technique.

And in spite of agreeing so definitely with Madge's remarks, I still want to be a moralist. Or rather, I want first to be clear in my mind as to the relation of the moral to the social question. At present, I still feel that I want to write so as to help other people to live, and I still don't quite believe that it helps much simply to 'delineate the relationship of an individual to his class'. I still feel that it is more important to teach how to understand and to love one's fellow beings; and how to develop 'a sense of existence'. That, at any rate, is what Chekov did, before delineating the relationship of his characters to their class, though he did that also.

'*Quand je n'écoute que moi, je fais des merveilles*' —

Yes, but what young writer nowadays dare listen only to himself? Twenty years ago perhaps it was different. Gide, Proust, Joyce, etc., cannot have felt under any moral compunction to affect their readers in any particular way, or

80

to integrate fiction and history or deal with the relationship of the individual to society. They simply wrote down what they thought was the truth about this and that (marriage, homosexuality, jealousy, a Dublin Jew), because they wanted to. Katherine Mansfield, in her journal, for instance, though constantly worried about her ability and the amount she wrote, never for a moment seemed to doubt whether she *ought* to write about people and things as she did.

It may be that one ought not to let oneself be too much concerned with these questions, just as one ought not to be conscious of the peculiar psychological mechanism which causes one to write about one thing rather than another . . . Anyway, it's more than likely that I shan't produce anything worth very much till I'm about forty, if I ever reach that age. But I do believe that if ever I reach the goal which is now gradually taking shape in my ambitious mind, I shall be among those who will have helped to set literature going in a quite new direction, corresponding to a new direction of society — not socialist realism (of the 'May Day' kind), nor surrealist romanticism, but propaganda for being equally conscious of oneself and of society, of the dream and of reality, of the moral and of the political. Meanwhile, one must keep one's nose to the immediate grindstone.

11.IV.37

Artist: poet. Poet, artist: someone with a special sense of existence. *'La poésie doit être fait par tous. Non par un.'* Everyone should be a poet in that everyone should have a (special) sense of existence. When everyone living is fully alive, the function of the professional artist as he is known today will be extinct.

Last Friday, saw Audrey Beecham again: delighted by her sudden occasional lapses into a seriousness almost confidential. Feel perfectly at ease with her. We might get to know one another very well if it were not that she works in Oxford all the time. Some day, perhaps . . . One never knows who are going to be the important people in one's life when one first meets them . . .

Later (at the end of an exhausting day most of which was spent wandering about doing nothing), met Philip. We went to Dorice Fordred's together. Josef Bard and Eileen Agar, the Farjeons and the Potters were there. Eileen wearing a dress with AMOUR written all over it. Stephen Potter delivered a mock lecture on Sir Thomas Browne in the spirit of *The Muse in Chains* and J.B. told stories about the Emperor Francis Joseph . . .

Philip. I keep congratulating myself on having an intimate friend of my own age, with much the same background, the same enthusiasms. Have become extremely fond of him. There are so few people with whom one is glad to share oneself.

Seem to have fallen today into a lax, demoralised state of semi-torpor, chiefly due I think to sheer physical fatigue, a thing I seldom admit to. The thought of all the human energy necessary to keep the world going makes me feel faint.

Ashamed to admit that I have written very little this week, and *April* is still unfinished. I *must* get it done with by Tuesday. Tomorrow I shall have to use a little discipline and determination. Get up at 8.30. Write from 9 till 1. Rest after lunch till 2.30. Write till 4. After tea, write journal, letters, etc. Write again after supper till 12.

No hope of ever getting anywhere except by *incessant* work.

12.IV.37

The arrival this morning of a postcard from George Barker has rather upset my plan to finish *April* by Wednesday. I am going to meet him tomorrow morning at 11.30 on the British Museum steps.

I have not done nearly enough work today! I always seem to fall asleep in the afternoon; and if I do, I dream. Yesterday it was about what Audrey Beecham told me about Spender and Tony H., but I can't remember it distinctly; today's I can't remember at all. (Extraordinary dream lately about a Flying Cow, which landed in a quiet twilit field on the edge of a wood, at each of the four corners of which stood a *double sheep!* i.e. two sheep with a single head, and with long ears like a judge's wig.)

How very remote the memory of going to Barcelona last October has become! It seems like a dream, or something I once read. Turning out a drawer yesterday and coming across some photos that Roland took there reminded me of it. I should like to write down everything I can remember about it before I forget too much. But there isn't enough room here for everything.

In the Barrio Chino in Barcelona there was a cabaret which we went to several times. They did the Quadro Flamenco there. It was a large room with a square platform in the middle, and balconies round the walls with boxes beneath them. The cheaper seats consisted of chairs grouped round the platform. In the boxes lurked stray whores, though there was a notice up to say that they did not belong to the building. The audience, as far as I remember, was made up chiefly of militiamen and sailors. One evening Mirravitles, the Propaganda Minister, came in (an intellectual friend of Dali, with whom he was once implicated in a plot to assassinate

Alfonso) with a lot of people from the Propaganda office where I worked, and sat in the balcony. Our party, in which were Roland and Valentine, Christian Zervos and Yvonne, Fernandez and Tzara, were sitting underneath.

In one corner of the balcony, above the performers' entrance, sat the orchestra — a curious, tinny little band of about five instruments, which played a kind of jazz so naive in its arrangement that the effect almost had something of the sophistication of Kurt Weill. They struck up a tune, and one of the girls came running on to the middle of the platform, wearing the sort of thing one might have expected to see in Paris cabarets in the 'Twenties (top-hat, brassiere, short black silk knickers, etc.) and sang a nasal song. This was repeated for about an hour. There were only four or five girls, none of them had much of a voice, and their songs, their gestures, their 'dances' — a sort of quick walk round and round the edge of the platform, bending the knees occasionally or kicking in the air, moving the hands fanwise, etc. — were all exactly alike. (Except for one girl, quite unlike the rest, who had a simple, rather touching face, and who came on wearing an Andalusian peasant's costume and sang an urbanised version of an extraordinarily sad, angry plaint of a folk song, in a good clear voice, with expressive movements and a tragic contraction of her black eyebrows.) After a time, the effect became hypnotic, and oddly pleasing. There was one gnarled and ancient sailor-man in the audience who, whenever one of the plumper girls passed by near to where he was sitting, in her prowl round the edge of the platform, would stretch forth his bony decrepit hand to touch her legs or belly, to the huge enjoyment of the audience. (The Zervos' afterwards said that he must have been paid by the management.)

Then came an interval, during which a man wearing a pair of bright green trousers, which looked as though they had been made from the cloth of a billiard table, mounted the platform and read a long Governmental proclamation about the rules to be observed by those presenting variety entertainments during the Civil War. In at least one clause — about 'excessive frivolity', whatever that implied, being strictly forbidden — the influence of Anarchist morality, which tends towards puritanism, was clearly apparent. When he had finished, everyone applauded and cried 'Salud!'

After the interval, chairs were brought on to the platform, and the Quadro Flamenco team appeared. There were three men, a guitarist, a dancer and a singer, and two women, wearing the authentic Spanish costume — combs, shawls, heavily flounced skirts, carnations behind the ears — and laughing and chatting rather nervously as they sat down. They were an amazing contrast to the little singers who had gone before, and immediately made the first half of the entertainment seem trivial and quite superfluous. These were *women*, strong and finely built, — elementally feminine. One had a gross, rather terrifying face, with a slight squint, and wore a permanent expression of grim merriment; the other, though taller, seemed more dark and fine and had a subtler smile. The guitarist began to plink-plink-plonk, and the singer and the dancers to clap their hands and stamp their feet in time with him. When they had all got thoroughly 'warmed up', and were shouting intermittent remarks to one another, one of the women suddenly sprang from her chair and began to dance — crouching, stamping, then drawing herself up with superb defiance, her head thrown back, one hand on her hip, the strong fingers of the other hand clicking in the air. When she had subsided, the man danced, drumming his heels magnificently, turning his body at the hips with lean ferocity; and then the other woman, the taller one, whose arms moved like threshers, and whose face wore an extraordinary sphinx-like smile, both blissful and savage. The clapping and stamping grew louder, the shouts of encouragement more frequent (they generally cry: 'That's the way they dance in Sevilla!' but this time we heard one woman calling out: 'That's the way they used to dance where the Germans are!'). And finally, both women took up castanets and danced together, with ultimate abandon, crossing and crossing, sinking and tossing, now back to back, now round and round, now face to face, the ebonies rattling round their heads. They were more like mountains dancing than women! I have never seen anything so aweinspiring. When it was over, all too soon, they ran from the platform and would not come back again however much we applauded. There was a pause. Only the singer and the guitarist were left; the lights were lowered and the other chairs taken away. The guitarist began to strum softly. The singer was a small, dark man, wearing a black jacket and tie and a plain white shirt, and sat huddled slightly forward, with his hands hanging between his knees, looking at the floor in front of him. He had the pathetic appearance of a Charlie Chaplin without the moustache. After a time he raised his head, fixed the back of the hall with weary eyes and opened his mouth: the sound did not come out immediately, but seemed to linger in his throat. There is nothing else quite like the improvisations of these popular singers, with their long, apparently aimless phrases and intricate jerks and convolutions, at the end of which, if the phrase is a particularly good one, the audience cry 'Olé, Olé!' They have the same profound melancholy and *Sehnsücht* as is to be heard in the songs of the Russians, or the call to prayer from an Arab mosque.

On the following Sunday, the 17th of November, we were watching the five-hour-long procession in honour of the Russian Revolution passing by; among the contingents of the various trades unions, I noticed that of the variety-performers; many of the singers and dancers we had seen at the cabaret (though not the flamenco ones) were among those marching.

In an interview reported in tonight's *Evening Standard* the Infanta Eulalia states that Alfonso gave £2,000,000 to the cause of Franco. 'Ex-King Alfonso', she added, 'is as bewildered as anyone else. I am very sorry for General Franco, who is a nice intelligent boy, and an idealist who believes he will win.'

The last words of Virginia Woolf's long new novel, which rambles on from 1800 into the present, are: 'The sun had risen, and the sky above the houses wore an air of extraordinary beauty, simplicity and peace.' I suppose she's right in a way; but how many novelists nowadays could end a book like that? I wouldn't dare to.

13.IV.37

This has been the most extraordinary day (or rather yesterday was — it's the 14th now, about 4 in the morning). Nothing definite happened to me personally at all; in fact in many ways it was a deplorable day, one of the kind I usually dislike most; and yet a great deal seems to have happened to me inwardly; I seem to have *understood* a great deal more. The effect, possibly, of seeing a lot of people after a practically uninterrupted solitude of several weeks. Yet this solitude and withdrawing is *good*; I ought to take other people — or most of them — only in small doses at a time.

87

Met Barker and had lunch with him and had a long, difficult talk. At last began to make him see where I am trying to get to, and why. (Could say more than this, but it is very complicated.) Arranged to meet him again, with Antonia and Emily, at 7.

Left Barker at Faber & Faber's at 3 p.m., and walked to Piccadilly Circus, where I was just about to ring up Antonia, when who should I walk straight into but:

Dylan Thomas and Caitlin Macnamara.

Walked with them as far as Villiers Street, where they were going to a cinema to see *The Golem*. (On the way, in Leicester Square, Dylan got a lump of dust in his eye and we had to take him to a chemists to have an eye-bath. Really rather repulsive as he sat there with his inflamed eye and ugly nose, his face thrown back, the boracic dripping between his corduroyed knees; but one did not feel repulsed, all the same.) He apparently intends to marry Caitlin M. in a few days' time. She is small — florid in miniature, with an incipient Roman nose — blonde, *almost* fluffy, wearing a brick-red coat and skirt. She says very little. My first impression was of a hard innocence, obtuse, hermetic, and a concealed but very precise knowledge of how to deal with anyone she might want to deal with. (This may be all wrong; I have never pretended to be a good judge of character, and am often very unfair to people on first impressions.)

Until quite recently, Dylan has been living with Emily Coleman who was 'in love' with him. Yesterday or the day before, he confronted her with Caitlin M., whom he announced his intention of marrying almost at once. — To put it baldly.

Rang up Antonia, to tell her I was meeting her and Emily and George at a pub in the evening, and to tell her about encountering Dylan. Emily has just met Humphrey J. again for the first time since they quarrelled.

To go back further: Emily was at one time in love with George, George is (or was) attracted to Antonia (at any rate, they are very close friends), and a strong undeveloped sympathy exists between G.B. and myself.

(*Je m'en fous de* human relationships of this kind as such: I have not got a gossipy mind: but the web of circumstance and coincidence has become so peculiarly complicated that I cannot resist recording it — what I have written down here is necessarily a mere shorthand skeleton of something which has impressed me far more deeply than the rather futile mix-up in the lives of a group of literary people which it appears to be.)

Went to the London Library, read the April *N.R.F.* (more pages from Gide's *Journal* — the poor man can no longer write anything else — some new short poems by Eluard; and a very good review of Breton's *L'amour fou* by Roland de Rennéville), and took away Drieu la Rochelle's *Journal d'un homme trompé*, I don't quite know why, and Henry James' *In the Cage*, chosen finally at random from a whole row of shelves full of James, whom I have never been able to read before.

Went and had tea at the Kardomah in Piccadilly and started to read James. *Enormous* pleasure, from the very first page. This was probably the most important encounter of the day. I've already got masses to say about him — but more of J. later. One particularly good sentence thrilled me: 'After the long stupors, at all events, there almost always suddenly would come a sharp taste of something; it was in her mouth before she knew it; it was in her mouth now.'

Went off at 7 in a mood of high exaltation to meet the company at the appointed pub. Met Barker outside and found Emily already waiting inside. Antonia arrived shortly afterwards. Then the evening began.

I really cannot think what made Emily arrange for us to meet in Fitzrovia (which I heartily detest); suppose she picked up the habit from Dylan. The usual blurry chaos ensued. Ruthven Todd arrived, very drunk, with a long story about fighting a gang of toughs; and Nina Hamnett, of course, also drunk and with long stories about everybody one has ever heard of; odd lesbians; vaguely literary young men; a rather nice sculptor called Richard Hughes; a young upper-class Cambridge friend of apparently everybody — and God knows who else! One's head went round. George very wisely left less than half way through the evening. When the pub closed we all went to another, then in a taxi to the Café Royal, then to some Soho café-bar place, Ruthven getting more and more maudlin and incoherent, and the subject of Emily and Dylan and Caitlin M. incessantly recurring. (Emily seems to be 'bearing up under the strain' marvellously well, as they say, but Antonia seems to think this is a danger signal.) This sort of thing usually overwhelms me, I get more and more depressed and dumb and finally go home feeling quite dead. But this evening I somehow managed to keep my head and to take in everything that was going on all around. It was extremely complicated. For once, I even quite enjoyed it all, in a detached and wondering way.

The whole point being:

(a) the impingement of worlds;

(b) the illusion of human intercourse ('There is no conversation').

One hardly dares to use expressions so forbidding; and naturally I haven't worked it all out quite yet. But walking back to Waterloo across Hungerford footbridge at 1.30 ('*L'énivrante monotonie du métal, du marbre et de l'eau*' etc. '*Ce matin encore l'image, vague et lointaine, me ravit.*'), and coming back in the slow journalists' train, had an intense conviction that I had tracked down the germ of what may develop into enough material to get me started writing for good. I mean, if I can get this clear, I shall have 'found myself' and whatever it is that I am meant to do.

14.IV.37

The impingement of worlds — peculiar that I should have chanced upon Henry James like that (of course, it all fits in), because I have a feeling that this is going to turn out to be what I shall discover to constitute the *underlying* theme of all his work. It is a theme very closely connected with the ideas of *A Quiet Mind*; unexpected disturbance into awakenedness caused by the impingement; all the oddly uncomfortable sensations caused by the breaking of familiar habits, moving into a new house, seeing the dawn come in, and so on. The peculiar upsets caused by the intrusion of — what? — well, say sensitivity, 'sense of life', genius, etc. — into mediocrity. The life-long complacancy shattered by the chance acquaintance. The unbalancing effect of foreign travel upon a bank-clerk. The employer suddenly made to see himself through the eyes of one of his employees . . . It is a theme of endless fascination, with countless possible variations and sub-divisions, and a most effective vehicle for disguised subversion. (It might be used with a purely aesthetic purpose: but that is not enough.)

The related theme, 'there is no conversation', is the accessory negative to its positive. The tendency of all disturbances to subside. (Nothing is quite the same again afterwards, but — .) The impingements are always *accidental*. One's course may be altered, but when one resumes one's way, one is just as alone as before. In the James story, for instance, the other world impinges even through the bars of a cage; but the bars remain. It is really shocking to see how everyone collides about in their own world, completely oblivious, almost all the time, of everyone else's. What impressed me most last night was the way everyone was so utterly at cross-purposes, unable to understand anyone else's objective even for a moment. Emily and Antonia misunderstanding one another, Emily not really understanding Dylan or he Emily, Barker unable to understand Ruthven, and everyone else around making the most fantastic mistakes at every moment, and nobody, except Antonia, having even the faintest idea about me . . . I don't in the least complain; that's how it always is. Perhaps they were all inwardly impatiently wringing their hands over their inability to make themselves understood; but I think not. After all, one has to resign oneself to being hermetic; one can even be thankful for it, I feel, so long as one is not unconscious of the possibility of an 'impingement' now and then, and is ready for it when it comes.

The only remedy: Cast out Fear.

Human beings are at present unable to understand either themselves or those outside them, because they are too *afraid* to. From a Marxist point of view, I suppose, this fear is the inevitable result of a system of ruthless competition.

17.IV.37

Finished *April* yesterday afternoon, with great relief, after having worked on the last chapter the whole of the previous night. Took the MS up to Cobden-Sanderson in rather an exhausted state. Masses of white blossom and fresh green all along the line going up in the train; pale hazy sky. In the evening met Sheila Legge and wasted precious mental energy in talking to her too much, with no returns. Unsatisfactory.

Under the surface I am getting very restless again. Must keep this greed for people under control; it's not good for one's work.

Warning: when you think you've got hold of a new idea or point of view, don't dissipate all your enthusiasm by talking about it to everyone you know. (This is what Humphrey Jennings does, though, and it doesn't seem to do him any harm; or perhaps he would produce more work if he could check the verbal flow a little more?)

19.IV.37

Kay came down today, and after lunch we walked from Richmond back along the Thames to Teddington. The Spring full out, in wild exuberance of fresh leaf and blossom everywhere. Felt not *quite* at ease with Kay, though I do not want to say so, for she is very dear. But somehow — why is this? Firstly, I think, because, as I said to her, our relationship, which began as the relationship of what were then hardly more than two children, has gone on and on with hardly any change, when it is not really possible now that it should be the same. Secondly because our outlooks intercept but do not meet . . . I feel that somehow how she does not fully appreciate the things in me which I most want her to appreciate. On the purely human plane we can communicate, but I want someone with whom I can also communicate on the *inhuman* plane, which is something she will never reach. I can speak her language, but she can't speak mine. It sounds selfish and arrogant to say this perhaps, but I know it's true, and I want no illusions about it, because I believe that the only fully satisfactory human relationships are those in which *everything* is both shared and appreciated, communicated and understood; and since I have always believed that my relationship with Kay was something important and enduring in my life, I want to make up my mind as to whether I can continue to believe it is so in spite of this handicap. . . After a time perhaps, if I were married to her, I could teach her my own difficult language (which I can speak, for instance, with Antonia and Philip — and possibly Roland C.); but at present she seems quite satisfied as to the adequacy of her own: and after all, why should she not be?

— 'D.G., incessantly on the self-regard . . .'

— 'That may be so; but have you never thought that it might be more satisfactory for other people in your relations with them if you knew a little more about yourself ? '

Il s'agit, en premier lieu, de tout remarquer, en soi comme en dehors de soi: Il s'agit de donner ainsi à toutes les énergies, l'occasion de se creuser les canaux dont elles ont besoin pour leur action.   Keyserling

It is a question of learning to suffer life: *not* in the sense of *passively* suffering it to happen to one, but in the sense that suffering (pain) is one's most *active* experience, since it forces itself upon one's consciousness more definitely and inescapably than any other state.

What I mean by the *inhuman* plane, above, is the plane of *knowledge*, of knowing and judging other human beings with the hardness that must accompany an absence of illusions; of accepting this kind of hardness; of accepting the essential bitterness of life (which does not mean to say that one can perceive *only* its bitterness or that one is necessarily a pessimist); I say bitterness with the same intention that I say suffer: one is *most aware* of a sharp, bitter taste.

(It is on this plane that Kay, for instance, does not wish to or cannot accompany a person of whom she is fond only in the expectation of mutual warmth.)

20.IV.37

'Something great but obscure is striving to express itself through me', I once quoted before. The whole development of my thought during the last few months seems to me now to be leading in a direction from which one might form the conclusion that I was meant to be a teacher, or preacher: one who makes propaganda for a morality or a personal philosophy. That's what I meant when I said that I wanted what I wrote to help others to live (and to be honest, this is not pure altruism — the idea of influencing other people or exerting some sort of power over them alarms but fascinates me more and more). 'How seriously he takes himself !' one would say, and of course it is difficult enough not to see the absurdity there is in suggesting such a rôle for oneself — (but why, *enfin*, should I trouble to excuse myself to those whose imaginary objections could result only from a narrow incomprehension: for it is really a question of not taking oneself seriously at all) . . .

All through history there have been those who taught *the Way;* and it is not difficult to see that all these Ways, of different epochs and peoples and civilizations, are essentially the same. It seems to me that modern man is in dire need of having the Way redefined for him in terms that he can understand, terms that include all that one can think of in the way of the steadily increasing objective knowledge brought in by this century — Marx and Freud, etc. There can be no hope for the Revolution unless it is accompanied by a great *spiritual* awakening and rebirth. This cannot be accomplished, I am convinced, until the last remnant of the official ideology of Christianity has been swept away.

Everything is forming a gradual coherence in my head.

The Way is what Keyserling calls Creative Understanding.

The Way is in its nature dialectical. Thus it is both active and passive, and sees no contradiction in apparent opposites; out of its active acceptance of both love and hate, creation and destruction — of both exterior and interior life — of both faith and disillusionment, pride and humility, — of both the conscious and the unconscious — of both the political and the moral — it creates a new unity and integration, a new and deeper sense of life, which alone can give back to human existence that full significance which has been lost in the disintegrating process of the decline of the old society.

Not an intellectual, but one who experiences knowledge, or rather, thinks with his whole self, not only his brain. The intellectual mind does not understand creatively, but only follows the superficial appearance of a given problem; it does not learn or experience. Intellectual activity should balance, reinforce, accompany the activity of the emotions, not suppress them or form a substitute for them.

Extract from a letter from Antonia:

The only trouble with you is that you are too lady-like: you make us all feel coarse. James was lady-like too, and it made him fall into the trap he most feared — vulgarity. It stops him from being a first-class artist. He made the mistake of selecting *beforehand*; one must accept everything and select *afterwards*. In the end, James' books are eunuchs: they produce no new *life*. What you can learn from him is a superb *method*. He confuses *chastity* and *castration*.

I believe for once I quarrel with the New Testament. I think it is better to be damned *whole* than saved with only one eye.

Extract from a letter to Antonia:

Very good remarks about being lady-like, chastity and castration. But they really don't apply to me! If there's one thing I *do* refuse to be responsible for, it's for making anyone feel *coarse*. The difference between 'coarseness' and 'refinement' is entirely artificial; and if anyone really does 'feel coarse' (which I can't quite believe) that's their lookout (outlook?) . . . But of course, all that side of James is simply laughable: the idiotic conception of refined society — and so on. But it's possible that he intended it to be so. A great artist must be capable of dealing with the nuances, the excitements and disturbances *within mediocrity*; and if it's in the nature of mediocrity to think in terms of 'coarseness' and 'refinement', then he must make use of such terms, if his reflection is to be a faithful one.

21.IV.37
Completely deserted by all *élan vital*.

Must *work* tomorrow.

22.IV.37

Yesterday *was* a bad day (but I think I know why: and it's *not* going to happen again). I'm in the middle of an article in French *(Notes sur la poésie en Angleterre)* which I should like to get into the *N.R.F.* Can't get on with *Oliver Middleton's Confession* till I've finished this, so I must try to get it done with today.

It's grim determination that is needed. To hang on by one's teeth. To push and push. All other difficulties fade into comparative insignificance so long as one does not *waste time.* There is nothing more exhausting than inertia. So long as one keeps moving, one is more or less safe. I must try to evolve a technique for getting out of ruts as soon as I fall into them.

Finish letter to C.

Write to G.L.M.[*]

Write to Eunice and send article on Barcelona.

Send poems to Grigson.

26.IV.37

The matter with me is that I've never learnt to concentrate; and am too apt to make excuses for myself.

An Adventure

One day last week, went for a walk down a road where I'd never been before. Past deserted playing-fields on one side and large ugly houses with unkempt gardens sloping down to the river on the other. It was about six o'clock, a windy evening, with a tangled conglomeration of clouds in a wet sky and a queer light in the air. In one of the gardens I passed by

---

[*] Guy Lévis-Mano, poet-publisher.

were the remains of a demolished house and a couple of men were quietly engaged in pulling down a tree. Presently came upon a backwater of the Thames, at right-angles to the road, with two rows of gardens and large, dreary, empty-looking late-Victorian houses backing onto it, on both sides. Conservatories and wooden balconies and so on, and weather-worn paint-work. But what struck me most, apart from the sluggish water and the dilapidated unused boat-houses at the bottom of the lawns, was that the house at the end nearest the road by which I had come had a sunken garden with a green pool and a leaden Cupid and a lot of tall trees standing round, in the midst of which was *a magnolia tree* in full bloom, with its pinky-white yellow-stained petals dropping profusely all over the flagstones and the water of the little pond. As I stood there looking, it began to rain, very gently. It was all most strange.

Kew. Went yesterday to Kew with Philip and saw a lot more magnolias, and early rhododendrons and flowering prunus and cherry and double cherry and in fact masses of blossom of every kind, of every conceivable shade of pink and white. Sat by the edge of the lake in a semi-dazed condition, staring at the young foliage of the trees on the island in the middle and vaguely observing the Chinese waterfowl. There was a white feather hovering in the air just in front of us, I don't know where it came from; suddenly a small bird dashed onto the scene, snapped at the floating feather in mid-flight and bore it away to line its nest with!

Philip has decided to stay on at his job, as he will get the editorship later. So we shan't be going to Cornwall after all. I never really thought it would come off! Am thinking of going to stay near Plymouth for the summer instead. It's money that's the devil!

Have been reading Plato's *Phaedrus* and am just going to read *The Banquet*. Must have been a Platonist all along and have never known it before!

Have made friends with a charming brother and sister who live just round the corner here. The boy is 19, the girl a year or so younger. Both sensitive, intelligent, impressionable. She: 'I don't know why, but I always seem to end all my sentences in the middle with "I don't know"!' He: 'Oh, that's just a phase you're passing through . . .' He occasionally has a curious violin-like note in his voice, and has very attractive eyes. We all went down to the weir the other night and sat on the island till two in the morning, talking and watching the moon scatter its light across the water — then withdraw behind a film of cloud. There was a mysterious fire blazing in the middle of the Ham gravel-pit fields on the other side of the river.

27.IV.37
Tedium vitae.

29.IV.37
Djuna Barnes (in conversation): 'I looked out of the fucking ship, and there was the whole lopsadaisy sea upon its ear . . .'

5.V.37

Depuis quelques jours je néglige ce journal. J'ai tort: je traverse actuellement une crise sentimentale dont je serai content, un jour, de posséder quelques documents.

Il est probable qu'alors j'aurais de mes sentiments d'à présent
une opinion différente, comme déjà j'envisage ma liaison avec —
tout autrement que je ne l'envisageais quand — vivait encore. Mais
à cette époque j'avais dix-huit ans et je prenais plaisir à vivre
d'illusions ou plutôt je n'avais pas encore appris l'art difficile de
la franchise envers soi-même. . .

Valéry Larbaud: *Journal d'A. O. Barnabooth*

10.V.37

This, then — the interruption of a carefully sustained regularity
in keeping the entries in this journal going — is due to my
having *fallen in love*. Back pages could have shown that it
was coming — even though not quite *how*: *that* was too oddly
complicated for prediction. So here we are! The grand old
impatience once again upon its rocking-horse; the not so
grand difficulties — which seem to have got both of us, this
time (Joan and I — and I hadn't even mentioned her name in
this book before!) upon skewers; the old sense of being
dangled on a string above the enigmatic future . . . the whole
conspiracy, in fact. Economics as always, always, are the
impasse, the familiar cul-de-sac. What *am* I to do? The hole
seems desperate — perhaps only a wild leap can get one out.
And this is what comes of having continually evaded the old
problem of financial independence. *Everything would be*
solved, if that were solved — life, love, work and all. I must
have been mad to think that I could go on like this until
'something happened', as though it would happen of its own
accord.

It looks as though I shall again be hurling myself at
London, in one of those expeditions in search of help which
sometimes seem more than anything like the futile fluttering
of wings against the bars of a cage, very shortly. If only the

whole place were not so utterly engrossed in all the ugly, exasperating stupidity of its Coronation celebrations! I feel like running away to sea, except that that would solve nothing at all, but would be simply a very spectacular repetition of all the previous evasions.

Ugh, ugh, ugh!

Profound restlessness and dissatisfaction — almost as bad as last September. But it doesn't do any good to keep on hammering at the thing.

Just a fortnight ago today, I simply walked out of the house in a sudden fit of exasperation, and walked nearly all the way to London, with some vague idea of going to try to see Cobden-Sanderson about money. By the time I got to town, it was past five and C.S. had all gone home. Met Antonia and, at Henekey's, got involved with her in an evening with Norman Cameron and Dylan, which ended, as I too well remember, in a gruesome scene at A's flat (Norman was not there, then) with A. and Dylan pretending to play 'wolf-dogs' on the carpet and altogether getting on each other's nerves in a bad way, till I blunderingly tried to stop them and succeeded in putting Dylan's back up. 'Where are the halo and the wings,' he asked, 'of Tony's guardian angel?' ('He is *not*,' she remarked, of Dylan, 'a child of light.' We none of us felt like one. It was very miserable.)

6.VI.37

Etre un grand homme et un saint pour soi-même, *voilà l'unique chose importante.*

Parce que je comprends une existence glorieuse, je me crois capable de la réaliser. O Jean-Jacques!

Donnez-moi la force de faire immédiatement mon devoir tous
les jours et de devenir ainsi un héros et un Saint.   Baudelaire

Seem to have been through a lot during the past month: to have reached the bottom of something: to have got *beyond* depression, melancholy, etc. But seem also, somehow, to have lost hold . . . Back again in the pit: hatred of the existent world, revolt, impotence, disgust —

At heart I must always have been an anarchist. Hatred of mediocrity: my most profound ambition to escape from it. It is not however, tragic to be enmeshed in futility while knowing all the while in what nobility consists: it is still futile. One escapes from futility only by *constant energy, constant work* (perhaps not even then). To plead 'fatal' weakness, physical incapacity, does not raise one's case to a tragic plane.

Energy is a form of love. Is it to be attained by the exertion of the will? Supreme effort.

In Dejection

Misery of my life. Profound dissatisfaction with myself and circumstances. This continual plaint! During the past weeks have I not often thought of suicide? *Mais je suis un lache!* Or is it that I have never quite lost faith in the possibility that I have a destiny to fulfil, the fruit of which can only be reaped by holding on through all the periods of blackest fog? Absurdity! Accomplishment, success, acknowledgement seem so endlessly far away and my capacity for application so very small: but it is not that I want these things so desperately for themselves, but rather that I must in some way *justify* my *amour-propre*. (No-one would know how complete a failure it would be for me to come to nothing, since no-one but I knows how immoderate is my ambition . . .) Ever since I was a child I have secretly believed myself to be an exception, someone unlike the rest, someone set apart to do something, get somewhere. And what have I done to prove this so far? Nothing, or next to nothing. I have *got* somewhere, yes, I believe I have; but that is purely intimate, there is nothing to show for it to the world. (But you are not ready for that yet, I tell myself . . .)

Everything I have produced so far, every small success, seems to be ridiculous and contemptible. And at the same time, how weary and impatient I can get of my own grandiosity! Nevertheless, I know quite certainly what I want: to achieve significance and coherence, to achieve spiritual greatness; not to betray myself, not to appear ridiculous or futile in the eyes of my judges. To be worthy of Pascal, Kierkegaard, Dostoievski, Baudelaire, Rimbaud, Nietzsche . . . (And perhaps these names will change during the course of my development and it will no longer be of them but of others that I shall wish to be worthy.)

Meanwhile, there are terrible warnings. My worst enemy, whom I fear the most: myself. All that weak, contemptible side of my nature, which is continually standing between me and my ambition, which has no stamina, which is continually wanting to go to sleep, to dream comfortable dreams, I have come to associate with my grandfather. How I wish that I could have known him before he died, and what a curious affection I have for him, whom I never even saw and about whom I know so little! Had I known him, I might have a more precise knowledge of what I have to combat; I know quite enough, however, to get seriously alarmed at times.

To remember: the life of Haydon. To check the insidious canker that is vanity. Moral rot. The Catholics are perhaps right in making spiritual pride one of the deadliest sins.

('Pride counterbalancing all miseries. Man either hides his miseries, or, if he disclose them, glories in knowing them.' *Pascal*, 405) Not that I care about sinning against a God in whom I cannot believe. But if God is in a sense oneself . . . ?

Present necessity, it seems to me, to win a moral victory over myself, to strengthen my character. Immediate opportunity to do this: in 'facing up to' certain things I have for too long preferred not to consider, which I *know* at the back of my mind but which cause me pain to think about: 1. That I should do myself a lot of good by conquering my childish cowardice about going to the dentist's. 2. That I ought to admit that I am not in love with J., that I have made a fool of myself, duped myself with a deliberate wilful illusion about my feeling for her, and generally behaved like a stupid college-boy. 3. That I could, if I really wanted to, by means of determined effort, get a foot into the 'necessary' world through the half-open door of 'N & D'.

7.VI.37

L'aube fait son apparition à trois heures du matin ces jours-ci — c'est un peu trop tôt. Combien l'habitude m'est devenu naturel de rester éveillé toute la nuit! Quelle vie irrégulière je mène, à la fin. Il faut la régler un peu.

The rate of one's growth is alarming; how I have matured during the last year. Ripe at last — once the sorry affair of last month is disposed of — for an *adult* love affair . . . Pondering this, also, I realise my tendency to lag behind long after the event in acquiring experience. Moreover, I *learn* instinctively, very quickly, but it takes me a long time to be able to make use of what I have learnt in practice.

Have been thinking again a great deal, lately, of Roland C. Half against my will, am forced to consider that *that,* perhaps, is the most real thing that ever happened to me. Against my will, because I *wish* to take a success first of all of the 'normal', the other is too easy, too *lache*. None the less, the strong feeling I have for C. — physical and intellectual, curiously combined, 'tested' by the sort of scepticism which accompanies it (being detached from and almost hostile to him in some ways makes no difference and this very fact that it does not, proves the strength of the attachment) — still continues; and if he returns next winter, it is possible that the whole thing, reciprocal this time, will flare up again into — Ah, Roland, Roland, why are you not here, and why have I not written to you? Truly there are some people who are quite incomprehensible, even to themselves.

Still bruised by the fall to earth out of the illusion that I was in love with Joan S., find myself still as unsatisfied as ever. This ridiculous, pernicious valve, the heart! (And how we all revel in the havoc it plays with our lives!) What makes the possibility of satisfaction a thousand times more unlikely than it should be, is my perversely restricted capacity to find 'the right face'. 99 women in 100 leave me quite indifferent, without a quiver of sexual emotion. All the more, then, do I need to find the 100th. She exists (and obviously there is more than one 100th woman in the world). — Striking image of the condition of my sexual life: On a Tube platform the other day, my attention riveted by a young woman talking to an elderly man. Followed them into the carriage, and found myself standing a few feet distant from them. *Coup de foudre.* Gracile limbs, a certain appropriate neat *fantaisie* in dress, easy movements, and the face and eyes! — full of extraordinary animation and intelligence. In a wide-ranged, very slightly strident voice, she was arguing with the man in a foreign language (Italian? Central European?). Type: Maureen

O'Sullivan, without that hint of a broad nose, that tendency to heaviness of the eyes and forehead. Dark hair, tall, slender, light. She was so engaged in her conversation that she did not once return my stare. At Piccadilly, they got out. Ever since, have been cursing myself for not having followed her and *somehow* or other — a word, a note slipped into her hand — attracted her attention, established communication. Absolute certitude that *there,* at any rate, resided happiness. But irrevocably snatched away. Ah, fate, — cruel existence! And then, a few minutes later, just to make the whole story true, found myself standing opposite a young man: who threw me a profoundly disturbing look from the depths of his attractive eyes: a mixture of dream, unhappiness and provocation. Further emotion. Then he, too, vanished; for ever, I suppose . . . What an exasperating farce!

But Joan! Never again, never, will I declare love for a woman without first experiencing a strong and unmistakable impulse of *physical desire.* To think that I could once more have plunged gaily into that sort of platonist cerebro-sentimental experiment which I should have finished with in 1933! I know perfectly well by this time what love is, and it is not *that,* and yet I insisted that it was. On a bench on the Chelsea embankment, in the nocturnal rain, she dazed or half-asleep in my arms, I kissed her; and how well she must have known at that moment — from the reluctant pressure of the lips and teeth, the hand's detached caress, the gaze wandering over the shoulder — the chilly truth! Yet I still protested.

To remember in future: *'Ne fais de bêtises que celles qui te font réellement plaisir.'*

8.VI.37

The chilly truth . . . 'Things are as they are . . . a spectacle it would be bad taste* to show to a young girl of twenty except in brief glimpses.'

To get out of this ill-conceived affair: be unscrupulously realistic, destroy all the false romantic aura, and propose straight-forward 'love-affair', *genre mondain,* putting the proposal in the most adult possible terms; *she will not be able* to accept this proposal, if she even understands it. Then: we have made a mistake, we (you) are not yet 'ripe' for this, but 'one day' we will make something of it.

Learn to be more conscious and deliberate in handling these matters. To develop a certain amount of sexual cynicism; always to remember (or at least pretend) that the loved person (this does not apply to mature and conscious women: but these appear to be rare) is in one's hands; to be conscious all the time of the 'art' of handling an affair — to know how to obtain the desired result deliberately.

Am aware today of being illumined by having gradually arrived at a decision which is now definitive: my romantic days are over. To know this seems like a fresh source of energy. It entails in the most literal sense: 'less sleep'. *Stade dépassé;* new period. Increase in creative production.

It is a question of 'taking over' and putting into practice, from now on, a body of knowledge, an attitude to life, *already* acquired but until just recently only incompletely, bit by bit. The suit is now ready to wear. Before, it was not that

---

* If one were in love with her. Otherwise the question of 'taste' does not arise; only that of necessity in this case.

I could not *see* the truth most of the time, but that I could not make any consistent use of it.

All this expressed itself, in the still unfinished state, in protesting to Joan, for instance, that I was 'an ex-romantic' (which was not then quite true); in the original but, I think, mistaken idea that in order to make the affair 'work', I should first have to corrupt her mind. Mistaken, because though an impressionable young girl picks things up with alarming rapidity, the knowledge thus acquired remains completely superficial unless accompanied by a radical shifting of the deeper layers of consciousness, etc., which is only produced very gradually in most cases. She is not corrupted by being confronted with the facts of corruption. My pessimistic insistence on the essential misery of humanity, etc., (exaggerated in reaction against her cloudy-headed Health and Beauty attitude — very natural, *d'ailleurs,* for a girl of her age, and which if I had been really a non-romantic I should have taken for granted with a shrug of the shoulders and not struggled against) only distressed J. and put her on the defensive.

At the back of my mind, two names have been repeating themselves, creating a sort of friction of curiosity and interrogation: Audrey B., and Cécile Eluard. Shall I write to the first, as she once asked me to? Will the second be accompanying her father to stay with Penrose next month in Cornwall, when I shall be there?

Extraordinary and upsetting dream last night:

To begin with, walking beside a young girl through lamplit deserted streets on a hill (Richmond: reminiscence of previous evening), when a number of members of the Twickenham branch of the C.P. went by on the opposite pavement, going the other way, apparently homewards after some meeting further up the hill. Some of them appeared not to see us, others made signs of chilly recognition.

Next, travelling with the same girl, still indistinct but I think almost certainly Joan S., on top of a bus along a country road (imagine the journey from Richmond to Kew if there were no houses, only countryside; also reminiscence of previous, long-forgotten dream-landscapes: Wiltshire?). Strained conversation. Descended to the platform in premature anticipation of getting-off, the bus still in full motion. Suddenly aware of the pressure of a hand upon my hand which was holding the vertical nickel rail. The conductor. Strange expression on his face. Confusion.

We alighted among trees. People standing about in groups. It had been raining. Scene in a kind of shelter where Joan tried to do something to her shoe(?)* which annoyed me so much that I turned impatiently aside. At this, she burst into tears, and with a sort of voluptuous increased annoyance I began to walk away from her. Weeping, she ran away past me to the other side of the road: question of catching the 'last bus home' though it seemed still daylight. Trying to follow her, found myself obstructed by large puddle of rainwater; bent down to attend to the soaked bottoms of my trouser-legs; — as though the puddle were a trap. Joan more and more indistinct. Moving again in her direction, found myself crossing a sort of vestibule like a tent. Odd scene: a lot of absurdly dressed spinsters and antique gentlemen taking part in a sort of gambling game or lottery; apparatus of numbered leather-pockets, books of tickets, I don't know what. The old people's faces flushed with excitement.

_____

* At this point she seemed to resemble the girl of the tube-train episode.

Smartly-dressed bookmaker in grey top-hat: 'Won't you join us?' But I went on.

Into the interior of a café, apparently. The memory of this part is slightly blurred; next clear scene, sitting at a long café table on a seat against the wall and talking to the most incredible idiot with a newspaper in his hand, about, as far as I remember, newspapers. As I sat gaping at this fool's nonsensical assertions, two men went past on the other side of the table, and one of them (nervy, fair-haired Nordic type) leant over and contradicted him scornfully. Angered by this, the first speaker turned to me and said something to the effect that *he* couldn't talk, anyway, he was one of those men who'd been in a Carmelite monastery where they do you-know-what (incomprehensible). Found the Nordic and his companion sitting next to me. Our hands met on the seat. Turned to one another, leaned towards one another. Swiftly accumulating desire. His companion tried for a moment to interrupt but was gestured angrily away. Momentary diffidence: I, my glasses, unshaven, etc. Took my glasses off. Embrace. Mouth locked to mouth, we went down on the seat, hands convulsive, almost unconscious. And then suddenly, in excess of passion, he was vomiting: into my mouth, over my clothes. Reacted to this only with amazing gravity, tenderness and absence of disgust.

* * *

(Interpolated for publication in 1980:)

Here the earliest volume of my Journal, or rather notebooks, comes to an end, with a peculiarly Freudian dream, for printing which I must apologize to those people who find accounts of others' dreams particularly boring. The first entry of my next Journal opens with an entry dated

19.VI.37, but it might be as well here to take the opportunity of adding a note to explain how I came to go to Paris not long afterwards. I had been wishing all summer increasingly to get back to France somehow, and when the plan for a holiday in Cornwall fell through, another scheme came along from my friend Philip M., who had arranged with his close friend Joan S., to whom he had first introduced me, and who I have already referred to, to go across to Paris, for a long week-end, to see the great International Exhibition which was shortly to be opened there. (As it turned out, the opening kept getting postponed, because of strikes by construction-workers, so the planned trip did not finally happen until August.) So it was decided that I should accompany them.

My friend Roger Roughton had made the acquaintance of e.e. cummings during his recent visit to America (he soon afterwards published a short booklet containing the first selection of cummings' poems to appear in England), and he had kept in communication with him since then, and he now gave me cummings' Paris address. Which is how, when I finally did go to Paris with Joan and Philip, who left me behind there after a few days, I was able to find a cheap attic bed-sittingroom at the top of the house where cummings was living, 11 rue de la Bûcherie. I do not know why I never referred to him at all in my Paris Journal 1937/9; but he was a very quiet, reserved man (with a most beautiful photographer wife — they were like a last example of an ideal Paris-American couple of the 'Twenties), and I never got to know him very well, though he was very friendly when I went to see him in New York during my American tour with Kathleen Raine and W. S. Graham in 1951/2. By an odd coincidence, he then lived just opposite Djuna Barnes, in Patchin Place.

II

19.VI.37

Have been through a shocking week; it hardly seems possible to sink further into depression, to suffer a more acute moral misery. The immediate cause is now removed, and I know there is only one solution: work; but one is left feeling so dispirited and exhausted that the energy necessary for creation seems quite beyond one's reach.

Depression: an absolute dissatisfaction with the state of one's existence; a frantic desire to change it; an awareness of one's inability to do so. Lack of courage, hope, faith. Vicious circle. Continual gnawing apprehension of futility. Fatigue. Urgent physical and emotional need of love in the absence of any conceivable love-object. A sense of separation from one's friends ('impossible to love those who suffer'). The added sting caused by the social necessity of dissimulating one's misery.

Was going down to Chinatown in a taxi with Penrose, Mesens, Ernst and Leonora Carrington, and feeling just as desperate as could be. Everyone was very gay and conversational; but all the while I was clutching the window-handle and wondering whether it would be possible to get up during the meal we were going to have and go out and get rid of myself somehow. Just then, Leonora Carrington turned away for a moment from excited conversation with Ernst, and exclaimed beamingly: 'You don't say very much, but I can feel you're most extraordinarily happy, aren't you?'

25.VI.37
(Inward)

Intellectual synthesis: Integration of the neurotic personality.

Personal conflict: masculine and feminine sides of nature: rational and intuitive sides of mind: ice and fire.

Does integration of personality = *fixing* of concepts? Surely not. Surely integration does *not* = resolution of conflict? Creation arises only out of the conflict; if this is resolved, the mind stagnates, fastened upon a single aspect of the true (unknowable?) whole; one enters the commonplace. I do not *want* to feel solid ground, or rather the *illusion* of solid ground, under my feet; but to go through with the experience of struggling in the void to the end. The whole meaning is in the struggle.

* * *

If it is nothingness that awaits us, let us make an injustice of it; let us fight against destiny, even though without hope of victory; let us fight against it quixotically.   Unamuno.

29.VI.37

It has been predicted that when I have reached a certain age, I shall receive power. A sudden influx of force, 24¼ days before 29th birthday (4 p.m., Sept. 15th, 1945)! I believe nothing of it! *But*, in spite of almost totally clouded outward aspect at present, — débris, exhaustion, — I cannot deny the possibility that after long and incessant struggling and painful development, one might reach a state of this kind: force to

enable one to make *coherence* of oneself; to *see*, — not the
answer to any Sphinx's riddle, or Solomon's Key, — but
something like a finally convincing image of the significance
of one's life, an *assurance of destiny*. Coherence: a
gathering-together of the dispersed powers of one's
personality. Such a state could not be lasting, but might,
nevertheless, permanently alter the *level* of one's life.
Attainment to a lasting deliverance from the trivial and the
unmeaning: from the quicksands.

Strange, long-recurrent image of mountains (Austrian
Tyrol?) — spiritual experience in the mountains — love, death —

It may be that some natures are fulfilled only in a sort of
slow, manic-depressive turning of the inner wheel from dark
to light, to dark, to light . . . Gradual evolution. If so, the
tormenting question would be: at what stage does the wheel
stop? Can one hope for a last triumphant blending of
darkness and light?

Morning World
All day yesterday, the wind blew. In the evening, clouds
closed in around the mournful sky; a cold grey glare made
everything balefully distinct for a few moments at eight
o'clock; the wind shook grieved rustlings from the trees and
turned back the pale undersides of their leaves. The rain
began to come in gusts, as the night fell. — I went very late to
bed.

Woke up full of energy at dawn, watched the clear light
grow, pearl-coloured bands of dispersing cloud stretched
across the sky; wrote a little; then went out into an early
morning miraculously fresh, clear, clean. Absolute
transparency of the air. A virgin world. — Walked over the

115

river, through Ham, through Richmond Park, down Richmond Hill.

Landscape of pristine, newly-washed summer colours, uninhabited except by larks, cats, dogs and solitary cyclists. The intense light gave significance to every leaf, flower, blade of grass. — In the Park, at the top of the tree-grown slope, sat on a bench in the sunlight and cleansing wind and drank in the whole perfect morning as though it were a tonic draught. — Have never seen the view from Richmond Terrace look more beautiful: all the rich-foliaged trees, the winding surface of the river blue but ruffled, sharp white of a few distant boats . . .

Within, deep singing: happiness? Still the conflict and division, aspiration, weakness; — yet a sort of sostenuto resonance *(Stimmung)*.

8.VII.37

June	26th	To Leatherhead with Priaulx Rainier to hear Purcell's *Dido & Aeneas*.
	27th	Saw Philip Marsh.
	30th	Reception at the Dorchester Hotel.
July	1st	Letter from Audrey Beecham.
	2nd	To the Caledonian Market.
	3rd	On the river with Roger Roughton.
	5th	Journalism
	6th	" "
	7th	" "

12.VII.37

An Epitaph

'Possessing a vague imaginative talent and of a literary inclination, he was endowed with an enormous seriousness, which made him exaggerate the importance of everything, particularly of himself.

'His generally weak character and indolent disposition preventing him from taking any firm foothold in everyday life, he wasted his time in making plans which he was unable to carry out. It seems unlikely that, had he lived, he would ever have accomplished anything of interest or value.

'When at last, realising the hopelessness of his destiny, he killed himself, the first thought of his friends was: a pity he couldn't first have managed to pay off his debts!'

13.VII.37

I have stopped writing poetry since more than a year, I tell my friends, because the writing of poetry seems to me to be a dishonest occupation *(viz.* Pascal), a compromise, a deception; or at best a pleasant pastime or hobby for those with nothing better to do. It would be better for everyone, I argue, if nine out of every ten poets at present writing became silent. — Whereupon they reply: Oh! it's all very well for a *Rimbaud* to talk like that; at least *he* had written superlative poetry before he decided to dismiss the Muse. But if one has written only mediocre verse, and is capable perhaps of writing only a little better, then *one has no right* to treat what one has not yet shown oneself capable of doing as not worth the effort. And so on.

What! because I have never written poems as good as X's, which make me impatient, am I therefore to persevere, knowing all the time that no matter how fine the phrases, the ecstasy, the spell, it would always be *something else* that I wanted to say?

1.VIII.37

Terrible August again here. Is it to be even worse this year than it was last? it seems so . . .

It is useless to say 'nothing could be worse than my present state', because every time one says this, one immediately sinks further. At least I can say: never in my life have I felt so isolated, so utterly petrifyingly solitary. What frightens me is the realization that lassitude and inertia have landed me at length in the doldrums of a perfect calm: there is no longer left even the desire to batter one's brain against the wall — nothing, nothing but a profound calm disgust with human kind. I am convinced that the next step is insanity. Possibly I am already half insane?

Even those nearest me, my family with whom I so unwillingly live, have not the faintest idea of my despair — seem perfectly indifferent, engrossed in their own fatigue, their inability to make up their minds whether to go away for a holiday, or where to go. Careless incomprehension could not be more manifest . . .

If this gets any worse, if I do not manage to get away, do something, explode, during the next few days, only the most contemptible cowardice and weak-will can prevent me from suicide.

Untethered, uncontrolled, lashing wildly from one side to the other at the least provocation.

But now that I know how to get hold of a revolver easily —

17.VIII.37

Paris, rue de la Bûcherie

My window looks out over Notre Dame. I have been here for more than a week. Am I more, or less, alive here than in Teddington, for instance? Ten days of dispersion, distraction, confusion . . . Does one *ever* become entirely solid? Can one in towns?

Before I came here, I had seen where I was: in despair: despair, physical and metaphysical, *into which one does not enter of one's own free will, and from which one cannot escape without deceit.* Can this ever change? Yes, it *can* change (but not at will) because despair teaches one that *all* things (solutions) are possible: *On croit savoir des choses; mais on se trompe; car on ne sait* jamais *rien . . .*

* * *

What is to become of me? I stake the craziest of wagers. In spite of everything, my complete lack of means of support, all my weaknesses, the moral blackness which surrounds me at present, I still cling to the irrational hope of becoming great; I care for nothing but *l'argent, l'amour, la gloire,* and have absolutely no honest grounds for believing that I shall ever attain any of them. Nothing can help me but the most improbable good fortune, in which I have no faith whatever. Exterior portents, however, for what little they are worth, are undeniably favourable for the future. — Which is only a more pompous version of Mr. Micawber's little maxim, after all . . .

17.VIII.37
4 p.m.

Extraordinarily clear dream: A ballet. During the first part of the dream, was seated near the stage watching a *pas-de-deux,* the subject of which must have been Love and Death, *L'Amour Agonisant,* or something equivalent. Most poignant music; powerful emotion. The setting Gothic, sacramental; the man's costume a mixture of knight and vampire, the women's less distinct, flame-coloured drapery. Slow, voluptuous, cruel movements. They were singing a duet while dancing;

magnificent strong tenor of the male dancer; a desire to join in the song, as though his long-held notes were in *my* throat. The audience in tears . . .

During the second part of the dream, I seemed to have arrived somehow in the wings of the theatre, while some lighter, gayer ballet was in progress. Two dancers, on their exit from the stage, called me by my name, took me by the arms, made me dance with them. — 'Are you coming tomorrow? Ah, you must come tomorrow!' Tomorrow was to be a gala night, a farewell party on the stage. 'I invite you to come,' said one of them, the man, 'You must come as my guest, I'll see to it.' Then he had to hurry away, leaving me with the girl, his partner. Hand in hand, we went down corridors. In some remote corner of the theatre, we sat down; she sat down on my knees. 'Is it really true, does he want me to come tomorrow?' She was serious, nodded. 'Yes, of course. You must get a ticket.' — 'But they are all taken? I didn't know, I would have got one before . . .' — 'Never mind, I'll get you in.' — Incredulity. — 'I, a poor intellectual, though with a certain sense of reality, have always thought of dancers as remote, god-like beings — and here you are on my knees!' — 'They all seem to think like that.' — She was English, quite unlike anyone I know, a personality to herself, self-possessed, authoritative, intelligent. It was like an actual relationship, not like a dream or a wish-fulfillment. 'We must exchange addresses, telephone numbers, you must ring me up in the morning, then we'll arrange it.' — Several people went by, on their way to a box-office, apparently in a great hurry to get the last seats for the gala; among them was Philip, who seemed astonished to see me there with a dancer, but who had no time to stop or speak. — 'After the farewell performance, we're all going away together on a holiday, a

120

voyage de noce.' — 'Why a *voyage de noce?* It is not you who are getting married?' — 'Oh, no, it is someone in the company, we are all going, you must come with us, we like you, you might do some work for us . . .' — Here the dream ended; I woke up.

2.IX.37

When is this going to end, and how? The pillory of penury, — *la supplice de la misère?* It surely cannot last forever? To have half-starved for a week, to have waited breathlessly for each post for days, and when the urgently awaited letter at long last arrives, to read: 'Sorry to hear you are again in financial difficulties, but — '; and then to be faced with absolutely *no* solution except suicide; — and all this in an indifferent foreign city, in complete solitude; — surely this must be about as far as the screw of material misery can turn? If ever in my life I have had a valid, actual reason for putting an end to my life, it must have been last night: and yet I could not bring myself to do it. Cowardice? remnants of an irrational hope? I wandered in a dazed state about the streets, unable to decide *how* to do it: whether to throw myself from the window of my room, or into the Seine, or in front of a train or lorry. I have no poison, or weapon, and am no longer in a room with gas . . . I got only as far as bursting into tears while writing the last letters of farewell and explanation — (which I may still need . . .).

I say 'absolutely *no* solution', but I suppose there always is *some* miserable solution if one searches hard enough for it. Going last night through my papers, in a state of desperation, came upon a letter from poor R.F.W.: 'Remember I'm still on the spot old Dibs . . . as long as I live it's "yours to command" so to speak — ' So have had to write to her for help, which I could never have done in any situation but this.

If I have a whole assortment of personalities, I certainly have a distinct pair of them: one, when I am penniless, — another, when I have a little money, even borrowed, in my pocket. The difference is very remarkable.

But it is shocking, when, after a week or so of more or less uninterrupted solitude and gloom, I chance once more to 'go out into the world', — friends, cafés, conversations, (and above all: food and drink), — to find how far in comparison, I have been sunk in my own depths, inescapably locked in my own egoism. What is it, after all, my miserable small misery, of which these pages stink! Shanghai is being devastated; women wail among the Spanish ruins. In the street outside my window, a child was weeping this afternoon because his father could not be prevented from fighting with the rag-and-bone merchant who had cheated him, and they all had to be carted away by the police . . . At St. Cloud, the distraught Basque children refugees smashed the windows of the dreary factory where they were lodged, because they had been mocked with the cruel news that Santander had fallen to Franco . . . All day long, and every day, the real world agonizes in its all too actual suffering, — and I, in my stiflingly closeted little world, imagine that the end of things has come simply because I happen to be stranded without money for a week! . . .

One has need of a little more *sang-froid*.

* * *

A week or so ago, received a letter from Kay Hime. 'My precious D.— Quite mad, but I'm going to be married. He's rather like you (of course!) and you'll like him I think. I like him *very* much.' (Extraordinarily, charmingly naive, and so

122

Kayish, the last sentence.) This evening arrived an official invitation to the reception, with the scrawled note: 'Please come and stand by me — ' How is one to understand such an orientation of mind??

Curious, it was here, in Paris, very nearly four years ago, that we first met, and here I am again, now to learn of her marriage, and we were so very nearly married here, then. I shall always regard those days, I think, as the happiest of my life. By this time, something in me has become so estranged from her (her innocence, candour and naiveté), that the strongest emotion I feel on learning of her marriage to someone else (in spite of the fact that at one time we seemed to be *the* couple, and everyone thought of us as being together), is above all that of a 'man of letters': an egotistical curiosity as to how I am reacting to the circumstance. (If I were like that through and through, as the genuine professional is supposed to be, I should indeed be dead!)

* * *

Later: Received a second letter:

'Where are you? There is such a packet to say. But oh darling I am frightened. Must *must* be a success. Pray by all the Gods you know for me and love me very hard and *write to me.*' — Somewhat of a problem in psychology, this! In face of the above, would it be very complacent of me to imagine that — ?

8.IX.37

I have for a long time been tormented by a desire to know: have I a *destiny,* and if so, what is it, and is it fulfilling itself? *To be,* in the most absolute sense: to be that which I am *meant to become.* — But what does this mean? *Meant* by what, by whom? Is it possible that certain men are 'sent' to be, to do, something on this earth? — The mysterious words: 'Many are called, but few are chosen.' And can 'the elect' ever know that they are elect, or even 'in the running'? What is the balance between 'being elect' and the Will? It seems impossible ever to see clearly here, yet to see clearly is my greatest wish. The most grandiose absurdity is evident. (Victor Hugo!)

* * *

Nevertheless, I feel something forming, a certain 'line' attempting to make itself clear, out of all the confusion of my thought and action. This autumn . . .

* * *

'Les Chefs d'Oeuvre de l'Art Français':
Made a discovery at this exhibition: Georges de La Tour (1593 — 1652). Four magnificent paintings: *St. Jerome, St. Sebastian Mourned by Saint Irene, Job and his Wife,* and *The Repentant Magdalene.* (This last, in particular, almost makes one think: a French Rembrandt; chiaroscuro, meditative *depth,* etc.) Have seldom been so moved as by this scene of the discovery of the death of St. Sebastian:[*] smooth candlelight on craning tragic faces brown with darkness; clear drops of blood on the youth's abandoned body; a sombre red dress; the writhing candleflame petrified with the stillness which hangs over everything. Out of this same smooth nocturnal stillness and *depth,* Job gazes with the meek calm of despair at the light held by his weeping wife, the Magdalene gazes at the dim but solid skull before her . . .

* * *

---

[*] Saw another magnificent St. Sebastian at the *Exposition El Greco* this afternoon, but how different! The one so placid in death, the other tortured, fleshly, neurotic, exposed!

Has French painting ever excelled, in the particular qualities one associates with it, the standard attained by Jean Fouquet in the superb *Virgin & Child* he painted five hundred years ago? It seems impossible. For once the authorities have been right in 'starring' a picture (it is this one that one sees on posters all over Paris at the moment). There is practically nothing in the exhibition to compare with it.

* * *

Among a host of other lovely things, particularly enjoyed the paintings by Clouet and Corneille de Lyon; — Watteau (among the Watteaus there is one from Leningrad which resembles, curiously enough, a Rowlandson); and Fragonard (interesting to compare the large-sized, broadly painted panel: *Fête de Saint-Cloud,* with the delectable, more subtle *Fête à Rambouillet* in the National Gallery) — Chardin, Oudry, (and how well the French paint food! Bonnard's succulent table-tops, for instance) — and another astonishing portrait of the bovine and enigmatic *Madame Moitessier* by Ingres, at which I could gaze for hours; — and several Courbet. On the whole, the French 19th Century school is less well represented here than in London, at the Tate and in the Gulbenkian collection at the Nat. Gal.

After the beginning of the 19th Cent., the work of individual painters seems to become remarkably *uneven* in quality. *Chez les impressionistes,* for instance, four or five more or less dead canvases to every single living one. This is true even of Cézanne. And the number of unsuccessful *ébauches* is even greater among the moderns, if one is to judge by the *Maîtres de l'Art Indépendant* exhibition at the Petit Palais. This show is mainly disappointing. I had always imagined that even minor French painters had *instinctive* good taste; but what shocking crudity and vulgarity of colour and conception one finds among the lesser *fauves*, the cubist and neo-cubist satellites!: Delaunay, Dufresne, Favory, Gleizes, Van Dongen, etc., etc. (Even of Braque I would say that I would give two thirds of all his work for half-a-dozen or so of his really superb *nature-mortes* of the best period: cloths of crumpled chalk, bruised apples, harsh green leaves and battered trellis-work.) It was a relief to find the rooms devoted to Matisse and to Picasso, as though coming out of a crude Neon glare into real sunlight.

* * *

Was moved to find in to-day's *Marianne* an article by Edmond Jaloux devoted to the *éloge* of André Breton. He is hardly the man to care anything for recognition of this kind; but at least the article gave him his due in terms of which his friends can approve:

M. André Breton a un visage pâle, d'une grande noblesse de traits, et dont l'expression la plus constante est une sorte d'intrépidité violente et lucide, comme un défi porté à toute obstacle; ses cheveux bouclés, rejetés en arrière, découvrent un beau front. La sérénité de ce regard, toujours tendu, même au repos. — Il est curieux qu'un si grand inventeur soit demeuré dans un tel isolement et presque inconnu, sauf d'un petit groupe de disciples et de lettrés. Il a cependant sur la jeunesse une vive influence; est-elle profonde? Je veux dire: 'Est-elle vraiment comprise par elle?' Je l'ignore. J'ai peur parfois qu'elle ne voit guère la réelle portée de son oeuvre et qu'elle n'en retient que sa part de bizarrerie, de hardiesse extérieure. — Cet isolement tient au caractère même de M. André Breton, à son humeur un peu farouche. Il n'a voulu obéir à aucune forme d'embrigadement. C'est un révolutionnaire à l'état pur; conception etrangère à une époque qui considère simplement la révolution comme le conformisme de demain, nécessaire à de nombreuses ambitions privées. — Peu d'hommes ont aussi

*courageusement défendu leur autonomie. M. André Breton est de
ceux qui méprisent le travail, tout travail régulier, comme ennemi
de la pleine liberté de l'etre intérieur; non par les chaînes
pratiques qu'il constitue, mais parce qu'il organise aussitôt une
routine, un esclavage de l'esprit, un pli professionel, et qu'il
prépare finalement une totale absence de soi. — C'est la notion
même de ce moi supérieur, agissant en vous comme un démon
sacré, se révélant quand il le veut, étendant son empire au delà
même de notre personnalité, que M. André Breton a toujours
dégagée avec un lucide courage, en ce temps où cette notion pure
a je ne sais quoi de choquant pour des milliers d'individus.*

* * *

Ambivalence of my attitude towards Breton (as towards
everything really important to me): at one time I had more
admiration and respect for him than for almost any man
living; then reacted against this rather excessive enthusiasm
and, on account of the train of thought aroused by my work
on Rimbaud, became keenly critical of his pretensions,
sceptical of his undertaking (Fondane); and now, again, I feel
attracted to him, but in moderation, and with, I think, a
clearer understanding both of his errors and of his great and
unique value. It would be impossible wholly to *deny* him;
although . . .

10.IX.37

Encore Moi . . .

My temperament: *fire and ice.* It is the latter ingredient which
those who do not know me well always see in me. (X, the
other evening: 'You make a negative impression. One cannot
imagine what you do when you are alone.') There is
something in this colder side of my nature which is almost
Jansenist; which hinders the freedom of my style, for
instance; which is completely non-sexual, completely cerebral,

127

and which would give me one of those hard, bespectacled faces which I hate, were I *only* that.

The chief cause of my laziness: a sort of *deadlock*. If only the energy always simmering in me *au fond* could find a direct, unhindered outlet, what a mass of work I should achieve! (Danger of such an explanation becoming a mere excuse.)

Not a case of 'schizophrenia', though; because, given a free choice, I should *invariably* claim the fire as my *true* self; or rather as the dominant element in the combination.

It is a question of constantly struggling to unseat the Jansenist. It is quite possible to get rid of him entirely.

24.IX.37

The wheel turns; the interior existence changes ceaselessly. In consequence, lack of centrifugal balance? Am I *still* unformed? (But there is no finality in life; and no growth, no solid accumulation without contradiction.)

Half against my will, in spite of my previous convictions, I am beginning to believe once more that I may be a *poet.*

What I wish first of all to say is all explicit; but I find there is still left over a margin of thought, or rather of feeling, which demands to be expressed *implicitly,* i.e. in poetry. The centre of my work will be in prose. The poetry, if any, will be secondary.

I cannot be satisfied any longer with work of mine that does not satisfy the highest of the demands I make of other people's work. Resolution: never to publish, to destroy, all poetry that does not reach this standard. But perhaps to continue the attempt in secret, all the same. (All that has been written, by Rilke, and others, about the long, painfully slow interior process that must precede all genuine poetic creation, is true: I think I only half believed it, before.)

Minor poets, minor poetry, exasperate me. The real thing — which is so rare — or nothing! I want to be a true poet — one of those rare beings, of whom I can only think of five or six alive today — or not a poet at all, but simply a writer. — *Ainsi soit-il*.

* * *

Until I wrote *Hölderlin's Madness* a few days ago, I had scarcely written poetry of any kind for well over a year. (The last poem I wrote, Summer 1936, the 'Elegiac Stanzas in Memory of Alban Berg', was perhaps a vague, only semi-successful attempt to find a new direction. I may now re-write it . . .) Anything of the kind I may write from now on will be entirely different: no more themeless improvisation, no more autonomous lyricism, no more 'pure' effect. I want depth, solidarity experience. Poetry that will say something definite. Emotion, a raised voice, but clear and coherent speech.

Certain elements that detach themselves from the line of thought I am developing in *Blind Man's Buff* may be destined to provide the *spine* for any poetry I may write in future.

Out of the discovery of the poetry of Hölderlin, and of Pierre Jean Jouve, and of the painting of de La Tour, and of certain Flemish and German 16th century artists, particularly Cranach, and of the German romantics, and the *idea* of Rilke's *Duino Elegies* (which I have not yet read), and the weather of the season (I want to go and see the autumn from the terraces overlooking Paris, near the forest of St. Germain), and the sediment of all the *chagrin* I have been through lately, — out of all this there rises a sort of ferment, and a desire to write a long poem called *Cortège and Hymn of Death*, which I have already planned out.

* * *

Chains which bind us:

A silly tune, a cheap perfume, the overheard low intaking of breath of a strange human being. — Sunlight and wind striking a puddle of water in the street outside the window through which one looks during a particularly acute moment of distraction. Again the wind in the trees, — again the dusty shop-window in the street down which one once walked with someone now irremediably absent. And again the 'sharp taste' — unwanted, forgotten, — rises to the mouth; and for the rest of the day one is dissatisfied and restless.

* * *

Have heard from Cyril Connolly that Kay is actually in Paris. On the day before her wedding, Freddy arrived in England from America, drove to Brighton, where the ceremony was to take place, rang up Kay and asked her to come out and speak to him for a few minutes. She sat down beside him in the car for a short talk, and he immediately drove away, took her back to her home in Surrey, broke into the house and snatched together a few of her clothes and her passport, and brought her straight away to France! — The aforementioned problem in psychology now becomes practically insoluble, and I am dying with impatience to see Kay and to hear her own version of the whole affair; but she and Freddy appear to be more or less in hiding.

5.X.37

My philosophy of confusion and uncertainty, at the same time authentic and suspect, — because it is the exact reflection of the condition of my own private life. Therefore, those who

130

would find it uncomfortable, or who had other reasons for wishing to evade its implications, would be able to say: True for *you*, but —

— All the same, is it only a personal distortion?

— Phenomenal difficulty of discovering 'the mean', in anything. To discover it in all things. Philosopher's stone.

* * *

Torn, shaken, bruised, carried precipitately up and down and round and round by the unending change of small events from day to day. Faces, people's personalities, recede into a hazy distance; then are shut out altogether from the black silence of an all-obliterating *cafard;* but with the return of an appearance of daylight, they loom up closer than life-size again, and with all the clarity of obsession. The idea of the past and future of one's life shrinks and swells like an erratic concertina. One day, one's work seems nothing but scribbles and scraps of paper; and the next, a sudden fecundity of thought brings it to life again. Meanwhile, the *moi* is hidden, and in its cell is trying to integrate itself within its own (predestined?) form.

O power of the self, or 'not-self', deliver us out of dissipation into concentration, for we perish in the quicksands!

* * *

The Chinese towns are blazing, the Foreign Office is disquieted by the report that still further detachments of Italian troops are being exported into ruined Spain, British warships are being torpedoed in the Mediterranean, the mounted police charge into crowds of demonstrators at another Mosley march through London, — and yet out of the very monotony of world-violence, a sort of lull has fallen, a

131

last or penultimate breathing-space before the grand-finale (which will perhaps never take place?).

And all over Europe and America, unknown and silent, engrossed in painful solitude, in *absolute* solitude and as it were almost invisible to their contemporaries, there are still living men from whom escape, from time to time, a few clusters of phrases dictated by a frantic and obscure compulsion; men who are writing pages that are alive because they cannot help being written, in spite of the general uproar and confusion going on outside. And these strange workers are perhaps preparing something like a great cry that must go up from the heart of our time.

> *Et plusieurs fois, sous la porte, du dedans au dehors, l'homme seul a fait glisser un billet. Ceux qui l'ont lu ont compris qu'il s'agissait de faire passer au reclus de la nourriture pour qu'il pût durer jusqu'à la fin.*
>
> R. Gilbert-Lecomte:
> préface au *Correspondance Inédite de Rimbaud.*

I could name one or two of these men. I know some of them. I too am trying to formulate some cry out of our common inner silence; the painful and disordained existence that I lead would have no meaning if it were not that I were meant to translate it into an articulation of this kind.

After having been ill and terribly depressed and without money to eat for several days I looked in the mirror and saw an ugly sunken face, and suddenly thought: I might die this winter. And I wanted to cry out to something for strength, but there was nothing *outside* I could pray to: there was only the thought of the depth *inside*, where the instincts are constantly struggling, — the hidden force of the blood, with which it is possible, for those who know how, to make a sort of contact, and so suppress the death which threatens momentarily to obtain a dominating hold over the centre of the *moi*. — (Jouve calls the hidden force *'le cerf sanglant'*. I wanted to call out: *Cerf!* give me strength never to succumb before I have uttered the great cry!)

9.X.37

Have at last seen Kay Hime (the 7th).

The story I had heard was more or less true except for one or two slight details. Apparently the English papers have been full of the affair. From everything she told me it seems evident that the man she was to marry was not in love with her, that she was unable to distinguish between a temporary physical passion plus the sort of affection she distributes gratis to almost everyone, and a solid desire for marriage: — elementary confusion. One might even say she wanted to marry him because for some reason he would not sleep with her.

She says that the nearer the day of the wedding came, the more strongly she had the feeling that he was a stranger to her. She suddenly realised that her closest friends, Freddy, who had become like a part of herself, were about to be removed to a considerable distance. She loathed the idea of a pompous church ceremonial, reception, etc., on which the fiancé insisted. When the admirable Freddy drove her away, she at first gave one or two conventional shrieks; — and then began to feel an enormous relief. — A very good thing someone had the sense to rescue her.

The abandoned bridegroom came across to Paris 'to talk things over'. There was an all-round display of self-sacrifice and nobility. 'But I shall never forget the look in his eyes as he went away.' — Then Kay went back to England for a week or so, to send back all the wedding-presents and tidy everything up, before returning to France to live here (with Freddy) for some time. She found my address and came round here to see me, but I happened to be out at dinner with Priaulx Rainier. She left a note to say where she was staying, which added: '*LOVELY* will see you. Oh Gods I have behaved bloody bloody badly.'

Perhaps she will now begin to develop a certain coherence and maturity. At least she is no longer so 'innocent' as I thought.

* * *

Julien Benda, in the Oct. *N.R.F.*:

'La guerre est ouverte entre l'esprit et la nature. Je vote pour l'esprit; le siècle pour la nature, non pas qu'il l'aime, mais parce qu'il hait l'esprit. Là encore, chacun est à sa place.'

Un Régulier dans le Siècle

But M. Benda! By casting your vote, you become a victim of the war! By trying to *submit* life, intuition, contradiction and the ever-becoming to the autonomous power of the mind, precision, logical clarity and parti-pris, you consign your thought to the rigidity of the mortuary. — *Il s'agit d'accepter l'opposition éternelle! La guerre est* ouverte: *il s'agit de ne pas la fermer!*

The weakness of the whole of Benda's work is betrayed by this phrase, which sums him up: *'Je vote pour l'esprit.'*

Benda: much the same sort of case as that of Wyndham Lewis. The 'persecution-mania' of the latter takes the form, *chez* Benda, of a suppressed sense of inferiority, owing to the fact that he is a Jew (— *le Siècle* is Gentile) — which leads him to assert an undialectical precision and singularity and assume

134

the role of a severe, clear-thinking *clerc* among an irresponsible flock of woolly-minded *laics.*

11.X.37

My 21st birthday yesterday. Am too engrossed in the present to be able to stand back and see myself very clearly. I have recovered enough hope, at any rate, in time to be able to look forward from this date with rather more assurance than was possible a month or so ago. Nothing is very certain, but I have got sufficiently accustomed to uncertainty by now to be certain of at least one thing: from now on I shall live permanently on my own, — that is to say, I shall never return to live with my family again, job or no job. Come what may . . .

* * *

The last few days have been extraordinarily beautiful, October at its best. On Saturday, on the Quai d'Orléans, Ile St. Louis: the fishermen's boats, the rhythm of their lines swinging slowly from side to side, and of the circling ripples on the quiet water, and of the piece of rope being twisted and shaken by a boy sitting on the cobbles of the towing-path. The golden plane-trees. The lovely gentle light on the tall houses across the river. Vistaed bridges — indigo and silver clouds climbed up into the soft sky behind the cathedral; it began to grow prematurely dark and presently there was a short fall of heavy rain. — (Went to hear Breton lecturing on *L'Humour Noir*. He sat at a little table in the middle of the platform, with a blackboard behind him and three readers grouped around. — Was chiefly interested in the young actor (J. L. Barrault) who declaimed Baudelaire's *Le Mauvais Vitrier* and an extract from *Maldoror*.)

Had lunch yesterday with Priaulx and Marianne Donhauser. We sat in the beautiful autumnal Luxembourg and looked at the rich green grass, on which leaves fell from time to time. The sun shone calmly on the afternoon strollers through the trees, and on a red balloon. — Wandered along the quais this afternoon looking for Flaubert's *Correspondance* (which I couldn't find). — Twilight in the Tuileries: the newly-lighted lamps were shining on the thick russet foliage of the trees and throwing the elegiac statues into relief and making the fountains glitter; the obelisk stood up clear and black out of the Concorde; the sky was dying behind the magic towers of the Exposition. — Went to have tea at W. H. Smith's in the Rue de Rivoli. Sat down at a table with three empty places in a corner and was waiting for the waitress, when there was a sudden stir in the room; I looked round, and there was Marlene Dietrich, with a woman friend, looking rather lost. There were no free tables. They came round the corner, saw the two empty places where I was sitting, and asked if they were free. I moved to the next chair so that they could sit together. — She looked paler and more drawn than on the screen, an expression of emptiness never left her face. She talked in German, in a low, quite unremarkable voice. She was wearing a brown fur cape, a round close felt hat surmounted by a red-brown plume (to give her height, I imagine). No-one in the room left off staring for a moment. I poured out my tea with great precision, and tried to pay as little attention to her as possible.

13.X.37
Stendhal

> *Mais le* si *de 'Si je m'étais présenté à la Polytechnique', 'Si j'étais riche' c'est, pour un homme qui a ses vingt ans sous le Consulat,*

136

soit sous le régime de la carrière ouverte aux talents, un si
superficiel, un si *commandé lui-même par un* si *plus profond,*
celui-ci: Si je voulais vraiment si j'avais eu, si j'avais de l'énergie!
La présence, le degré ou l'absence de l'énergie, voilà ce qui fait une
destinée. Le jeu comporte une direction, ou un dessous des cartes,
qui est l'énergie. Et voilà pourquoi Stendhal devait naturellement
trouver son grand sujet et sa grande oeuvre dans le roman de
l'énergie, Le Rouge et le Noir.

Thibaudet: Histoire de la Lit. Franc.

14.X.37

A letter from Antonia this morning:

> I have at last realised I can do without love, and you would be
> surprised what a huge relief this is. It gives one such a lot of time, for
> one thing. I shall however be as gay as possible and continue to buy
> things I can't afford until the bailiffs arrive which they will shortly do.
> But I will NOT be dim and virtuous and go into sackcloth.
>   — I'm not a bit frightened now when people tell me writers are
> useless and there's no salvation except in the working classes and
> mass-observation. I have one or two things to say and, in the intervals
> of being a female journalist or a governess in Greece, I shall shortly
> *and* briefly say them.
>   — Barker sends his love. He's frantically job-hunting. Oh dear, I'd
> give a lot for one of our nice endless talks!

I'd give a lot to see Antonia again, too. Of all the people in
England whom I miss, I miss her most of all.

My solitude here in Paris is not complete. I see people
almost every day. But there is no-one here with whom I can
make anything but a superficial exchange; and the comparison
between friendly acquaintanceship and the real thing is
painful.

Some evenings I lie on the bed incapable of anything because of the intensity of the hunger and thirst for human contact, physical and spiritual. Then I feel like going out and wandering about the streets in search of a human face; and if I stay at home, it is because I know I should not find one, but only the anonymous face of the mass. Or if I do go out in such a state, I come home feeling almost ashamed of having been born with an excess of sensibility.

I wish Philip were here too. I miss our weekend meetings terribly. He writes so seldom — At the end of this month I shall be seeing Kay, and Roland Cailleux again. But Roland in Paris will not be the person he is in London, and I'm afraid that . . .

Barker. A sort of contradictory ellipse has always prevented us from meeting, from really knowing one another; it continues to do so. His thought and development are not at all like mine. I don't know what he's up to now, but thought his essay in the last *Criterion* a rather boring waste of time and prim. And the more I think of his *Calamiterror*, the more impatient of it I become. And yet he really has so much in him, and of all the generation now between 20 and 25, it is of him that I expect the most; and I can't help regretting that there cannot be more exchange between us — Ubiquitous walls and partitions.

* * *

Work planned and begun, but still unfinished:

Rimbaud *(Diabolic Angel)*
Oliver Middleton's Confession
Paradise Lost
Blind Man's Buff
The Death of the Churches
A Sentimental Education

Theme out of Silence
Bride of Quietness
Cortège and Hymn of Death
Projects still to be begun:
The End of Fine Days (novel)
The Bitter Taste (story)
The City by Night

18.X.37

A Letter to Lawrence Durrell

Dear Durrell,

After having read those horrifying journals in *The Black Book*, I feel even more diffident about showing you these pages than before. The first part of your book particularly made me feel the writing of journals to be such a miserable hole-in-the-corner sort of game that I hardly dared to open this *cahier* again. Yet none the less there are still two reasons why I would rather present the foregoing to you than to almost anyone else, and they are: (1) because I can see that you are engaged on a sort of adventure of experience to which documents of this kind are particularly relevant; and (2) because you are an expert on the English Death, and what I have written here seems to deal almost entirely in one way and another, even if not deliberately, with precisely that.

The simple fact of having read your wonderful objectivisation or projection of the absolutely universal spiritual squalor and disintegration of the inhabitants of the British Isles, seems quite suddenly to objectivise, to stand outside of and examine the latent content of the year-cycle of experience recorded here, in a way that otherwise I should probably not have discovered for a long while.

It seems obvious, doesn't it, that there has been a conflict going on? And it occurs to me now that this struggle can be explained in two different ways. Firstly, it is between the side of my nature which by instinct, heredity, environment, circumstance, what you will, is altogether *implicated in* the English Death, and the other side, which somehow, blindly, is trying to struggle towards absurdity and life. And secondly, though not so clearly, it is between me as a whole and the English Death as a whole that I have been pretty conscious of the existence of the E.D. all along. The thing is that my relationship towards it has kept changing. I seem to have had some very odd notions as to what one should do about it.

I should think that the greater part of this book will make you wince: it makes me wince most painfully to reread it. A lot of it is dreadfully portentous; there are all the distressing symptoms of a late or protracted adolescence trying to eat its own tail; and then, a frustrated, inhibited personality always has something curiously unpleasant about it: — I'm afraid a lot of this stuff must give the impression of a dank and feeble creature with great fish-like masturbatory eyes.

Moreover, it's shockingly badly written, packed full of clichés, platitudes, naiveties; there are no flights of fancy, no sugar and spice; a great deal of it consists of mere reportage of the flattest kind. I do not claim though, of course, that it is of any interest except as a photographic record of a small cross-section of the E.D. at work in myself and in the lives of the people I know (I mean as near photographic as possible).

It seems at the moment as though I were in the draughty and uncomfortable position of being half in the womb and half out of it. Don't ask me whether it is my head or my feet that are in or in which direction I'm moving, because I haven't the faintest idea. One can only try to keep moving all the time, and perhaps if one manages to keep it up long enough, one will find out something.

Yours, etc.

29.XII.37

Since the last entry in this book, so much has happened, the interval has been so rich: in people, events, unexpected happenings. I don't regret that I haven't recorded it all in detail. It is only the *interior* existence that matters.

I have been practically happy. I have had things I wanted. It is strange, — almost everything that I wanted so desperately during the summer has come, in varying measure. I could face solitude again now, feeling richer, stronger and more certain — I feel that I am *in* life, at last, in my *own* life; that there is no longer an obstruction between me and the possibility of things happening to me. Things are within reach of my hands.

More than anything else, I am happy because I have regained belief in myself. Before, it was always the urgent question: *who* am I? *what* am I? what is going to become of me? And now I no longer ask, because I know that no-one is hard and defined, but an essence perpetually in process of becoming more and more itself.

10.II.38

Désillusion. Un Monde Désert

When I got out of the lift, I heard exciting music coming from the other end of the corridor. I began to look for door no. 55. Then I found that the music was coming from Anaïs Nin's room. She had it all rigged up inside to give a Moorish effect, and there was a smell of burning incense . . . — We went downstairs to talk in the hotel lounge.

141

She asked me when she would be able to see more of my journal, and I had to confess that there was nothing to see, as I had not written any more since the time when we first met and I read her own diary.

That time was the beginning of a period of excitement and activity that has by now quite died away. Perhaps Anaïs's influence had something to do with the way I felt then. 'Let yourself go', was the gist of her argument; and I thought, well, I will let myself go, spend money, get into debt, see a lot of people, go about, probe into people's personalities. And for a while I lived at a great speed. Engagements for lunch, tea, dinner; the telephone ringing all day long. I started two unimportant love-affairs purely out of a feeling of expansion and curiosity. Neither of them led anywhere, or taught me anything new; both left a sediment of futility behind — (two more evaporative beings than Isobel and John I could hardly have chosen). During this time I created a sort of illusion of flight and speed, and seemed to be quite happy.

At any rate one satisfactory thing remains out of it all: new friendships that mean a lot to me: with Anaïs, Renata Borgatti, Audrey Beecham, the Durrells. (Also Buffie Johnson; and perhaps Jean le Louët.) It was also in October that I began going to see the Jouves.

Then, just after Christmas, Antonia came over for a week; and, as I had secretly known it would, that pricked the bubble.

Recently, I have had a return of the old fits of depression and *angoisse*. Now, I work only with great difficulty; seem to be waiting for something; suffer from a sort of weakening of the will which makes me put off the writing of letters, paying of debts, etc., keeps me too long in bed in the morning, makes me restless, then inert. (Lack of money, therefore of food, therefore of regularity, is, as usual the chief cause of all this: but the trouble is that I seem incapable of doing anything about it.)

Life takes its course, and everything seems all right for a while; then suddenly a rift forms under one's feet, one catches a glimpse of hell: *le monde désert,* a terrible fundamental boredom, a terrible sense of being alone among people who are all alone with themselves and inarticulate, a terrible dry interior sobbing. Night and rain, and the endless electrically-lighted street, and the burning, burning . . . — A sense of a world of beings who each one carry the burden of their own void about with them behind their mask, and do not know how to communicate their need and suffering.

* * *

More than ever the romantic in me, that part which thirsts incurably for the Absolute, centres its nostalgic dream round the idea of an ideal love in a setting of mountain-heights. More than ever I look forward to going to Switzerland in April, to stay at Schloss Berg, in a white room in a tower. An impossible hope is breeding in me, which I fear can bring only one more disillusion. . .

12.II.38

I sometimes dare to believe that I am destined to realize, to undergo and express, certain higher states of consciousness. Need of great humility and simplicity. (If only one were simpler and more natural, it would be easier to accept this: it is the quick, corrupt, sophisticated intelligence that so often hinders spiritual development. A certain kind of intelligence is one of the worst enemies of the simplicity inseparable from greatness; it can prevent the development of greatness from the very beginning, by cleverly making one's aspirations seem absurd.)

* * *

Le coeur divin en haut
Tout devenant immense et irradié
En haut plus près du bas
Seulement si l'on est à l'intérieur et si l'on joue
Tout pour le tout.

Jouve

22.II.38

La souffrance est une méditation, l'étude des mystères de Dieu.

Drieu la Rochelle

23.II.38

I wonder every now and then, whether it is really worth it, — this endless poverty, borrowing, uncertainty, frustration, — all for the sake of a possibility that I may one day write something that will have value. Is my talent big enough to justify my leading this sort of life? If I were never to become a writer of very much importance, what would be the sense of my making this attempt to live on nothing but what each day brings, to devote myself to nothing but trying to understand the sense of existence and to make words live on paper, — this prolonged refusal to submit to everyone else's way of life? What small excuse, then, would there be for not coming to terms with the world, and gaining the security of an income earned in an ordinary way? How far more sensible it would be to work in a regular job, as everyone else has to who has no means of support and no other *raison d'être* — if I do not succeed, if I end by having nothing to show for all this struggle, the disgrace will be twofold, I shall be doubly *raté;* and the responsibility for a wasted life will be all my own.

26.II.38
Je suis un désespéré qui cherche Dieu dans les ténèbres . . .

1.III.38
Impotence: tedium vitae. Sleep, bad dreams.

* * *

Yet, in the evening, the energy of Poetry returned.

(Saw the sun setting over the Seine from the clear large-windowed living room of Anaïs's barge.)

7.III.38
Went on Saturday afternoon to see Mathilde M. She has fairish hair, frail appearance, high forehead, Jewish profile, a slightly forbidding manner, a good sense of humour. What did we talk about? Music, 19th century painting (a portrait of Wagner by Renoir), English novels, haunted houses . . . I chiefly remember eating a very good tea. — Left there at quarter to six, and walked up the Avenue Foch towards the Etoile just as the sun was setting: many people walking, wonderful light, opulence and calm. Arrived at the Avenue Wagram to give Michel Dreyfus his lesson, only to find the whole family away in the country; they had sent a *pneumatique* which I had not received. Found myself standing on the doorstep, *sans-le-sou*, having been counting on getting them to pay me a week in advance. — Walked down the Champs Elysées, wondering what to do. Crossed the Seine, deciding to call on the Durrells; but as I was going along the Boulevard Raspail, ran into Ivy: went back to her hotel with her, and was finally asked out to dinner with her

and Stephen and the Bunn. We went to the 'Nègre de Toulouse'. Went to call on Princess Loewenstein afterwards, at her suggestion, but there was nobody in. Went home feeling very low-spirited; fell on the bed in the dark with my coat still on, and immediately went to sleep.

Walked to the rue du Colisée next morning to lunch with the Bunn, Ivy and Stephen, as arranged. Wonderful weather, like May — Spent the whole of lunch discussing a fabulous imaginary project to cross Africa by car, from Cairo to Johannesburg! Afterwards we went to the Louvre: looked at the mediaeval French sculpture, then at the Flemish pictures, which never fail to thrill me (*Loth et ses Filles* by Roger van den Leyden!). Then I left, and walked back alone along the towing-path on the left bank in the most glorious afternoon sunlight, which seemed to have created a sudden efflorescence of the human everywhere: people busily engrossed in strolling, fishing, painting, pissing, making love, all along the river . . .

Freda and Jean Jacquot came to tea. Presently the light began to fade. Went back with Jean by bus to the Porte d'Italie, where they live, and then walked along the outer boulevard to the Parc Montsouris to see the Durrells. Strange fleeting lyricism aroused by the still leafless branches of the little palinged trees along the pavement, seeming to be straining upwards in the sunset light, among the dust raised by the swift procession of cars returning at the end of the day from the country, towards the darkening depths of the sky, like humble praise; to one side the hopelessly straggling zone, and to the other, Paris, smoking away in the descending night, and all her teeming and endlessly intricate life . . .

15.III.38

Last Saturday, went to Versailles for the first time, with the Bunn.

Long, somnolent ride in an autobus after lunch. When you get there, you walk a little way, then you find yourself on the edge of a sort of miniature Sahara: a desert of cobblestones and gravel, stretching away on all sides into the distance, out of which, in front of you, the vast walls of the Palace slowly appear. It takes quite a long time to cross the desert, then the courtyard. The expanse of brick and windows is almost too much to take account of. You pass through an archway beside a rococo chapel, and then the tremendous view begins to unfold itself from the terrace beyond. The Palace, quite as long as the *Queen Mary*, if not so high, is behind you; before you, the balustrades and lawns and trees descend to an extent of ornamental water that stretches, literally, out of sight. I have never seen a place that creates so profound an impression of size and space. That afternoon the sky was lofty and absolutely clear: one of those beautiful March skies swept clean by the wind; a globe of dead white ash was floating in it. The staring white of the walls, the statues and the moon, the sombre green of cypresses, the azure overhead, the brooding quality of the declining sunlight: this combination, and something, perhaps, in the very proportions of the place, make it impossible to escape from the obsession and nostalgia of the past; the atmosphere is thick with it; the space of every perspective is weighed down by it. No wonder people see ghosts there.

* * *

Returned to Paris in one of the new double-decker trains, reading the news of Hitler's occupation of Austria.

147

For the last three days, have been constantly haunted by the shadow of this most recent crime of fascism, whose power now looms right over the heads of the rest of Europe. The atmosphere of this putrid continent becomes every day more horrifying and more impossible to breathe. How can one's mind escape any longer from the constant menace of irrational, *meaningless* violence and destruction? It is beyond my understanding how anyone can remain indifferent and undisturbed at this moment. — Perhaps what is most difficult to bear is the uncertainty and suspense.

I refuse to accept that my life and my work and the quest upon which I have set out, should be interrupted by the insanity of another war. Nothing is more important to me than that I should be able to fulfil that which I firmly believe it has been consigned to me to do, no matter how insignificant that function may appear in an immediate light. I have been given the materials with which to make a *whole,* and what else matters to me beside the attempt to make it? But what a task, to persist in the pursuit of one's *destiny* in face of (among) the conditions and environment of a time like this! How can one's voice attain to more than the most infinitesimal of whispers, or all one's fervour and desire seem more than a faint pinprick of light in an ocean of engulfing darkness?

18.III.38
Lutte et Destin.
What I have suffered during the last week is too intricate to be put into words: it all seemed to crystallize today — tonight, above all, when I was walking down the Champs Elysées after leaving Kay, and the cold spring moon, and the lights, and

the budding leaves on the trees, were all blurred because of the tears of self-pity swimming in my eyes.

This morning, a letter from Renata: '*pour vous annoncer que, hélas, avec le prochain envoi, la somme qui vous était destinée est finie. Il m'a été impossible d'obtenir des collaborateurs. L'unique chose qui me rassure, en partie, c'est —* ' etc., etc.

And then at lunch-time, at the Durrells, when we were arguing, futilely, about war and war-resistance, Miller said: 'Yes, Durrell's probably right; because he's a man, if ever there was one, who's so strongly favoured by Fortune, that even if he were fighting in the front line, he could be pretty certain of coming through without a scratch. But you're not like that; you ask for trouble; your destiny can only be a tragic one . . .'

Faced by acute financial crisis, spent the afternoon trying to think of a way to get to England until the time to go to Switzerland. Kay having bravely volunteered to get me a return-ticket, I have now worked out a plan for the immediate future, but it's not a very comforting one . . .

In the bathroom of Kay's hotel apartment, washing my hands, struck by a sudden indescribable desolation while listening to her cross-channel telephone conversation, in the other room, with Freddie 'Do you love me? Yes, but' (shouting) 'Do you LOVE ME? — SAME HERE!' Standing in one of the basins was an enormous bouquet of daffodils and narcissi that he had had sent to her. (I had never thought that I should one day reach the point when the spectacle of other people's happiness would arouse only bitterness in me. — And when they don't even realise their own happiness!)

We went out and had a rather gloomy dinner, overshadowed by the horror of the Barcelona air-raids, news of trouble on the Polish-Lithuanian frontier, and the general foulness of the European outlook. Afterwards, went to see Garbo in *Marie Waleska*, which did nothing to calm one's emotions. When we came out, I was feeling so wretchedly lonely that what I wanted more than anything was a long talk with Kay and a certain amount of human sympathy. But no, she was resolutely determined to go immediately back to bed; and though she must have vaguely sensed how I was feeling, this only seemed to have the effect of making her shut herself off completely. 'Now don't go and do anything queer', she said, as I was saying good-night at the door of her hotel — I don't know why, unless my expression was strange. (She meant, I suppose, don't go and get picked up by anybody —) Walked away alone, at the end of my tether. '*Le pauvre jeune homme,*' said somebody in a group I passed in the Champs Elysées. Violent resentment of self-pity at gratuitous pity from outside.

14.IV.38
Teddington
Have been back here three weeks, in a state of mingled torpor and uncertainty. I couldn't stay more than a week longer: a good thing my return-ticket to Paris expires at the end of next week. — The how and when of the future is still horribly obscure, which is chiefly due to the sort of paralysis that has prevented me from doing necessary things since I have been here.

I don't belong here any more; I am a stranger; I am absent. No other experience than this short return could have given me more convincing proof that my life belongs elsewhere, and is on a different plane.

Does one become progressively more sensitive to atmosphere? Impossible to do any work here; impossible to do anything.

The spring advances, but I only want to sleep. I have no centre and no strength; almost no hope. Perhaps I shall wake up a little after I have returned to France.

18.IV.38

Am hard at work now on the translation of a book on China by a M. Dennery, for the *Penguin Special* series; and in consequence, with the added prospect of a little money to come and of returning to Paris at the end of the week, am feeling slightly more alive. — There are also the disturbances of Spring at work in the air and in the blood — a wind in the trees at night, a fitful breaking of haggard light through the restless clouds towards evening, a periodic welling up of images, dissociated memories and only half-glimpsed intimations in the mind, as though the subterranean depths of the emotions were in a state of equinoctial flux or overflow, — producing that momentary, but piercing, sense of expectancy, of 'anything-might-happen', which occasionally seems to lift for one a tantalizing corner of that mysterious curtain which conceals the future; a sensation that used to visit me much more frequently when I was younger.

There seem to have been certain evenings, in those days, in Spring, when I was a prey to a particular kind of excitement that I would give much to recapture now. — The sky was the colour of warm lead, yet the atmosphere was full of a latent silver-greenish light; it was as though it were about to snow. The shadows in doorways, the empty spaces of open windows, took on their greatest power of suggestiveness. An imperceptible smell of sulphur in the air. How finely attuned

151

the nerves were to the least possibility of the miraculous! It seemed that at any moment one was going to be able to *walk right through* the screen of surface appearances, as through a mirror, into a strangely violent but exalted world of poetry and revolution. It seemed to be only some inexplicable, too human, weakness of the will and the imagination that prevented this other world from instantly, but permanently, taking its sombre revenge against the wretched mediocrity of the world that human beings have built up to defend themselves against it.

5.V.38

Paris — rue de la Bûcherie

Have finished the translation at last — what a strain it was — and have been back here now almost a week. Beautiful Paris. I'm so glad to be back again. But the future, as usual, — so uncertain. Suspense. How long am I going to stay here? Shall I go to Switzerland, Italy, Greece?

And as soon as ever I return, I find myself plunged in an — *embêtement de coeur*? The antennae of the emotions, after semi-monastic seclusion, were extended greedily in the most taut expectancy. And then . . .

The present situation could not exemplify more perfectly that frustration which is the most outstanding characteristic of my life. Perhaps I am at the moment too impatient; everything may resolve happily if I wait. — But I'm always waiting; it's unbearable. Yet I can't see what action to take! Extraordinary perversity of fate, that just what I've been looking for and waiting for so long should be in question. — And the delicacy of it all! What a strain on the nerves! There's every excuse for jealousy and bitterness on my part, yet under the circumstances they are quite reprehensible reactions. —

This miserable business of being *in love:* and that is undoubtedly the state I'm in; the symptoms — restlessness, sick-feeling, shivering — are quite unmistakable, this time.

11.V.38

Cette fois, alors, c'est vraiment l'amour dont j'avais rêvé. C'est extraordinairement beau. C'est beau. Tant de bonne chance et de bonheur m'étonne! Ce sont des choses qui m'étaient devenus tellement infamiliers! Bien entendu, il y a encore des difficultés; mais la partie la plus importante est déjà gagné. Il n'y a plus de doute. C'est un amour pur, grand et passioné. Une de ces rares rencontres fortuites, mais de toute apparence prédestinée, de deux âmes solitaires faites mutuellement pour se comprendre.

Bent von Müllen est un jeune Danois, au regard bleu, ouvert mais rêveur; grand, et d'une allure fière et noble, comme est son caractère. Il a le front clair, la bouche charnue; les mains fortes d'un homme d'action. Sa voix est chaude et douce. Il peut bien s'éloigner de l'extérieur; il sait s'entourer de silence. Il est très généreux de nature, et d'une politesse naturelle exquise. Dans tout ce qu'il fait il est d'un bon goût impeccable; il a une sensibilité très fine, une intelligence incorrompue, un esprit qui n'a pas peur de ses propres profondeurs. Il n'est pas vaniteux, quoiqu'il ne soit pas sans orgueil. Il est d'un tempérament imaginatif vif et perturbé, melé d'une admirable austerité nordique. C'est un artiste.

La difficulté qui s'est presentée à nous jusqu'à présent, c'est d'être seul ensemble. Nous sommes accompagnés toujours de son ami (que j'avais connu à Londres et qui lui m'a presenté d'abord), et nous n'avons eu que très peu d'occasion de nous entretenir. Hier soir, c'était particul-

ièrement intolerable. Mais ce soir, nous échapperons peut-être ensemble de quelque façon, je ne sais pas encore comment. Demain, en tout cas, nous allons nous rencontrer, sans Michael, pendant l'après-midi, quelque part.

13.V.38
Encore de l'amour, qui continue, qui devient de plus en plus grand. Comme si j'en étais obsédé.

Ce qui est difficile, c'est de comprendre ce qui s'est passé. Une expérience si grande et si extraordinaire, — il n'est pas facile de la sentir jusqu'au bout au moment même de la vivre. Pour cela, il faut être conscient en même temps que d'être exalté, déséquilibré, intoxiqué. — (Non, il ne s'agit pas de l'intoxication, mais d'une état d'existence plus intense, plus profonde et plus vraie que la vie quotidienne.)

Je me croyais toujours être prêt pour cet amour. Je l'ai tant désiré. Mais quand il est enfin venu, alors seulement je comprends combien de force spirituelle et de pouvoir créateur cela demande pour être vécue: pour être transformé de l'imagination dans la réalité.

* * *

Last night we sat alone in the Place Dauphine, under the chestnut trees. It was so warm, the sky so blue and clear. A perfect May night. (Even the *pissoir* nearby sounded like a fountain playing in an Italian piazza!) The white steps of the Palais de Justice glimmered like a more romantic marble balustrade in the background. — We were silent most of the time. Some people went by with their dog. We were there for perhaps an hour. I shall never forget it.

20.V.38
It is raining today. Bent stayed with me here last night again, but he has gone to the atelier now, and I am alone.

I have done no work since I returned to Paris. I have been entirely consumed by the intensity of the experience of Bent. Today I wanted to produce a poem; but I have not yet recovered enough force. — I see the Light, beyond, but I cannot reach it; I know the Voice is always speaking, but I cannot hear the words.

To be alone; to make the sacrifice. I wish to become an Instrument, but I am suspended. Will the Energy return? How can I attain the power that would enable me to *speak* what I *know?*

Flesh, spirit. *'Le combat spirituel est aussi brutal que la bataille d'hommes.'* All states reside in me, but they are unresolved. All I can do is wait. I still have faith; I shall always believe that there is *another plane.* I also know that in order to be able to reach it and to speak of it, one must lose everything, and be destroyed: I am trying to prepare myself to accept loss and destruction, even to desire them.

The power of Poetry alone redeems the world, and reunites the blind, confused and fragmentary elements of universal experience within the circle of significance. The supreme task: that of synthesis. How to invoke the welding flame?

Ideally, the poet's destiny is the most glorious of all. And in a period such as the Present, when death and the diabolic are manifest on every side, most difficult of all.

30.V.38
(*'Dramatique du Moi'*)
Still tongue-tied (I have not written a line of verse or a page of prose for months), and with lost time flowing past at an

155

increasing rate, I sit down this morning again in an attempt to perform the operation of *crystallisation:* the concentration of the forces of the self, with the object of clarifying the confusion and obscurity of one's life as it passes, and of seeing it *objectively* but *from within* . . .

Turning the pages of such a book as this, following the past in retrospect up to the present, the difficulty (the essential) is to grasp the continuity and understand the sense of the development (perhaps they do not exist, *a priori*, but are created by one's own attentive effort).

Looking back, at first it seems that all that has happened has been fragmentary, and that I have done almost nothing. But gradually, I see this: that the period in Paris from last August till the end of March falls into three parts, like an arc, — those eight months brought a definite enrichment and an *approfondissement* I did not have before, — a greater understanding of solitude, poverty and despair, and of the nature of human relationships. I wrote *Hölderlin's Madness*, and 'Despair Has Wings'. — The short time when I went back to England and was working on the translation was like a hiatus, which taught me nothing except that I no longer have a home or country, that I shall never have lasting roots; (I knew this before, but now I know it positively). The last month, in Paris again, has brought something new, longed-for, but unexpected, and I am rich with it. I have what Bent has given me in my hands, and nothing can take it away, but it is still as though it were something too bright for me to see it clearly.

If Bent were to be killed today, or were to send a note and disappear, I should still have had an experience of inestimable value: the materialisation of my most secret dream. (How can I write these things? When I wrote about

156

Bent before, it was in French — because of a sort of unworthy *pudeur.)* How hard it is to be ready to equal one's own dreams when they come true! I am afraid of not having enough strength to live through in reality an experience I anticipated so intensely, often and often, in imagination.

For a whole month I have done nothing except be in love. It seems far longer than a month, the time has been so full. One should be able, though, to let time pass without anxiety, and thus give the Present its real intensity and spaciousness. One should be glad to be able to let a month pass by with nothing to show for it except interior gain.

Now Bent has proved to me that one's dreams *can* come true, I shall never again be able to put *only* a black mark against existence.

I have been unable to write; I wanted to write poetry again, but nothing would come. Then one evening, since the last entry in this book, it occurred to me that I might be about to begin a period of prose-writing, and that I ought not to try any more verse just now. I have had the idea of a novel vaguely in my head for weeks; today it is beginning to take form more clearly; I have an accumulating urge to start. I must make notes, write a full synopsis. If only I could finish it this summer — What I want to do in it is to extract the essential from my own experience up till now, to present the *zeitgeist* as I feel it, and to state the attitude of the generation born during the last War. Penetration: dynamism: poetry.

5.VI.38

Saw today in an English paper a notice of somebody's journal, recently published, containing a sort of daily account of the year's events described from a personal angle: which led me to reflect that, considering the extraordinary and momentous

157

nature of 'the times', (apart from the fact that this is a quite different type of journal in its intention), these pages contain singularly little reflection of contemporary history. Demonstrations in London, Spain, the Anschluss, do appear, but only in passing. It's true that I've lost most of my former interest in politics during the last year, but I've never been at all unaware of, or indifferent to, the things that are going on; and I have a very strong general sense of the present state of the world. I've never altogether been able to decide whether or not I wanted this book to be published some day. I suppose it's not uninteresting to read, but quite what its interest is I find it difficult to say: a record of the late 1930's; or a '*mon coeur mis à nu*' sort of confession? Perhaps not quite either one or the other: there's not enough general contemporary detail on the one hand, and it's not really sufficiently intimate on the other. I've given most of my most 'hidden' self away, I think, but have confessed to singularly little of my factual life, so that the self-portrait, insofar as this is one, tends to be rather too flattering. I ought to force myself to be much more painful about money and love, for instance — In the end, perhaps, the real reason for keeping a journal is vanity or narcissism, unless one is absolutely determined that no one shall read it; which I am not.

9.VI.38

Last night, went to a concert of Stravinsky at the Salle Gaveau, with Bent and Winnie B., and heard *L'Histoire du Soldat*, concertino for str. quartet, the wind octet, and the first performance of the new concerto for chamber orchestra. Stravinsky conducted, and strengthened the impression I have always had that there is something diabolic in him, — a streak of real evil in the R.C. sense, — cold, heartless, intellectual. In his appearance there is a mixture of mediocre respectability, of a Victorian melodrama-villain (or the 'sinister master' in Jean Vigo's *Zéro de Conduite*), and of a rat. Expressionless face, pokily precise movements of the wrist, a crouching backward slink followed by the calculated pounce of a little fencing-master spy. I am sure, too, that there is something 'bad' about the music of the *Soldat*, with its acid waltzes and raucous ragtime (*'c'est abominable'*, hissed the lady in the loge behind us) and its wicked parody of a Bach chorale. The new concerto, though, is undeniably most attractive, particularly the delightful second movement, a sort of Mozart minuetto. It is gay and witty. But unfortunately, there is no longer anything inventive or original in S.'s work. The new opus is really no more than brilliant *pastiche:* of Bach, in the 1st movement, Haydn or Mozart in the 2nd, and 19th century romanticism (Weber) in the last.

* * *

This evening, went to another concert in the same hall, conducted this time by Hermann Scherchen and consisting of Bach's *Musical Offering*, a Mozart divertimento (one of the less interesting ones) and Satie's *Death of Socrates*. Quite a different and less numerous public than last night. The Satie is extraordinarily pure and fresh, though a little monotonous, — like Vichy water. I am ashamed to confess that I went to sleep during the Bach.

5.VII.38
Tuesday Night
— Bent went away last Sunday morning. Ever since, it has been raining. I feel as though a lump had been torn out of me somewhere.

* * *

— *Seul enfin, encore seul, toujours seul.*

— *Déchiré. Horrible manque de force, de centralisation. J'ai soif. Horreur du monde quotidien des gens, de la vie bête, insignifiante, menée par tout le monde que l'on connaît. Soif de la transcendence, d'expérience spirituelle, d'assurance. J'ai l'envie de m'échapper du vide.*

— *J'ai envie de quitter Paris, d'être seul avec moi-même dans une ville nouvelle; de travailler; de me purifier du contact des gens que je méprends.*

— *Absence irréparable de Bent. En même temps, certitude consolante de l'indestructabilité de ce qui existe entre lui et moi. Même si je ne le revoyais plus jamais — Pendant le dernier mois, j'étais devenu peut-être trop dépendant sur lui, il était devenu pour moi tout à fait le centre de ma vie; et voilà pourquoi la solitude m'est tellement difficile à présent. Il faut que je m'y habitue.*

— *Que la vie se répète: en spirale: ascendante?*

* * *

What I have definitely realized about myself recently is that I belong to the same category of men as the Wandering Jew, Don Juan (not in the vulgar 'amorous' sense, but spiritually), etc. Never to find lasting repose in any place, on any breast, never to see the final vision nor to grasp the object of one's search . . .

10.VII.38

Last Thursday: went with Jessica H. to take Buffie to the American Hospital to be operated on for appendicitis. Came home early. Friday: lunch with Michael M. and a friend of his, tea here; went to swim at the American Club; met Odette P., dined with her at the Grenouille; spent the evening at 'Le Joker' — Saturday: Georgette Camille came to tea; went out to dinner with her in Montparnasse; spent evening at the Select and the Flore. Sunday: met Georgette, Michael M. and Henny for lunch; went to see a film; dined at the Select; spent the evening with Jacques Givet; later went back to the Select and saw Melcarth, among other people, and an American boy called Fred; came home at half-past two. Today: a heavy, close, grey day, with occasional drizzles of rain; went to visit Buffie at the American Hospital (difficulty of buses — endless traipse down an interminable empty avenue —); met Odette there; went to tea with Monsieur Georges C. and afterwards went with him for cocktails at the apartment of a Monsieur Marcel R., who lives in the house where Beaumarchais used to live and owns some nice paintings, among them two Chiricos; dined alone; came back to my room, where I have been lying inert on the bed in a state of deep depression, weighed down by an aching heart.

What a life! I am half-dead these days. No letter from Bent. The insoluble financial problem as urgent as ever. The weather sad and grey. I always hate July, August and the first half of September. If only I could get away to the South, but I see no means of leaving Paris at present.

Underneath all my present deadness and depression an obscure anger and revolt is smouldering — there seem to be no means for it of expressing itself. If one could shift even only a little of this great load of torpitude and mediocrity and wretchedness that weighs everything down!

21.VII.38
Grèz-sur-Loing. — Hôtel du Vieux Pont.
Arrived here the day before yesterday. Calm, peace, sleep. I do not care or worry about anything. Only at night, when one hears nothing but the soft, continual sighing of the tall trees

in the garden (or is it the whisper of the distant weir?), does the familiar restlessness and depression try to come back. Next morning there is sunlight on the white walls I can see from the window of my room, there are larks in the blue sky. In the afternoon, one can take a little boat out on the river at the bottom of the garden, one can bathe. The hotel is rambling and almost empty. A little way down the river is the house where Delius used to live. There is a big black dog that wanders about. In the evenings, when it gets dark after dinner, one doesn't know what to do except go to bed; there is only the wireless, or a book; the electric light high up against the ceiling of my room is too dim to work by. — Altogether, everything is very restful; and I certainly needed a rest after the recent strain of Paris, which I couldn't have borne any longer. I don't know how long I am going to remain here, but I wouldn't mind staying on until the end of September.

26.VII.38

Have decided to stay on here for a couple of months. — Yesterday morning, went back to Paris to fetch clothes, books, etc., and arrange various affairs; returned here this afternoon and am glad I didn't have to stay in Paris any longer.

Ridiculous scene with Anaïs yesterday evening: just as I had only half-seriously suspected, she really is one of these hot-blooded vendetta-loving Spanish women like the elephant (a baby elephant) that never forgets. *C'est une amateur de sensations fortes.* I should admire her exaggerated pigheadedness as a sign of passion, were it not that one has the suspicion that she has deliberately to force herself to act in this way, out of a taste for the theatrical and the picturesque, such as is evident in the Moorish décor with which she surrounds herself, the 'barbaric' jewellery, the incense-burning, the glass tree, and other exotic stage-properties that she requires in order to convince herself that she is leading an intensely interesting 'inner life'. (Oh, *miaouu* — !)

After dinner, went with Georgette Camille to a *séance extraordinaire* of the International Association of Writers for the Defence of Culture against Fascism. Met Aragon for the first time. Practically the only breath of genuine life about the meeting (which was held in a most sumptuously decorated salon somewhere in the Faubourg St. Germain) was the unexpected arrival of La Passionaria, who is superb, and the speeches of Ernst Toller and Anna Seghers. Theodore Dreiser was in the chair, looking rather like a depraved headmaster in retirement; next to him sat Rosamond Lehmann, who smoked a lot of cigarettes very elegantly and took a nice kindly interest in everything that was said. The English representation, disgraceful as usual, consisted of Cecil Day Lewis and Rex Warner, who made feeble, hesitating, thoroughly embarrassing speeches about their impressions of what ought to be done about 'saving culture' and 'advancing the frontiers of democracy'. Stephen Spender, who had spoken during the afternoon, was also there, and did his best to avoid seeing me; apparently because, as he finally blurted out, he has had to write a 'rather severe' review of *Hölderlin* (which I have not yet seen). Really, his social manners, or rather his lack of them, are very hard to put up with, though one realizes that much of his boorishness is due to abnormal shyness and nerves.

No one could care more passionately about the things discussed last night than I do. But the strongest feelings with which I came away were impatience and disgust. What good

163

do they do anyone in the end, all these earnest speeches full of vague and abstract phrases about liberty and culture and democracy, beyond giving the speakers the pleasure of hearing their own voices and of making noble but indefinite appeals?

Altogether, left Paris feeling very glad to get away from *tous ces gens*. What a lot of resistance everybody must require in order not to realize that they are all incurably disgusted with themselves. I can no longer pretend to be amused by this sombre farce that all the intellectuals one knows insist on performing continuously, in spite of all their boredom with their roles.

27.VII.38

Reading a novel such as Jean-Paul Sartre's *La Nausée*, one is forcibly led to speculate on one's own existence. My existence: that is what is supposed to be the matter of these pages. But is it? Does this journal give the least suggestion of what *my existence is?* or rather, has the writing of it helped me in the least to *realize* my own existence more strongly, more deeply? To a certain extent, yes; but not in the special sense of the word, only in the superficial, not the 'metaphysical' sense. When one begins to think of one's existence in this particular sense, one does indeed begin to experience a sort of sinking feeling in the pit of one's stomach, as though all the familiar furnishings of one's life were suddenly becoming dislocated and displaced . . .

To try really to experience one's life, that is to say really to feel one's existence, is like trying to build a house with rags and bits of straw with a strong wind blowing. One is constantly beginning again. This journal, for instance: I am continually sitting down to try to realize on paper my existence, to concretize it, to look at it. But the 'real thing' slips away from under the pen, one is left with unfinished, inconclusive fragments, trickeries, illusions, approximations. Then one stops trying to live until the next time.

Apart from what is fragmentarily recorded here, can I sincerely say there have been occasions in my life that I have lived completely, when I have been in immediate contact with existence? There have perhaps been moments. I believe such moments do arrive from time to time, unexpectedly, sometimes at the most banal instigation, preceded by a slight shiver of excitement, a sickening tension of the nerves accompanied by a deep conviction that one is never going to forget whatever it is that is going to happen, that one is going to see. With the same sort of temerity as that with which one takes a head-long plunge into an icy bath, one loosens one's habitual grip on the normal surface of everyday life, and at the same time, a sort of fluid antennae inside one begin to unfold their tentacles and to grope outwards into the vast, chaotic, senseless flux of the existent world. This is what happens in the state of poetry. Sometimes, if one is lucky, very rarely, the feelers close round something that is hard and satisfying, one has the impression of having at great odds saved something against eternity. More often, the obscure exaltation fades away, the moment reassumes its habitual insipidity, one forgets what one was thinking and everything is just the same as before, except that one feels rather more bored than usual.

There was the moment, for instance, when Bent and I were lying on the bed together in his hotel room, on a dark Sunday afternoon when it had been raining; through the muslin curtains I could just see something of the shivering leaves on the plane-trees on the *quai* outside and of the

165

silverish grey light reflected on the surface of the flowing Seine; and he said, 'What are you thinking about, you look so sad?' and I told him I was thinking of all the poor human beings shut up together in rooms like the one we were in and not knowing anything about the future and unable to prevent anything happening to them and defenceless against the endless flowing of existence that carries everything remorselessly away, no-one knows where to. — Then there was the moment I wrote about previously. — And suddenly now I remember a moment that happened in November 1933: It was a wet evening, about six o'clock, and I was walking along the Boulevard St. Germain (on the righthand side, — I had just passed the *pissoir* near the Metro entrance outside the church —) and was looking at the long reflections of the lights on the shiny pavement, when suddenly I had an extraordinarily strong feeling of being alive, and I told myself that it was a very important moment and that I should never forget it as long as I lived. I no longer have the faintest recollection of where I went or what I did after that.

29.VII.38

Was ill yesterday with some sort of stomach trouble. Spent the morning typing; woke up from afternoon doze feeling terribly heavy and sick. Went out with Prince, the dog, for a dreary walk to the next village; the sky was grey and lowering, it drizzled with rain from time to time; unpleasantly conscious of the damp sleepy vegetation on either side of the road, of empty fields and rubbish dumps and gravel pits among the trees. Came home feeling a wreck, lay down on the bed in my room and got up later only to be violently sick. Couldn't eat any dinner, the very idea of food intolerable. Went to bed reading Julian Green's Journal.

Woke up this morning feeling perfectly all right again. After lunch, went for a little row. It is very pleasant on the river here, with calm, sculptural clouds crossing the sky and reflected in the faintly rippling water on either side the boat, the dense and contemplative trees, the occasional women scrubbing clothes at the water's edge and the charming French houses with their towers and shutters, dreaming peacefully away among the untidy riverside gardens.

* * *

Last Sunday wrote the first two pages of a novel, but now I find it horribly difficult to continue. Great determination and perseverence needed to get it under way. If only I had the facility and the enthusiasm that I had when I was sixteen! At that age I had no experience of the doubts and difficulties that assail me now. *Opening Day* seems so remote that it might well have been written by somebody else, so that I have the feeling that it is my first novel that I am about to write: as in many ways indeed it is.

The more I ruminate upon this book, the keener I am to get into the middle of it, and at the same time, the more alarmed I am by the formidable demands that it is going to make on all my faculties. I ought to be pleased, all the same, to have at last found a theme which gives me an opportunity to express all the loneliness, despair, disgust and revolutionary passion that I feel. The treatment of it calls for irony and bitterness as well as lyricism. I shall have to put into it everything that I know. The whole of modern European madness and disruption has to be evoked as background. The hero has to be firmly situated right in the middle of his time. London, Paris and revolutionary Barcelona form the principal scenery. Among the psychological problems to be dealt with are virginity, sterility, the love of a

167

middle-aged woman for a boy, and homosexuality. There are also the financial problems of what to do when one has no money, and what to do with money when one's got it. There is an enormous cast of characters to be created. The book ought to run to four or five hundred pages. Goodness knows how long it will take me to write.

I always used to think writers were pedantic and unreal when they talked about 'the problem of style'; but now I see how all-important the problem is. To give cohesion and continuity to what one has to say, to find the natural rhythm of the sequence of events, to put words into sentences, sentences into paragraphs and paragraphs into chapters, — that is what presents all the difficulty, not the *matter* of the story.

5.VIII.38

It has been extremely hot for the last few days, but last night the sky was full of summer lightning and the moon was veiled, and there was quite a strong wind blowing this morning so that it is cooler today.

The hotel is full of flies. One is also pestered all the time by wasps.

Audrey Beecham has been staying here for a short while. This afternoon I went with her to Fontainebleau, where she caught the train back to Paris. We wandered about in the grounds of the château, and watched the ancient carp fighting for bits of bread in the lake. (Unfortunately, the place was swarming with grotesque American and English tourists.) — Rode on a tram to the station through the sleepy summer-afternoon town streets.

Before I got up this morning, dreamt that someone was calling out my name in the courtyard underneath my window.

In the dream J., whom I haven't seen or thought of for at least a year, had come to the hotel to see me. With tears in his eyes, he took my arm, embraced me with extraordinary affection. It appeared to be J., but his personality had quite changed. The strange emotion evoked by this dream has been haunting me all day.

Dear Bent, how I wish you were here! The passing of time is coloured only by your absence.

Will anyone ever be able to cure my disease of melancholy once and for all?

8.VIII.38

Yesterday evening, went for a walk in the woods. Taken back in memory to childhood by the damp green smell, the filtered light, a narrow meadow walled by trees. Scattered piles of dead white wood, like bones on the floor of a monster's cave, awakened for a moment at the back of my mind an echo of the child's sudden terror of lonely places. The wildflowers' names, all of which I once knew by heart, came back in recollection, though I thought I had forgotten them: St. John's Wort, Ragwort, Toad's-flax, Campion, Lady's Slipper, Vetch . . .

* * *

This morning received by post three volumes of new poetry from Fabers: Auden, Spender and MacNeice. More and more, I feel the existence of a great gap between their generation's conception of poetry and my own, and feel the need to explain in writing all that this gap means. Auden I admire because of his mastery over words and because of the sincerity of the best of his utterances; Spender I am moved by because of his real passion; but MacNeice generally irritates me with his slick technique, his trivial imagery and his

169

cultured whining. And the kind of thing that passes for poetry in MacNeice is also common to the other two. To me, MacNeice's poetry, typical of what in Auden and Spender is raised to a higher level only because of the quality of feeling behind it, is never anything but verse.

Poetry is not verse, it is not rhetoric, it is not an epigrammatic way of saying something that can be stated in prose, nor is it argument or reportage. In England, the whole question needs to be cleared up and restated. What I call poetry is not understood in England, but I believe it to be something of far greater value than what is at present understood there. The tradition of modern English poetry is really something quite different from the tradition of Hölderlin, Rimbaud, Rilke, Lorca, Jouve. — I belong to Europe before I belong to England. The values I believe in are European values and not English ones.

10.VIII.38

Apart from endless money problems, perhaps the chief cause of my perennial melancholia is my inability to carry out promptly enough all that my mind plans. My body cannot fulfill the demands of my ambition and my will. Physical lassitude is like a chain tying my hands. Sometimes, the thought of the enormous number of things that I must do, that I should have done already, is like the terrifying weight by which one is crushed in nightmares.

The life here at Grèz is very pleasant, but the air of the place is far too relaxing. I have no energy, and seldom want to do anything but doze.

* * *

Yesterday and today, wrote two poems: 'Fortress', and 'Insurrection' — Must revise 'Despair Has Wings', and make another effort to find a publisher for it.

11.VIII.38
Remarkable coincidence; J., whom I dreamt about on the 5th, has written to ask where I am, because he wants to come and see me during his holiday.

* * *

Have decided to write my Rimbaud book in the form of a novel.

17.VIII.38
There has been a *fête* in the village over the week-end, and a fair, with shooting-ranges, a roundabout, and a *bal*. Every day, while the fair lasted, Roberte, the little maid at our hotel, would come in with the breakfast in the morning demanding eagerly: *'On va aller à la fête ce soir?'* And all day long, she never missed an opportunity of reiterating this request. In the evening she dressed up in her Sunday best and we took her with us. On arriving at the fairground, she made a dash for the roundabout, and all the rest of the evening sat whirling round in the royal carriage, or else perched sedately side-saddle on a prancing horse. Her little face expressed only a desperate sadness, a grim determination to get the last drop of enjoyment out of the occasion. When we waved to her as she went sailing by, she was too preoccupied by taking in every detail of the music, the movement, the scenes painted on the panels round the engine in the middle, to be able to give us so much as a glance. When at last we wanted to go back to the hotel, she could hardly bear to be torn away.

20.VIII.38

The other morning I heard Peggy saying, as she walked across the garden underneath my window: 'The summer is over before it has really begun.' So at last it is the end-of-summer, that season which I hate so much. A kind of invisible darkness hangs in the sunlight, even when it is fine. Strange configurations of cloud pass slowly over the harvest fields. In the afternoon, everything seems to be waiting, undecided: whether there should be rain, or thunder, or wind, or sunlight; the weather of the season seems unable to make up its mind, and stillness reigns.

Spent yesterday wandering about by myself in the forest, almost happy to be alone. It was a beautiful warm day, and the forest was superb; one could not have guessed that it was going to be so wet and dreary this morning.

J. is not coming here after all, having gone on a motor-tour of Germany instead.

Am reading Briffault's *Europa*, most of which is trashy and unreal, but which has given me some ideas for *Son of the Evening*.

At night, behind the heavy curtains of my bedroom, with its pink-striped grey wallpaper, where the flickering electric light is reflected in the long mirror and on the shiny sides of the pinewood wardrobe, I lie tormented on the yellow eiderdown, a prey to acute mental conflicts and disintegrating doubts. A sort of dialogue goes on inside my head.

'You call yourself a writer, and what've you done to justify such a title? You've had 5 books printed in 5 years, and not more than one of them is worth a flick of the fingers. And for the last year, you've written nothing at all but a few dozen poems for which you haven't found a publisher. You always say that it's 'conditions' that prevent you from working, yet for the last month you've had ideal conditions and what've you produced but a few pages and a lot of plans which you'll never have the energy to carry out?'

1.IX.38

The day before yesterday, Rollo Hayes gave me three cachets of opium, which had been given to him by M. de C. When I went to bed that night, at one o'clock, I took one of these cachets and fell into a light doze. Awoke at about three, feeling very slight effects of the drug, and took a second cachet. Agreeable sensation as of warm waves radiating outwards through the body from the solar plexus, tingling of the finger-tips. The only effect on the consciousness seemed to be an intensification of the auditory sense: the dripping of a tap in my wash-basin became so exasperating that I had to go and stuff it up with a piece of cloth, and the least sound seemed to penetrate one's whole body. The intelligence appeared to be dimmed, if anything; one's thoughts slowed down, repeated themselves stupidly, with occasional sudden 'revelations', such as: Arthur Rimbaud loved his brother Frédéric, — Monkey Brand *se vende seulement à Grèz-sur-la-Nuit!* — Took the third cachet at 5 o'clock, hoping to increase the action of the drug as far as the visionary stage, but shortly afterwards fell heavily asleep. When Roberte woke me up in the morning with the breakfast-tray, the very sight of the coffee made me feel violently sick. For the rest of the day, was unable to take a bite of food; the stomach could not retain even a cup of tea. Felt wretched all day long: the experiment wasn't worth a whole day's nausea!

* * *

Everyone has gone away and the hotel is almost empty. This morning I have moved into Rollo's and Peggy's studio in the garden, which is quieter and more pleasant than my hotel-room. Leona returns here this evening. — Am glad to have made friends with Charles R., a young Swiss artist who has a studio in the village and who first made the acquaintance of Rollo Hayes and Peggy Lipp when he came into the hotel one evening to sketch the gypsies who were playing some music in the bar.

4.IX.38

Wrote yesterday to Cobden-Sanderson.

* * *

The present political situation is almost comic, diabolically comic, if one has enough detachment to see it that way: the whole of Europe waiting with bated breath for the 'inspired' utterances of a madman! Everything seems to depend on what Hitler will say at Nuremberg this week. All these diplomatic conversations, and 'exchange of views', and sending of notes, and 'attempted conciliations', — all this flurry and nervous chatter in the international henroosts, — because of the lunatic whims of a paranoiac little mediocrity of a German housepainter! — The newspapers talk of nothing but the possibility of war. It's all too desperately futile and disgusting to meditate on, our Western civilisation! . . .

* * *

It goes on and on, as though there could never be any end or issue to it, this daily tension and conflict between what I am and what I want to be, between what I possess and what I want to have, what I do and what I want to achieve. No-one can ever know, or care, what I have suffered alone in lodgings and hotel-rooms, faced with the horrible contrast between my sterile dreams and reality.

11.IX.38

Last Monday, recommenced work on *Son of the Evening*. Have been writing for a week — Leona Ryan is in Paris, but have seen Charles R. several times.

he other day, conceived the plan of a new novel: *The Anointed*, but I suppose I shall have to try to finish the other one first. *'On n'écrit pas les livres qu'on veut'*, as one of the Goncourts remarked. — One needs tremendous determination to do creative work of any sort in a world so disordered and uncertain as the world today. *Crise de la politique, crise de l'homme, crise de l'esprit . . .*

12.IX.38

Cafard

Cannot work because of a gnawing feeling of hopelessness, and anxiety about the future. Time passes so quickly; the days slide one into another, and nothing is accomplished, no decision made. I am incapable of looking after myself, — totally inadapted to the circumstances of my life.

I am beginning to want to get back to Paris. The hotel is now entirely empty except for myself; everything has a dreary sort of 'end-of-the-season' air; even the countryside looks desolate. If it were not for Charles R., between whom and myself a real friendship has developed, the solitude here would be unbearable. (How well I understand Valéry's remark about *'cette transparence d'une vie trop égale qui à travers les jours identiques laisse distinctement voir la mort.'*) — If I could have what I wanted, I would find someone to live with when I got back to Paris, for one thing, and would also get some sort of regular work to do, — in films, if possible. It would be absurd to expect anything of the sort to happen, however. I am so incapable of any effort to help myself, that I cannot even bring myself to write the letters which might have some favourable effect upon my future!

The sky is the colour of dirty skin through which is diffused a sick, discouraging, whitish glare. Every leaf on the trees in the garden which I can see from my balcony is motionless. In the chicken-run on the other side of the hotel, a cock begins to make an intermittent noise like an idiot child with whooping cough. The ensuing silence is broken again by the tuneless meanderings of a throaty falsetto: Roberte is relieving her soul in the kitchen. At the foot of my bed, Chi-chi, Leona's chow which I am looking after during her absence, grunts in her sleep, chokes, and turns over on her side making revolting sucking noises. I then doze off into a sleep coloured by senseless dreams (about Peter B. among other people — why?). The afternoon passes by without anything happening. I drink some coffee, then sit on the balcony reading Dostoievski. Presently a flock of crows start careering round and round the tallest tree in the garden, and their tumultuous caws sound like the squeaking of dozens of rusty wheels clattering along a stony road.

13.IX.38

Awoke at dawn this morning and finished reading *The Idiot*. Went to sleep again and dreamed I was having a long talk with Antonia. When the *petit-déjeuner* arrived, a familiar-looking blue envelope lay on the tray. It contained simply this one sentence: 'How . . . where . . . and why are you? Much love, Tony.' I have not once written to her since I last left England. When I rang her up to say goodbye on the morning before I returned to Paris, she sounded so indifferent and remote that I imagined I should never see her or hear from her again. But there has existed between us an intimacy so strong and so deep that traces of it will perhaps always endure.

15.IX.38

Terrible day yesterday: war seemed inevitable. Sick feeling of hopelessness and disgust all day long. Today's news is slightly more reassuring, though Europe remains nearer to disaster than she has been for twenty years.

I suppose we are 'living at an historical moment'. As I write, Chamberlain and Hitler must be having tea together. Charming scene! — This business of heads of governments stepping into aeroplanes and flying off to talk things over with one another may well start a new era in diplomacy.

* * *

What is so detestable about war is that it reduces the individual to complete insignificance. Our private destinies are swamped by the lumbering destinies of nations.

16.IX.38

Received a pathetic letter this morning from Bettina Shaw-Lawrence:

> I think it's wicked and beastly that we should be forced into a war we have nothing to do with and don't want, and I'm not afraid of saying I shall be terrified, not only for myself but for all my friends, and Peter and you. — I have had such a glorious day today, and I was so happy and then suddenly I saw the placards reminding me of war, and it made me feel so terribly unhappy I wrote to you.

Also an anxious letter from home, enclosing press-cuttings about *Hölderlin*, amongst which a bad-tempered and conceited article by Spender, who permits himself to make patronizing remarks about my 'charming talent', which he compares gratuitously with that of Christopher Wood! No wonder he looked so embarrassed when I ran into him last time I was in Paris . . .

* * *

Am reading Denis de Rougemont's *Penser avec les Mains*. Apart from the somewhat arbitrary nature of the central thesis, I am almost entirely in agreement with him in his analysis of contemporary disorder: divorce between thought and action, culture and society, absence of 'measure' (spiritual unity, or rather unifying element), etc. His attack on the moral detachment of modern intellectuals no doubt contains a misunderstanding of the essential nature of the artist, which is amoral; and his conception of 'the person' and what he calls 'personalities' is a little vague. But have found the book remarkably stimulating so far.

As I grow older, I become more and more convinced that my real function, insofar as I may have one, is to synthesise and enunciate the principles of the spiritual revolution which is imminent in the crisis of society. I see my own spiritual and intellectual development as a *filtering process.* What the residue of that process will be I can already see with increasing clarity; but the ability to pass from the plane of accumulative understanding to that of definition and exposition will no doubt come only with complete maturity. And only then shall I be able to decide with what form to embody the principles I conceive: poetry, fiction and direct critical statement all seem equally attractive at the moment.

The chief difficulty one has to face is perhaps that of overcoming a certain scepticism as to the efficacity of enunciating any 'message' at all. Paradoxically, this scepticism, this feeling of hopelessness that one has when one contemplates a public deafened by the shouting of innumerable voices, confused by a plethora of contradictory vocabularies, harassed and vitiated by countless partial and intermediate causes, is based on a consideration which, bound up with others, forms the very source of the argument which, having overcome one's doubt, one feels bound to put forward. On the one hand, one has to accept the risk that what one has to say will only add further to the general contradiction and confusion; and on the other, one has to have the belief that a voice is always heard in the ear so long as it is that which the need of the epoch calls forth. Also, the confusion of contemporary thought is not perhaps so absolute as it appears: behind it there are probably a quite limited number of tendencies, and each writer who tries to make a really serious analysis of the situation, helps to clarify and reinforce one or another of these tendencies.

Probably the deepest and most formative intellectual influence I have undergone so far is that of Marxism (no doubt inescapable for a young English intellectual of today); which explains why I feel that I have to express all my ideas in the form of an *argument against Marxists.* For two years now I have been fully aware of the insufficiency of Communism as a solution to the great contemporary problem; but I have never doubted that it was a far better solution than any of the others that have so far been put forward. Once one agrees to this, it would appear to follow that one is morally obliged to act in favour of Communism, *faute de mieux,* on account of the pressing urgency of the situation. But this is no longer so, as soon as one can clearly define *why* it is insufficient and at the same time propose a solution more truly satisfying to actual human needs.

179

18.IX.38

'Europe, ma soeur, ne vois tu rien venir?' asks *L'Oeuvre*, this morning. The high tension of the last fortnight continues; it is still impossible to say with complete certainty: there will not be a war. Apparently arrangements are being made for the evacuation of Paris . . .

Went out this afternoon for a Sunday stroll through the fields along the river, heavy with the inner burden I have been carrying for years and which sometimes seems, on days like this, too great to bear any longer, particularly when augmented by the hateful futility of the outside world such as has been forced into everyone's awareness during the present crisis.

I wonder whether one is made to suffer so acutely during one's youth in order to prepare and strengthen one for what one has to achieve when one is older. Otherwise — but enough of self-pity and self-dramatisation.

* * *

Charles R. has a curiously-shaped head, not unlike a pear, with a strong, broad forehead; quick, friendly dark eyes; a small, rebellious, slightly childish mouth. From time to time, he stammers painfully. He wears a grey, belted overall, which makes him look a little like a shop-assistant. He is 26 yrs. old, but might be said to look younger.

To reach his studio, one goes through a door in a creeper-covered wall, crosses a charming secluded garden-courtyard and mounts a little narrow staircase with dark red walls. The studio is quite spacious and has whitewashed walls, a ceiling-light, a large balcony window overlooking the garden and a smaller window looking onto the street. In one corner of the room there is an open brick fireplace. There are two or three easels; paintings, colour-sketches and drawings stand about everywhere or are pinned up on the walls; the white room seems brimful of sunlight and clear colours. As a painter, R. seems to belong to the 'intimate' school, and his work, which is very talented, has an affinity with that of Bonnard.

I often go to visit him after dinner in the evenings. He then draws the curtains, places a lamp on a small improvised table made of a stool and a drawing-board on which a red silk handkerchief is spread, and very often, since the nights are already beginning to be chilly, makes up a smoky wood fire in the brick hearth. We talk and smoke, and talk. A great deal of the conversation is of a highly philosophical nature, as we share the same interest in Kierkegaard, Dostoievski and the 'existential' school. Presently he gets up and makes tea or coffee on a little spirit stove, and after a while we notice that the hour is late.

Last night, R. made me sit for a couple of portrait-sketches. The first, done in thin, wispy lines with thumb-blurred shadowing, had the remote and dreamy look of a *pierrot lunaire*; while the second, bolder and more harsh in style, made me look like a Parisian *noctambule*, haunter of cafés, slightly 'diabolic', probably drugged: a vicious, androgynous face with enormous eyes and a sensual mouth. — I was amused because, although I don't really look like either of these pictures, I like to imagine I look alternatively like both; it flatters my romantic susceptibilities to be represented as a murderer *à la* Pierre Blanchard or Peter Lorre, or a degenerate, or a lost soul, or a St. Sebastian!

21.IX.38
Disgusted by this morning's news. England-France being blackmailed by the threat of immediate war, one had hoped

that Chamberlain would at any rate arrange nothing worse than a compromise with Hitler; but instead of that, all Hitler's demands have met with unconditioned acceptance. The 'democratic' governments have flung all their supposed ideals to the winds without a moment's hesitation. Was peace only to be bought at such a price? Last March, after the violation of Austria, I wrote: the power of fascism now looms right over the heads of the rest of Europe. This is ten times more true today. Practically speaking, democracy in Europe has now entirely ceased to exist as a vital factor, and that the decline of the British Empire has definitely begun cannot be doubted any longer.

Wrote yesterday to Allen Lane to suggest that I should write a documentary on Modern France for the *Penguin Specials*. Argument of the book: only a reawakening of the French masses to a united consciousness of their revolutionary tradition and historic mission can save French civilization from disintegration. The same might be said of England; but France has always represented the vanguard of Western thought, and it is in France that one can expect to see the first signs of a new determination and concentration on the part of progressive forces. One can only hope that the present strain and crisis will bring about a universal crisis of conscience. If only it has had the result of shaking the average Briton out of his habitual torpor and of breaking down the scrupulous barriers he has built up to defend himself against reality, the last few weeks will not have been in vain.

Mother and R. F. W. are probably coming over to Paris for the week-end on the 30th.

I still haven't the faintest idea of where the money is going to come from to enable me (1) to pay the bill at the hotel here, (2) to buy the new clothes I can no longer do without, (3) to continue to live in Paris during the coming winter.

23.IX.38

What a monotonous plaint this journal is! The first page of this volume starts off with a *depression,* and during all the pages which follow, the gloom hardly ever lifts for a moment. Anyone reading it would think I didn't even know what it means to be happy. But I do know what happiness is, though, and so well that perhaps that is why I so seldom achieve it.

'*Tu dois persévérer dans ton être!*' Terrible commandment, meaning: day after day, week in week out, for months, for years on end, to have to drag this heavy, lanky body about everywhere, and always this same turgid soup of thoughts simmering and bubbling in one's head! To have to keep endlessly chewing over the same stale bread-of-tears! Every morning to have to sit down to face the same unworkable equation: *Money* and where is it coming from, and how can I manage without it, and who can I borrow it from, and what can I do to get hold of some within 24 hours, and how can I pay it back, and how am I going to be able to live next week? And when it isn't money that's the rub, it's the dreary old problem of *self,* like a flea that one can't get rid of, or a stone in one's shoe, or an incurable boil on the back of one's neck: procrastination and masturbation, and I must *work* tomorrow, and why haven't I got more *energy,* why haven't I got more *will-power,* and what can I do to *discipline* myself, and why don't I answer all these *letters,* and why don't I make more *effort* on my own behalf? — Always the same old story, too-familiar disgust, interminable sterility and impotence, interminable futile floundering in an unlimited slough of despond! I'm sick and tired of it all, — sick and tired to death!

And it isn't any relief, either, to turn away one's gaze from the comfortless mirror of one's solitude towards the world of other human beings, or further still, towards the wide world in general. Practically every person whom one knows or meets is busily brewing their own private stew of misery, or engaged in trying hard to ignore the fact that they exist. Everyone knows that what is called 'love' causes at least twice as much wretchedness, of one kind or another, as happiness; and any other kind of intimacy between two people is bound to culminate in a moment of obscure frustration, the moment when one has nothing more to say, when there seems to be *something* important that one wants to communicate to the other person but which one can never quite manage to formulate, so that one remains silent, or forces oneself to talk of something quite impersonal . . .

As to the wide world of the nations and of history, it goes steadily from bad to worse, and man in general has probably never been in such a tragic dilemma as that in which he finds himself today.

Altogether, the most extraordinary thing of all is that somehow, in spite of everything, one manages to find the force to go on living, and to maintain a mysterious faith in the future.

After all, — the expression: *myself* indicates that my 'self' — the tiring body that one pushes around, the brain-box full of seething grey matter, the bundle of nerves continually being plucked and played upon by one's solitude or by one's contact with the outside world, and all the wearisome superstructure of conflicts and contradictions, the impulses and weaknesses that one calls 'character', — all this complicated muddle called 'self', is something that belongs, for better or worse, to *me,* and I am something different and apart from it all, perhaps even indifferent to it in the end.

I suppose it must be the idea of the future that keeps one going: that unknown future into which one projects all the nostalgia of one's dreams. But which never comes; because if it came, what would there be then to continue to keep one alive? So that perhaps in the end, the future for which one longs is nothing else but death . . . Perhaps that is the supreme paradox: it is death that keeps one alive.

But then, one must have had some experience of happiness in order to know what it is that one waits for from the future. One experiences happiness at those rare and unpredictable moments when present and future meet, moments of grace. — There is some music playing, perhaps it is only a jazz-tune on the wireless, or there is sunlight on the floor, or a red wall against a blue sky, or one comes across a few lines in a poem which seem to pierce through some screen shutting one out from a superhuman world, or else it is that fleeting instant when someone else's arms first close around one and another's mouth first falls upon one's own: and suddenly, one is happy; suddenly, something in one's breast that was cold and jagged melts away, and the wound of existence is healed, and a love of life that one had forgotten one possessed springs forward in a warm jet of enthusiasm like an unfinished bridge towards a vague perspective rich with the possibility of adventure and of buried treasure.

Evidently, the unblindfolded contemplation of existence, of one's own existence and of that of the universe in general, is a dangerous occupation, indulged in only by adolescents who have not yet learnt to be wiser, and by neurotics and other such suspicious characters. It can lead only to disgust, horror and despair; that is to say, only to indecent extremes.

I have gone to these extremes; I have looked at myself, and I have seen the void; I have lived in despair for more than a year, and I intend to persevere in it. I would not commit suicide even if I had sufficient courage (which I have not); because I believe that one can get *beyond*. '*Ce qu'il y a de plus surprennant dans le pessimisme, c'est qu'il conduit à les illusions.*' (Léon Pierre-Quint.) When I have reached the end of my life, I shall at least have lived it out; and maybe I shall have learnt something truly unpredictable from it.

(Nothing in this passage which I could not have written a year ago.)

25.IX.38
Impossible to reproduce here the confused train of reflections and arguments provoked in my mind by the European situation; it is too complicated. The deadlock of the Godesburg conversations, the general mobilization of the Czechs and the summoning of two divisions of the French army, made yesterday as gloomy a day as any during the crisis, quite as bad if not worse than the 14th. The high tension continues today; and everything now depends on developments in Berlin and Prague. I suppose we are in for another week of strain; if it goes on much longer, there is grave danger of the worst happening simply because people won't be able to bear it any more. But it all ought to be decided, one way or the other, before Oct. 1st.

26.IX.38
Another ghastly day today. Absolutely unable to do anything. Rained all day long, a heavy grey sky hung low over the earth.

One lives in an increasingly nightmarish atmosphere; life in Paris last summer, even here at Grèz before everyone went away, seems extraordinarily remote. Completely alone in this dreary little village (except for Charles R., who is a very great comfort), face to face with terrible metaphysical problems and with the reality of a world balanced dizzily on the edge of a precipice, in which everything seems to be preparing for 'extinction in circumstances of unspeakable horror', as Roosevelt said this morning. Never have I been so acutely conscious of the Void. — Fear, exasperation, impotence. — Where are we, what is this strange and terrifying world that we have woken up in and in which there is no longer any firm ground beneath our feet?

Listened to the wireless account of Hitler's speech to Germany tonight. One had quite clearly the impression of a madman speaking; his whole attitude and manner indicate an advanced stage of paranoia. It is quite unpredictable what he will do next, but otherwise the situation seems perfectly clear. Either he accepts the terms of the London-Paris agreement, in which case peace may be saved, or he insists on the complete destruction of Czechoslovakia by force, in which case there will undoubtedly be war. Everything is timed for the explosion, and unless some very definite change takes place during the next four days, it will go off.

In spite of everything, I still cannot believe that, of the two evils between which Europe has to choose, the disappearance of Czechoslovakia is the worst. One could not publish this opinion tomorrow morning without being accused of being pro-fascist. Very soon, people will cease to think any more, and we shall all be carried away by slogans and virtuous indignation.

Tant de choses se préparent sournoisement contre nous,
Quoique nous fassions nous craignons d'être pris au dépourvu
Et d'être comme le taureau qui ne comprend pas ce qui se passe,
Le mène-t-on à l'abattoir, il se demande où il va comme ça,
Et juste avant de reçevoir le coup de mort sur la nuque
Il se repète qu'il a faim et brouterait résolument
Mais qu'est-ce qu'ils ont donc ce matin avec leur tablier plein de
*   sang*
A vouloir tous s'occuper de lui?

Jules Supervielle: *Prière à l'Inconnu*

27.IX.38

Listened this evening to Chamberlain's wireless address. He spoke slowly, in a sad and exhausted voice, and expressed a pathetically sincere horror of war. However much one may have disliked, even despised this man before the crisis, and however true it may be that the futile policy of his government in the past is responsible for the present situation, one cannot deny that during the last few weeks he has done everything one could possibly expect him to do; and his attitude has been human and dignified, in striking contrast with the crude mock-heroic posturings of the Nazi villain.

There's at least one thing we can be thankful for, and that is that they haven't yet started in England a lot of jingoism and flag-waving and false nationalistic propaganda. They haven't yet started making passionate speeches about honour and the glory of heroism and sacrifice. No claptrap about the sacredness of the Empire, so far. — That's what I'm most afraid of: the stifling atmosphere of lies and distortion and hypocrisy that war brings with it. The atmosphere is appalling enough already, without that.

It will be a very strange war, if it comes: a war that nobody wants, for which no one has any enthusiasm, and which everyone knows at the start to be useless and unnecessary. A war by which there is nothing for any country concerned to gain, but everything to lose —

Can it be possible that Hitler seriously dreams of becoming the ruler of Europe?

If I had an 'aesthetic' type of mind, instead of a deeply 'ethical' one, I should perhaps better be able to record the fantastic element in the period we are living through; one needs a kind of *sang-froid* which I don't possess in order to describe its wonderfully dramatic aspect, the superb décor of dense black clouds pouring over the world-horizon (as in the Partridge cartoons one finds in old copies of Punch), the storm-tormented sky, resembling that which one sees in Dürer's *Melancholia*, or in Van den Leyden's *Lot and his Daughters*, or certain paintings of El Greco: the tremendous perspectives of horror and desolation, worthy of the biblical language of the Psalms or of Dante, which have opened up before us: the no less sinister scenes that are actually taking place today, children trying-on gas-masks, the hasty digging of bomb-shelters in the parks of London, soldiers disappearing silently into the bowels of the Maginot Line, countless anguished faces of people listening hour by hour to their wireless-sets. Are the scenes of H. G. Wells' prophetic film going to materialize so soon, — perhaps even next week? The spectacle of dense ranks of bombers zooming across the sky, of famous buildings tottering in flame and smoke, of masked stampeding crowds, the sinking of giant liners, would perhaps not be so difficult to bear if one were above all appreciative of the tragic-catastrophic-epic quality of the panorama from

the 'artist's' point of view. One might even console oneself by
repeating Rimbaud's lines:

> *Qu'est-ce pour nous, mon coeur, que les nappes de sang*
> *Et de braise, et mille meurtres, et les longs cris*
> *De rage, sanglots de tout enfer renversant*
> *Tout ordre; et l'Aquilon encore sur les débris;*
> *Et toute vengeance? — Rien! . . . Mais si, toute encore,*
> *Nous la voulons! Industriels, princes, sénats:*
> *Périssez! Puissance, justice, histoire: à bas!*
> *Ça nous est dû. Le sang! le sang! la flamme d'or!*

Poets are generally accused of exaggeration when they hold
forth in this tone; but Rimbaud's evocation now seems a little
pale, if anything, and *'mille meurtres'* becomes a very
optimistic under-estimation in the present circumstances.

3.X.38
Paris

Last Wednesday morning, was quite sure that war was about
to break out. Waiting to hear of German mobilisation when
news of Chamberlain's announcement to the Commons came
through on the wireless. Relieved, but still rather incredulous,
went to bed feeling very tired, and woke up next morning
with a high temperature, a headache and a heavy weight on
the chest. Stayed in bed all Thursday. Constant rain outside,
thin grey light in the room, rats rattling about in the ceiling,
the unmade bed damp with sweat and full of crumbs, a
mosquito buzzing around: — Purgatory! Determined nevertheless to leave Grèz the next day; which I did, feeling very weak
and shivery, accompanied by Charles R. On reaching Paris,
found temperature had returned. Lucky to find my old room
in the rue de la Bûcherie unoccupied. After lunch, read the

lunch-edition papers, with their headlines: Peace is saved! Horrible photographs of Hitler looking grimly triumphant, Musso and Goering grinning, Chamberlain and Daladier looking sheepish. Became more and more convinced of something sinister and shameful having taken place at Munich. What a peace!

9.X.38

Had lunch alone on Saturday at Chez Paul, and afterwards wanted to go to the Louvre, but found it closed on account of the war-scare. It started to rain. Wandered about the streets behind the rue de Rivoli, and ended up in the Champs Elysées, where I went into a news cinema. The audience applauded everything in the film about the crisis, even Hitler and Mussolini, and the film which followed, all about White Russians, was so disgusting that I went out in the middle in a chilly rage. A stupid, ugly, smug Saturday afternoon crowd was surging slowly up and down the boulevard under the dreary sky. Went home feeling dead and found C.R. in a similar state of gloom; lay down for about an hour in the dark, then went out with R. and had a good dinner and later went to Montparnasse, where Buffie appeared, just returned from Jugoslavia, and Jean H. and Melcarth. Came home with a fresh temperature; and woke up on Sunday with a second bout of *grippe*. Stayed in bed all day. On Monday had lunch with Leona, and dinner with Buffie, and later met Peter B., who persuaded me to go back to his hotel in the Avenue de Maine to listen to him reading the MS of the novel he is writing, an odd fantastic allegory about a lost angel. Feeling too stupid to react at all definitely, but expressed as much appreciation as possible, and walked home at two in the morning in a terrific wind, through a Paris which seemed to be at the bottom of the sea, along deserted streets where trees were roaring and waving their branches overhead, red electric blood flowed over the wet pavements, shutters and awnings squeaked and flapped and the lamplight threw wild shadows on the lurid walls.

15.X.38

The incoherent stupor of despair. Bewildered and inarticulate, silent and alone. Inert, tormented by the ruthless core of consciousness, I have no force to break the cold paralysis which prisons me. Complete despondency.

17.X.38
2 a.m.
Ill and without strength, but cannot sleep.

Have reached a state of complete paralysis, surrounded by walls entirely black, as in a dungeon. A state similar to that which I was in at the beginning of August last year. It seems impossible to go on living here, impossible to return to England. All hopes and expectations have failed. The future is completely void. And I have no force, no energy or faith with which to move, and am incapable of the effort and determination necessary to get me out of the pit I'm in. Only a sudden and *violent* solution is possible.

One of the most terrible things about this kind of state is the utter solitude in which one finds oneself. One seems to lose all real contact with other people; no one seems to matter. One may talk to one's friends, but they seem miles away, and all one feels is the futility of any attempt at communication. The shipwrecked man on a raft gets tired after a while of waving at an empty horizon the flag he has made out of his shirt.

This is worse than anything I went through at Grèz, because all the time I was there I was at least able to defer the solution of my problems until Paris and October: now I have been back in Paris for a fortnight and October will soon be finished, and there is still not the least sign of any solution, and the problem of how I'm going to be able to go on living becomes steadily more insoluble.

Despair brings one a new courage at first, and leads one to hidden sources, but there comes a time when these sources become all but exhausted, and when one can hardly move any longer beneath its crushing weight.

22.X.38

Last Thursday, started analysis with Mme. Jouve. Every two days. — Last night, letter arrived from Cobden-Sandersons announcing that *nothing* can be done about the financial situation, advising me to return home to Teddington and mildly threatening to prosecute me if I should arrange to publish anything with another firm. Final touch of irony: 'If there is any tone of severity to be detected in this letter, it is only because we are so anxious to see your name on our list once more.'

It certainly looks as though I shall have to go back home for a while, every hope of arranging some way of continuing to live in Paris this winter having failed so far; and maybe I really shall decide to go, unless something entirely unexpected turns up before the end of the month. This morning I had almost definitely given in; but since seeing Mme. Jouve this evening, feel far more decided to resist circumstances and stay here at all costs. — Having once begun analysis, which I feel is going to do me a lot of good, it would be a very bad thing to break it off after two or three sessions.

I have great confidence in Mme. Jouve, and already feel that with her help, and given a certain recovery of moral strength and, of course, at least a minimum of material security (depending at the moment on a quite hypothetical and unpredictable change of fortune), it may be possible, this winter, it I make a great effort, to break the vicious circle in which I have been hopelessly floundering for so long.

Charles R., who turned up unexpectedly yesterday morning, is really one of the best friends one could wish for: as soon as he knew what sort of situation I am in, he sat down at once and wrote off to some magazine editor or other who likes 'projecting artists' . . . I don't suppose that this will come to anything: but how rare to have a friend who when one is in trouble actually *acts* without a moment's hesitation. — One of the most *sympathetic* people I have ever known.

25.X.38

Still in the air. Analysis coming along nicely: unearthed a lot about Harrow and Florence Mole[*] this morning.

Spend most of the time nowadays sitting around in cafés writing letters, etc. (am writing this at the Select); find this a better plan than staying in my room and doing nothing but make tea, read fragmentarily and doze.

27.X.38

No letters, no developments. In order to stay on in Paris, I must get hold of Fr. 5,000 *immediately*. But how? This sort of situation has so often arisen before, in a less acute form; and past experience unfortunately gives me no reason to be

---

[*]   My godmother.

hopeful! I am getting so tired of all this waiting about the uncertainty and wasted time . . .

Last night, I was reading through the pages of this journal that I wrote two years ago. How I have changed, how I have aged! In those days, it seems, all experience was sharper, clearer; I took far more interest in the people I saw and went about with; the small details of everyday life appeared much more significant and interesting and worthwhile to write about. The things I write about here now are almost always abstract and interior. Now, it is as though I had become so worn-out, or disillusioned, that I can no longer be bothered to record the various lesser facts that go to make up my life. As though I were always tired, and lived in a semi-daze, and had come to believe that life is always monotonously the same, that the difference between people's personalities are only superficial, that there is no longer anything left to find out — *Mon dieu, il faut s'échapper de cet enfer étouffant!*

Jessica H. was talking to me about glands the other day (we were standing at the corner of the rue Delambre, just opposite the Dôme, in the growing dusk and a chilly wind, waiting for Buffie): I was suffering from an excess of pineal (I think), she said, and ought to have certain injections to counteract it; and I belonged, she said, to the type of person haunted by the idea of the futility of all effort and who has to have recourse to some escape from this vision of life, such as drink, or in my case (she said), dreams. But I don't dream nowadays — she's wrong; I read very little and seldom even write poems any more. I have tried, and perhaps succeeded, in developing a kind of asceticism which consists in constantly trying to see things as they are, that is to say from the most pessimistic point of view, at every moment of the day. Foolhardy seriousness? How can such a way of life *not* result in an overwhelming vision of futility? Something tells me that to see only futility proves a weakness in one's sight, and that what one must hope and strive and pray for is to be able still to *see things as they are* and yet see *more* than the hopelessness of everything. I had this thought a long time ago; and yet since then nothing has changed, I have made no more progress than a man who treads a wheel and who seems to be walking but who always remains in the same place.

I see all this, and there is no escape for me from what I see. Life is like a long and painful operation performed without an anaesthetic —

And yet, I know that I see life out-of-focus just now. One needs *money* and *love* to see it at its best, and just now I have neither. Money and love, the finest tonics in the world. Without them, it is almost impossible to make life seem worth living; I am unable to do creative work of any kind, I let myself float on a grey stream and stare without interest at the monotonous passing banks.

I sit writing this in a comfortable corner of the Café Rotonde, where I hardly ever go. The wall to my left is entirely taken up by a mirror, in which I see myself reflected, with my shabby blue suit, blue shirt and red bowtie, my sulky grey face, the hair which I have let grow far too long at the back of my head. Beyond my reflection is the reflected café, lit by a sort of diffused pink and green glow and full of people who do not make the slightest impression on me, for which reason I almost like them. Outside, it is drizzling slightly. The time is half-past six. Because I have been writing for more than an hour, there is a familiar kind of nervous tension underneath my lower ribs.

This morning I got up at ten, made tea, sat about smoking, shaved, and went out to analysis at eleven. — Rather a difficult session today: tried to talk about the impression made on me by a scene in a film of *The Fifth Form at St. Dominic's* which Florence Mole took me to see when I went back to Harrow to stay with her somewhere between the ages of 4 and 6. Also talked about my 'subterranean' fantasies. Ended up by describing a little dream which I thought was quite uninteresting but which apparently is simply *fraught* with significance. Then the Thursday midday hooters started going.[*]

Strolled leisurely to the rue du Bac, to have lunch with Buffie. We went to a large, cheap, dreary restaurant nearby, and Michel d'A. and Lee H. came with us. Somewhat laborious homosexual conversation during lunch which I entirely failed to find amusing. When we left the restaurant it was raining and cold; spent some time wandering about the rue du Bac with the others, visiting various shops. Went back to Buffie's badly-lighted, rather stuffily central-heated appartment and spent considerably more time doing nothing, that is to say helping Buffie and Lee move trunks and picture-frames, sort out an old portfolio of photos and reproductions, etc. Denham Fouts, or whatever his name is, a sumptuous, spoiled young man with a lot of frail and rather hard-worked charm, drifted in and out again with a young-old American home-companion. After a little more intermittent sitting about, made an exhausted departure, took a bus, and came here to the Rotonde, where I have been sitting ever since. When I leave here, am supposed to be going to Ed. Melcarth's studio in the rue Delambre for one of 'those sort' of parties. I know

---

[*] After Munich weekly air raid warnings had been instituted in Paris.

perfectly well what it will be like, but having nothing better to do — as long as it doesn't turn out to be another evening as dreary as yesterday, which I can't be bothered to describe. I suppose tomorrow will be another day of the same kind. I can only hope that next week I shall be able to spend my time a little more satisfactorily.

29.X.38

The Rotonde. 6.30 p.m.

Got up at 2 in the afternoon yesterday and spent the rest of the day at the rue du Bac. Had dinner with Michel d'A. and Pierre and Marcelle de S. Went to bed early, but was woken up before 1 by toothache. Miserably restless night. Went out to analysis late and unshaven, with a thick cold in the head. Difficult and inarticulate hour with Mme. Jouve. Too worried by the money situation to be able to talk much.

Had a long talk with Lee H. this afternoon but did not arrive at any closer intimacy with him. Am going this evening with Michel d'A. to hear the second part of Bach's *St. Matthew Passion* at St. Eustache's.

No letter this morning. Financial crisis remains exactly the same. If it were not for Mme. Jouve, I should be going back to Teddington next week. I have caught cold because I have no winter clothes; I have no change of linen, no clean socks or underwear, and whether I eat or not tomorrow is purely a matter of chance. Very much want to start writing again, but it is really impossible to concentrate or settle down to anything in the present circumstances. I have, however, written a fragment of a long religious poem, which ought to form the final part of 'Despair Has Wings' ('It is dark here and silent this dark place').

Want to write an essay on 'The Apotheosis of Lautréamont' (to mark the appearance of three new editions of L's works in France this year) stressing the importance of the 'magical' theory of poetry in the understanding of L.; the surrender of English poetry to rationalism, of English poets to rationalist critics and of the necessity for the poet today to create a super-rationalist faith *ex nihilo*. Reiteration of the idea that the practice of magic (in poetry) involves 'damnation' (Hölderlin goes mad, Rimbaud abandons writing, Lautréamont dies abnormally young):[*] i.e. the poet's destiny is to risk madness despair and death for the sake of a possibility of redeeming existence by means of the secret power of the Word.

* * *

30.X.38

Bach's *Passion*. Exquisite singing by the Leipzig St. Thomas's Choir. The lovely chorales I know so well because we used often to sing them at Salisbury, brought a lump into my throat and made me long to be able to sing them again. The lofty, shadowy-roofed nave, the calm iridescence of the distant candles, the voices climbing upwards amid the obscurity of the pillars, brought back a luminous recollection of everything that was most beautiful in the days when I was at the choir-school and wore an Eton suit and a white frill — days which now seem to belong to another life.

---

[*] Hölderlin's madness, (the pathetic folly of Gerard de Nerval), the final obliteration of Baudelaire by the powers of darkness; Rimbaud's desperate rejection of the Muse, the tragically premature and lonely death of Lautréamont; the broken heart of Housman; the suicide of Essenine, of Maiakovski, of Hart Crane; the murder of Lorca by the representatives of ruling-class baseness and imbecility; etc.

Bach's greatness in this work lies in his extraordinary power of transforming the great pain and sorrow of the rejection, betrayal, flagellation, crucifixion and entombment of Christ, into an unearthly calm and sweetness; of transfiguring grief and suffering into the radiance of a peaceful sky. This is the operation of the greatest art: resolution of the most violent contradictions, creation of harmony out of opposites — elevation, consolation.

31.X.38
Went yesterday to the Louvre, but having a cold and being weighed down by physical fatigue was unable to appreciate what I saw as much as I usually do. Purely psychological experience of communication with a young Florentine of the Renaissance portrayed by Botticelli. Spent longest time looking at that amazing French primitive of the Avignon school, the *Pietà*, with golden sky, strong reds and blues: the Christ-body arched poignantly backwards across the knees of the Madonna, whose features are stretched on an angular frame of grief, the halo like a jagged golden crown radiating sharply from the stiff, unseeing holy face. The nearest approach I have seen, in a work definitely belonging to the Southern French tradition, to the intense Gothic emotion of Grünewald.

Anne Goossens and Bettina came to tea; a pleasant change, the company of two such *jeunes filles*. We went to supper in the rue Delambre, and later went with a Russian friend to see *La Symphonie des Brigands* and *Pierre le Grand*. The only first-rate Soviet film I have seen for years; it has an admirable savagery and vigour, is packed with scenes of an astonishing richness of realistic detail, and is brilliantly acted in the best Moscow Arts Theatre manner. Outstanding scenes: a ball given to celebrate the founding of St. Petersburg, at which all the old *boyars* of the court have been ordered to appear with their traditional beards shaved off and wearing German wigs, and during which Peter, oppressed by the stuffiness of the rooms, throws open the windows and lets in the wind from the sea: the curtains flap, the candles flicker, and the dancers, with their heavy costumes and sweating, exalted faces, circle ever more wildly to the Tsar's clapping and exhortations, — their hair, the flowing locks of their wigs, blown back dishevelled from their heads. The ball is brought to an end by the rising of the sea: terrific scenes of flood, storm, drowning, panic (far more effective than similar scenes in the American film *Hurricane*).

* * *

In Montparnasse this afternoon met Tristan Tzara, who has asked me to translate certain poems of his for *New Writing*, and had a long talk with him: about poetry, about politics, the present situation in France.

The fundamental idea behind Christianity, he said, was that of *justice;* Christianity owed its success to the dominating power of the conception of justice in the collective unconscious. '*On a crucifié le Christ, qui était au fond un homme* bien, *n'est-ce pas,*' he said (my astonishment at hearing such words from the mouth of the founder of *Dada* was considerable), '*et c'est la protestation de l'inconscient contre l'injustice de celà qui a fait la religion.*' He spoke of the *St. Matthew Passion*, which he too had been to hear — '*j'en étais très ému*', he said, — as of a work concerned entirely with this all-important justice, first principle of the human.

He gave me a leaflet announcing a new collection of his poems, in which Jean Cassou says: '*Aujourd'hui que le scandale est passé et que l'esprit de rebellion souffle dans un autre domaine . . .'* And he himself said: *'Je suis convaincu que la période de l'experimentation est passée. Je ne puis faire aujourd'hui que suivre mon développement individuelle telle qu'elle se trouve à travers mes anciennes poésies . . .'*

We talked of war, of the political débâcle. Between people today who feel the social problem at all profoundly, there inevitably arises the impossibility of expressing oneself with the conversational vocabulary at one's command: one repeats words such as *'inimaginable'*, *'affreux'*, *'dégoûtant'*, in every other sentence, impotently.

6.30 at La Source, boulevard St. Michel.
Have just been to analysis. At present I have no clear idea of what is happening; today brought out what seemed only a muddled collection of images. Talked about the intermittent bursts of creative enthusiasm I have, which so often fall flat because I feel incapable of fulfilling them. ' *"La mariée est trop belle"*, as the proverb says,' Mme. Jouve remarked.

Have been thinking it might be useful to put down a few notes about *sex*.

Mme. Jouve says I have an exceptional faculty of transformation. I suppose this includes a particular aptitude for sublimating sex urges; because when I read novels about adolescence, confessions of sex experiences, etc., it seems to me I must be undersexed, if anything, so little have I suffered from the usual assault of tormenting carnal desires that most young men appear to have to cope with.

Every now and again, but not so very often, slowly and lazily a somewhat vague sort of sensuality wakes up; my imagination finds itself looking about for something lacking, for an object to which to attach the indefinite desire for

202

tenderness which is the strongest form of manifestation my sensuality generally takes. One could hardly call this being 'enflamed'. (The object looked for, I should add, has become exclusively male.) If nothing turns up, I usually find it quite easy to do without till the next time. All the same, I do attach a great deal of importance to the idea of love. But this is probably a mental idea rather than an instinctive one. It may be, also, that having somewhat high ideals of what I want, I have become accustomed to not expecting to get it very often.

At one time, I always told myself I was 'bisexual', and seemed unable to make up my mind as to whether I was attracted by women or not. After having lived in Paris for over a year, I realize that I never in my life had any genuine, unmistakeable sensual feelings about a woman; whereas I know by long experience that I can be physically attracted by men, that to make love with a man can give me great physical pleasure and emotional release. It no longer seems possible for me to make any reservations about accepting to be a homosexual. If a certain hesitancy about this is evident, it is not because I have ever had the slightest of moral scruples about following a perfectly natural inclination of my nature; but rather because I used always to have a vague feeling that I might be missing something by not loving women, that my inability to find any kind of enjoyment in a physical relationship with a woman might be due to a timidity surmountable with effort and experience; also, no doubt, because of a certain dislike of being classed by other people as a homosexual, because the average homosexual represents a type I do not care to be thought to belong to.

2.XI.38

I detest the kind of frivolity affected by a certain type of homosexual much to be found about the place. I detest the homosexual who is too visibly so, who exploits his role, who accentuates and parodies his abnormality because he is unconsciously ashamed of it.

For me, no real physical pleasure without emotional release. To be unable to find pleasure except in casual, ephemeral relationships with persons deliberately chosen for their inferiority of one kind or another, is to be dominated by fear and weakness. No emotional release without feeling of equality, mutual responsibility and understanding.

For me, love is the projection, the temporary focusing-point of a *perpetual* nostalgia. Nostalgia is a melancholy feeling; just as physical pleasure is a bitter-sweet feeling. Bitter-sweet: why? I can only say that I feel it that way, and that this is *not* because of any lingering feeling of guilt attached to the act of love, but because of something mysterious, the mysterious relation of Eros to Death which the conscious mind can take account of but cannot really understand. Nor can I accept the *omnia animalia* explanation for though it seems that the most intense erotic pleasure is almost always mysteriously mingled with melancholy and nostalgia, with a vague apprehension of the cruelty and tragedy of all destinies, yet if one accepts this darker side of love to begin with, one is far less likely to suffer from the usual dreary reaction afterwards.

Bent: my relationship with him was the nearest approach to my particular conception of love I have ever experienced. We were ideally suited to one another in so many ways. Why did it have to come to an end so soon? It seemed unnecessarily hard that we should have to be separated by his return to Denmark; though I suspect that if he had been able to stay, something else would have turned up to separate us before now . . .

In spite of my would-be faithfulness, now that what we were to one another is cut off from the present by what seems a long and tumultuous stretch of time, how can I help feeling that the old restless searching and waiting has to begin all over again?

Searching and waiting: imagine a life-time of only a such questing vigil. Always on the edge of life, in the margin just over the border, like money and love, lie beauty's undistorted forms and colours, and the eternal delight of energy, and the music that we long to hear. And in a purity of light we never see on this side of confusion, the real embodiment of all the images we give to our desires: golden flesh, the smell of hair, the tenderness of unfamiliar hands, moist warmth and gentle pain between the thighs, and eyes almost as near to eyes as mouth to mouth and full of disturbed depths and shadows; — movements of strength and grace, slimness and smooth resistance of a defiant, pliant body discovered in its final secrecy.

3.XI.38

My unconscious appears to have a very hostile opinion of Mme. Jouve, representing her as a witch with a pointed hat, a beard and horns! I am too polite, of course, to tell her so to her face; but I imagine she is wise enough to realize that each part of this composite image refers to a certain extent to her.

* * *

Met Tzara again on Tuesday afternoon: he gave me two new poems of his to translate, *Sur le Chemin des Etoiles de*

Mer (on the death of Lorca) and *La Face Intérieure*. Both are very beautiful, more simple and more logically constructed than his previous work, but still rich with a continual flow of new and unexpected images, animated by a continually renewed emotional force.

Il faut que la poésie devienne humaine,' he remarked, '*ou bien elle dégenérera en pur byzantinisme. J'en ai assez de théories. Je veux tout simplement m'exprimer, sans chercher comment ou pourquoi.*'

Whether one theorized or not, I said, there still remained the fundamental distinction, which he himself had made, between *poésie-moyen d'expression* and *poésie-activité d'esprit* (which corresponds roughly to the distinction between the English conception of poetry and the French).

'*Peut-être*', said Tzara, '*je sais seulement que dans mes poèmes les plus récents il y a tous les deux.*'

The Pit

I sink, I climb laboriously, I lose the thread, I fall. This endless groping, endless suspense. Everything is irrevocably hopeless, everything nevertheless is possible if one has faith, everything is uncertain: thoughts of hope and despair incessantly beating like hammers on the anvil of my mind. There must surely be a breaking-point, a moment when I shall not be able to bear any longer the strain? And then?

Courage, courage.

This is one of those days when I feel finally overwhelmed by the complication of existence, without refuge, perilously exposed to the assault of possibility and irrevocability, duration, consciousness. A sort of panic begins to rise. They were right to build the wall that I detest, the wall of caution and habit, blind prejudice and unconsciousness; when one has no wall to protect one, one sees that the world is at the bottom of an abyss, that it is dark and tumultuous here, that we are the helpless prey of an eternal, terrifying purposelessness, monster with staring empty eyes and all-devouring jaws. One is alone in this appalling shambles. One's only chance of salvation is to be able to cry aloud: but how faint is the whisper that one forces out when one would make the whole immensity of darkness ring with one's protesting voice!

4.XI.38

Absurd and tragic contradiction between one's interior and exterior existence: After writing the outburst above, I had my hair cut and went off to a cocktail party at Michel d'A.'s. Went out later, with a group of people left at the end of the party, to supper at the Select. Afterwards felt restless and did not want to go home, so accompanied Michel and Lee to Montmartre, where we wandered up and down the boulevard in the November wind, then went to a sad homosexual haunt in the hope of picking something up; or rather, where the other two hoped to pick up something. Dim lights, smoke, gramophone music, a huddle of dull and unattractive *habitués*. Sat there, bored and depressed by the scene, until Michel managed to secure about the most *canaille*-looking of the rough trade to be had, and then we returned to the Left bank in a taxi. Walked home alone along the deserted *quais*, where dead fallen leaves rustled on the pavement.

* * *

Continual desire to work, but there are so many things I want to write at once, that I end by not getting on with any of them. A page here, a few notes there . . . The only thing I can write regularly at present is this journal. I don't feel I can really get started with anything else until I've found some money.

Have decided I must finish and get published three books before I return to England: a novel, a non-fiction book and a collection of poems. And if I don't go back to England, I want to go to America next year. And if I have to return to England, I want to get some sort of job in the theatre and make a change from writing for a while.

Later

Had rather a shock this afternoon, and not an unpleasant one. Mme. Jouve was occupied, so I couldn't see her at 4, and went instead to call on Leona Ryan. We went to have tea at the Flore, and had been sitting there talking for about an hour, when I looked up and saw a familiar figure standing in the doorway and peering around the cafe. It was Roland Cailleux, whom I had not really expected ever to see again. Though I had imagined that all my old feeling for him was quite dead, I must admit a sudden twinge of it came back then. He sat down at the table and we talked for about ten minutes, and I have seldom known him be more charming or sympathetic. I am going to see him at his hotel tomorrow morning.

What is curious is that the other day at analysis I was telling Mme. Jouve about a dream I had just had about meeting a French doctor in a shop, and in talking about this dream, unhesitatingly associated the doctor with Roland, which led me on to talk about him for quite a long while.

5.XI.38

Had dinner with Maureen C. last night, and went with her afterwards to see Pierre Blanchard in Dostoievski's *Le Joueur*.

Not a bad film, but rather muddled; the settings and costumes excellent. Afterwards read anxiously through the winning numbers of yesterday's tirage of the Lottery, for which I had bought a ticket a few hours before; but no luck, of course!

Got up too late this morning to be able to see Roland. Must go and see him early tomorrow. He is going to England on Tuesday.

* * *

My plan to write a documentary book on France this winter having more or less collapsed, I have decided to go straight ahead at once with *The Anointed*, with the opening pages of which I am struggling today.

This decision seems rather absurd after having already started work on *Son of the Evening*: but for many carefully considered reasons, I think it is the best thing I can do at present. I must get on with something immediately, I can't stand this waste of time with nothing to hold on to any longer; at the same time, it must be work that I can finish within three months at the outside. *Son of the Evening* would probably take me about a year to write. *The Anointed*, on the other hand, will be a *récit* of not much more than 200 pages, and if Cobden-Sanderson won't take it, Dent's probably will. It is not an easy subject, but it is less rigid than that of *Son of the Evening*, and allows much greater freedom of treatment; it is a subject dramatic in itself, so that the plot does not demand a lot of incidental peripatation, but leaves me free to give more or less direct expression to the most important part of my own personal experience: metaphysical unrest.

The Anointed is the story of a tragic spiritual adventure; Mervyn Randle, an obscure young theological student preparing for the ministry, has a sudden revelation of the non-existence of the God of the modern Christian church, of the withdrawal and separation of God from the Church. The living God, into whose hands St. Paul says it is a terrible thing to fall, is the Unknown God to whom the Athenians raised an altar; He is mysteriously hidden in the confusion of the modern world, and man has lost the way to Him. The revolutionary inner upheaval which Mervyn undergoes, leads him to believe that he has been specially called to search for the Unknown God, that he is one of 'the Lord's anointed'; (the pure materialist would say that it unhinges his mind). His search subsequently leads him to seek for direct experience of the reality of Good and Evil. He goes to London, where he finds himself a bewildered stranger, solicited by secret dangers and inexplicable temptations. Exalted by his quest, led on by newly-awakened unconscious forces, he gradually enters a strange domain and becomes aware of an inner abyss opening up beneath him. He strays continually further from normal existence, until at last he realises he can no longer turn back and that he has to offer himself as a sacrifice by obeying a terrible instinctive power beyond his control: he commits a meaninglessly brutal crime and gives himself up to the blind and arbitrary justice of men, convinced at last of the existence of a true Light and of another and really profound justice.

7.XI.38
Went and drove about in the autumnal Bois yesterday morning in Roland's car. Spent the rest of the day at the rue du Bac. Went out in the evening with Buffie, Lee and some Americans . . .

Roland much the same *au fond*, but rather *adouci*. As fantastic as ever: wants now to find a woman to bear him a child! *'Je suis dans une période de gentillesse, à present'*, he exclaimed. Took him to see Buffie in the afternoon and he was *tout à fait ravi*. Unfathomable person. It would be hopeless to begin that all over again.

* * *

Am grimly determined to finish *The Anointed* this winter, but how I am going to be able to manage it is more enigmatic than ever.

Difficulty of starting. Such cold, deliberate, *uninteresting* writing is required to lay the foundations of the opening chapter. The introduction and scene-setting of a book I always find more difficult than anything else: one cannot let oneself go; the inner substance of the book, which is all one is really interested in, cannot begin to *flow* until the material framework of the story is firmly in place.

Have got the jitters again today. Holding on by my teeth. Can see the future only as a black and bottomless pit. If it weren't for analysis I positively shouldn't be able to go on any longer.

9.XI.38

Painful scenes with Mlle. David about the rent, which I've not yet been able to pay. Shall probably have to move. Can't stand all this useless arguing every month.

Mme. Jouve said yesterday that I was living through again at present a childhood nightmare. It certainly seems that I have been living in an abnormal state for some while past. The sense of suspense and unrelenting strain, the exaggerated proportions of small events, the violent inner ups and downs, all belong to nightmare rather than to everyday life.

Drinking coffee, smoking cigarettes with increasing abandon, sitting about trying to get on with *The Anointed*. Wrote a long letter last night to R. F. W. in a final attempt to get hold of 5,000 francs.

At Michel d'A.'s the other evening met Etienne C. de la Ferté, whom I first met at a luncheon-party about a year ago, for the second time. Went back with him and Michel after dinner to his very charming little apartment near St. Sulpice, where we sat in the firelight drinking cognac and listening to records of plainsong, Lully, Bach and Mozart. Etienne is slight in build, wears a slight moustache and has unusually sensitive eyes; he reminds one continually of Proust's Robert de St. Loup. When Michel had gone, I stayed behind for a while with him alone; the atmosphere became intimate; we discussed poetry, and he read aloud some early poems of Patrice de la Tour du Pin, who is a friend of his. Presently, when I murmured something about having stayed too long, he said: *'Ce sera peut-être le début d'une nouvelle amitié.'* — *'Je l'espère bien.'* — *'On va voir.'* — Am going there again this evening before dinner for a drink.

10.XI.38

Ran into Georgette Camille in the rue du Bac yesterday: she asked me to accompany her to a dinner given by the *Cahiers du Sud*. The restaurant was packed with very obviously literary people. Valéry, looking rather like an old white horse, was the guest of honour; Fargue and Supervielle were also there. Spoke to Benjamin Fondane, who seemed a little out of place, but was very pleasant, as he always is; also to that odd, pathetic little man, Jean Wahl, who introduced me to de Rennéville — a disagreeable experience. Sat next to a nice young French novelist called Magnane, and to a friend of

Tzara's called Berthelet. Met Roger Caillois for the first time, and afterwards he and Georgette and I all went and sat at the Flore and talked.

Caillois has a long narrow head, a sharp, pointed face; black, mephistophelean, mobile eyebrows, a small mouth. — Talked to him chiefly about Mass Observation and Charles Madge, of whom he reminds me a lot, both in appearance and because of his ideas. There ought to be a rapprochement between Mass Observation and the Collège de Sociologie. On the English side, excellent practical fieldwork, but general confusion and vagueness of theory; on the French, brilliantly developed theory, but absence of direct contact with material fact. Asked Caillois to send Madge *Le Mythe et l'Homme*, must write and tell Madge to send a copy of the *Coronation Survey* to the Collège, which is giving a séance soon on *Le Symbolisme de la Couronne*.

Went this morning to call on Mlle. Clairouin, who is trying to get me translation work to do. Had lunch with Etienne at his apartment, and spent the afternoon there, playing Bach: a joy to touch a piano again after such a long time! Etienne has asked me to spend the week-end with him at his home in the country; have naturally accepted very willingly.

Had rather an important session with Mme. Jouve this evening: beginning to get at things now. Apparently my censor is on too low a level, my aggressivity is too repressed, and I have a masochistic attitude towards my father, whom I imagine to be punishing me all the time!

Have a sudden crop of translations to do: an MS from the Centre d'Etudes Politiques which arrived this evening, and four radio talks by Georgette Camille which I'm going to do tomorrow. May also be going to help Stuart Gilbert translate *Les Thibaults*.

13.XI.38

Spent most of Friday at the rue du Bac, typing. Apéritifs *chez* Buffie, then went out to dinner with Georgette Camille and a friend of hers, rue Jacob. On coming back, met Buffie, Lee and Melcarth's sister on their way out to dinner, and accompanied them to Lipp's. Was feeling headachy and heavy, but at the Flore afterwards, after a lot of black coffee, began suddenly to wake up and to feel extraordinarily energetic. Quite unexpectedly, Charles R. walked in, with his friend Jean-Pierre, whom he has often spoken to me about. I was feeling very gay and conversational by this time, and we all talked animatedly for a long while. Scent of the eau-de-Cologne someone at the table was wearing: a *cold* invigorating smell, wind, night in the hotel: a wave of indefinite memories, *élan,* restlessness . . .

Returned to the rue du Bac, intending to work on a translation for Georgette, which I was supposed to finish and leave at her flat nearby that same night. Found Lee still up, reading; we began to talk: religion, politics, sex, travel; and the conversation went on all night long. Watched the grey November dawn percolate gradually through the long windows behind the Greek plaster torso, and left the flat at half-past seven. Went and had a large breakfast at the Dupont Latin, and then returned to my room, where a letter from R.F.W. was waiting.

She has decided to lend me the 5,000 francs I need, so the financial problem is solved for a while, I trust . . . This winter I must make a terrific effort to put my life on a new basis. With the help of analysis, and great determination, I may be able to put an end at last to this long dreary story of lack of money, depression and inability to work.

Packed a case for the weekend and at nine o'clock went off to meet Etienne at his flat. We left Montparnasse at half-past nine, and arrived at Dreux, which is on the edge of the Beauce, near Chartres, at about eleven. A typical large French country-house. We went into a lofty salon and were given porto, and then into another room to see Mme. la Baronne, Etienne's mother, who is *souffrante* and has to live in bed. A pleasant old lady with a round bespectacled face and white hair, propped up among the pillows, surrounded by screens and bedside-tables, little crucifixes, *objets de pieté*, medicine-bottles, gadgets; she seemed remarkably lively for a permanent invalid. Had lunch in a room leading through folding doors into one of the salons, at the end of which the windows, hung with long yellow curtains, looked out onto a bright green lawn thick with the gold of fallen leaves and surrounded by trees whose autumnal colours burned against a profoundly luminous distant sky. Sunlight poured into the warm room. Went upstairs after lunch and slept until five o'clock tea. Played the piano for a while, then went up and sat in Etienne's room until it was time for dinner, after which we went to visit la Baronne once more. She was sitting up in bed listening to Paul Reynaud's radio address about the new financial *décrets lois*; when it was over, a discussion about politics began. Familiar argument between an aristocratic and reactionary mother and an emancipated disillusioned son, into which I dropped only a non-committal word here and there. Presently we went up to sit in the library; on the landing, Etienne turned and said: *'Il y a une proverbe arabe qui dit: on est l'esclave des paroles qu'on dit, mais maître de ceux qu'on ne dit pas.'* Still cannot quite make out what he meant to imply . . .

Directly after breakfast this morning, we drove out through a rather desolate flat countryside of brown fields, scattered copses and deserted villages to the edge of the forest of Sennanges, where we walked for about two hours along muddy paths through melancholy glades in the pale end-of-autumn sunshine. Deer ran across the distance from time to time. I was feeling rather liverish and found it difficult to talk. The car picked us up again beside a lake on the other side of the forest, and we drove back to a late lunch. Slept in the library beside a blazing log-fire this afternoon until it grew dark and it was time to have tea and leave. As the Paris train left the little station, lurid streaks of light were dramatically fading on the Western edge of the sky.

Had dinner with Etienne at the Select this evening, and now that he has gone home, am writing this. I still haven't done Georgette's translation, and I really must return it to her tomorrow. It's going to be a busy week.

14.XI.38

One of the profoundest causes of our obscure perpetual frustration no doubt lies in the fact that we wish to give form and meaning to our lives, to live them like a *story*; while Existence, which is flux and confusion, continually thwarts our desire for clarity and significance; bewilders us with an endlessly growing mass of futile, irrelevant details; exhausts us with noise and strain to such a point that we have hardly ever the *force* that is necessary to *integrate* the raw material of our lives and to transform them into the shape of a reality less meaningless and transient than that perceived by the merely passive mind. Spiritual adventure of the *conscious* man, the 'artist in living': to enlarge the rare and poignant moments of perception and realization, to make them gradually longer and more continuous, until at last they cease to be interrupted. To be able to do this one must rid oneself of all fears, and above all of the fear of *burning with one's own flame*; one must be prepared for all emergencies, for the strangest, most unexpected and apparently pointless accidents; one must be completely *open*, which means accepting everything (not in the sense of *submitting* to the ugliest and petty facts of one's experience, but of accepting them as valid material and as necessary parts of the whole); one must learn never to be discouraged by muddles or disappointments, but always to preserve enough energy to begin again, (for to be able to give form to one's existence, to give it its fullest richness, demands continually renewed effort); one must learn always to answer *immediately* to the promptings of one's intuition, always to follow one's least initiative without hesitation, carry thought through into action without the loss of spontaneity which a moment's delay inevitably entails.

Grandiose, indeed almost superhuman task. Those who have undertaken it have very seldom succeeded. But there is something particularly admirable and moving about those who have sufficient obstinacy or courage to struggle continually in their personal lives towards the fulfilment of this task. One can in any case found a whole morality upon such a struggle.

The chief difficulty one comes up against is that the undertaking is bound to become increasingly complicated, since it entails ever passing to successively higher planes. As soon as one has learnt from A to Z, one discovers that A to Z is only the sum total of the A of a higher series; and so on. But perhaps one does reach a point, sometime, at which a transcendental revelation intervenes; though of course this would not happen unless one threw oneself into the enterprise to begin with without the least hope of benefiting from such a grace.

I have long been haunted by the desire to live my life according to this ideal. To a certain extent I have attempted it, and have been defeated numberless times. And now, perhaps, a turning-point has come. I have always wanted to get out from beneath a certain weight which seems to hold me down — to release the fund of energy which is buried in me somewhere, to live more positively, to penetrate fully into the world of action. Something has always held me back, there has always been some check. Now perhaps the time has come to find out what this something is, to face it and to overcome its domination.

During the recurrent periods when the exterior circumstances of my life seem as hopelessly difficult as they have seemed to be during the last few months, I enter a nightmare world, the terrible domain of black despair; but I do not believe that this is an unreal world, but one rather of abnormally profound depth and of more intense consciousness of reality, like the abnormal world of love. When exterior circumstances are easier, I rather tend to become *abruti*, lulled into illusion, deadened in sensitivity. As always, of course, what I must try to achieve is a firmer balance between these two extremes, by maintaining during the easy periods the intensity of experience of the periods of depression.

16.XI.38
Have reached the same sort of check in analysis as I am accustomed to meeting in my life. Feeling that there is a barrier between my conscious mind and the part that is being

analysed. Lay on the couch this evening associating words and images *around something that was hidden* and which I could not get at. Then silence. *'Est-ce que ce n'est pas l'orgeuil qui vous empêche de parler?'* demanded Mme. Jouve. Was finally forced to speak by a violent desire to urinate, the same desire that a ridiculous *pudeur* used to make me suppress for so long when I was a child and which used so often to lead me into painfully embarrassing situations.

* * *

Fantastic news: I may be going to be a husband in a few months time. Buffie wants me to marry a German girl whom she made friends with in Dalmatia this summer and who is desperately in need of a British or an American passport. Her name is Ingrid and she is coming to Paris after Christmas. Buffie having written to tell her I am willing, she writes back: 'David is now the hope-star on my heaven.' In her photograph she is very beautiful.

18.XI.38

Have got some money now, at last, and consequently some clothes, various necessities, etc.; but life seems just as *dangerous* and uncertain as ever. The pit into which one can so easily fall is always waiting just round the corner. That is to say: no money lasts for long, and there is always the uncertainty, or rather the unlikelihood, of getting any more. Now is the moment, however, to combine all my forces in one terrific effort to change the material basis of my life. (And as I write that sentence, I think of the lives of Balzac, Dostoievski, Baudelaire . . .)

Am going through a critical period in analysis at the moment, it appears, and shall be glad to get out of it again.

Lee, Etienne, Peter B., Jean-Pierre. Vague restless feeling of interrogation attached to their names. What will become of these new friendships? Is any one of them going to become more important than the others?

Had lunch and a long conversation about 'life' with France N. today, and afterwards went with her to a gramophone-shop to buy a record of Purcell's *Golden Sonata* for Etienne, with whom I had tea. To the tailor's, then to Mme. Jouve's, then to Montparnasse, where I had dinner with Peter B. Spent the rest of the evening talking 'literature' with Georges Magnane. Finished up at the Flore, where I saw Tzara and the Reichs; more talk. Altogether, enough talk today to last for quite a long while.

'*Si on le veut ou non, on ne peut pas s'empêcher de faire un tas de choses absolument ridicules tous les jours,*' remarked France very appositely this afternoon. *C'est écoeurant.*

Little by little, I begin to see how to formulate the essentials of *a new morality*. *Blind Man's Buff*, which at present is quite fragmentary and unpublishable, may gradually develop into a work expounding the principles I am beginning to see with increasing clarity.

20.XI.38

It is very fortunate for me that I am always attracted towards the books that I need at a given moment as though by a magnet. Yesterday, for instance, suddenly remembered the title of Marcel Jouhandeau's *Algèbre des Valeurs Morales*, and although I had never before thought I had any particular desire to read it, decided to go and buy it at once. It is for me one of those books whose importance for oneself one realizes at first glance, which almost make one feel one is familiar with them already, so close is one's sympathy with the author's thought.

* * *

Je fume trop, je me laisse trop trainer sans rien faire, je me cultive intérieurement et je m'observe (mais je n'admets pas qu'on peut faire trop celà).

Si j'ai un chemin à suivre, c'est celui qui mène chaque jour davantage vers une plus grande conscience de moi-même et en même temps vers une plus grande conscience du monde. Le chemin des abîmes.

* * *

Larry and Nancy Durrell have returned from Greece; I saw them yesterday evening and met them this afternoon. He is just the same, the same charm and the same old nonsense; but I have changed a lot. The world of Durrell and Henry Miller, *The Booster*, the Villa Seurat, etc., has not the same hold on me as it had last winter. The world I live in has become only my own, and I am alone in it.

22.XI.38

I wanted last night to be a test of something which it is always rather difficult to be sure about at first. I was watching Lee all the time, and watching myself watch him. Every moment had an enlarged importance, simply because he was there. All the time, I was waiting for the moment when I should be able to summon up my courage to say the phrase which would have made everything suddenly easy — or difficult? — for both of us. But the 'right moment' didn't arrive. At least there was something for me to be glad of, though: my reaction to everything he said, my growing exasperation at not being able to make him understand, were strong enough to make me realize the truth of what I have been suspecting for about ten days. When at last I managed to get him up to my room, I was almost triumphant; when he said that he had decided to spend a fortnight of strict celibacy, I was crushed; and when he finally and deliberately went away, I was left feeling desolate. As he went down the stairs, I was so miserable that I knew at once how much it would have meant to me if he had stayed. I flung myself face downwards on the bed, and began to recognize that unmistakable wringing of the heart which means only one thing.

Wrote him a long letter this morning, a thing which in such circumstances I have never done before. I have a horror of being importunate, and a horror of putting people into the kind of position into which I may be putting Lee; but I have also a horror of vagueness and indetermination in these affairs; I must know where we stand. I know what risk one runs in sending a letter of this kind to someone whose response is unpredictable; but I cannot trust myself to take any other action sufficiently quickly.

23.XI.38

After having left my letter to Lee at the rue du Bac yesterday morning, spent the rest of the day in a state of nervous exhilaration at having for once taken definite *action* and unhesitatingly followed an impulse of the heart. When I went home last night, found a *pneumatique* from Lee: 'I love you very much, David, but there are certain complications and I think I can best explain these by letter . . .'

Am suffering today, of course, from torturesome reaction. I suppose I prefer things not to be too easy; but I'm afraid — I'm afraid he cannot respond to the passion I have conceived

222

for him, he is holding back, and 'certain complications' are a kind excuse. I'm afraid, too, he would be out of his element in a passionate relationship with a person of such a voraciously, insatiably imaginative and introspective temperament as myself. I've never met anyone, except Antonia, with whom it would be so difficult to carry on a love-affair as with me.

In the end, though, success or failure, what does it matter? It is *my own* unique experience and all that I really desire is to *experience* it in its utmost entirety.

* * *

Everything has suddenly become coloured by this obsession: the streets, the weather, sleep, the passing hours. The exterior world is seen through an intensifying glass; the imagination is constantly alert; a latent magic force has risen to the surface of consciousness and seems ready to overflow at the first sign.

> *Il faut remonter du plus bas de la mine, de la terre épaissie par l'humus du malheur, reprendre l'air dans les recoins les plus obscurs de la poitrine, pousser vers les hauteurs — où la glace étincelle de tous les feux croisés de l'incendie — où la neige ruisselle, le caractère dur, dans les tempêtes sans tendresse de l'égoisme et les décisions tranchantes de l'esprit.* Reverdy

The destiny I have chosen — or which has chosen me — demands the most constant and determined effort, endless upward struggling, long weary vigils, and ever-repeated beginnings — again incessant concentration, intensification, purification — to make a diamond out of dust.

24.XI.38

Feel as though I had thrown a rope towards Lee, the end of which he has neither taken nor rejected, and which remains waving loosely in the air. I wonder if he realizes how unbearable is the uncertainty he is inflicting? He was there at Buffie's at lunchtime today, but made no sign at all: exasperating comedy of two people in a room together, one in love with the other, the other aware of this passion, and neither of them able to speak of it or show that it exists! If he is trying to avoid hurting my pride, I would prefer brutality; it is far easier to face defeat than not to know whether there is hope for one or not.

> *Que l'être que tu aimes soit docile ou indifférent à la passion qu'il t'inspire, qu'importe?*
> *. . . mais si tu es la victime d'un homme, quel qu'il soit, qui exercerait sur toi sa puissance de destruction, tu es jugé. Est-ce que tu acceptes d'être esclave?*
> *L'amour est un accident terrible qui n'est pas toujours à notre disposition.* Jouhandeau

26.XI.38

Went to lunch yesterday with Etienne, at his apartment, and in the afternoon to Buffie's, to find a note from Lee at last. Just what I had expected all along, I'm afraid. Hopeless. But it's a relief to have finished the uncertainty.

> Not being obtuse I have understood your feelings for some time. And had sympathised with them because I have been in the same place myself. I had hoped by inattention to avoid the issue and, if possible, to see you happily engaged with Etienne. I'm sorry it could not have worked out that way.

Meanwhile do not desert me, and please forgive me. The only alternative would have been some sort of false, insincere arrangement. Neither would have liked that. I find that almost always I fall in love with dull and worthless people. And vice versa. There is no sense in it.

I do regret that so much emotion is rewarded with so much coldness. The 'new society' will have to make love less illogical.

Why did this have to happen? I suppose it is good for me. I suppose one learns something, and that there is a point to it all? At least I know now how poor Antonia must have been feeling two years ago (I had a long letter from her yesterday, by the way). If my sense of irony were a little more strongly developed, I could see the whole thing as a perfect comedy.

After leaving Buffie's, was going along the Blvd. St. Germain, dropped quite by chance into a little *tabac,* and there was Roger Roughton who happened to be passing through Paris for less than 24 hours. Had a quarter-of-an-hour's completely insincere talk with him: insincere, because it was someone else talking, a stranger, and not myself at all, only Roger's idea of me as I used to be.

Afterwards, met Desmond and Leona Ryan at the Flore, with a party of other people, including Brian Howard and Tony. Had a very good dinner at Calvet's, during which Brian, I must say, was extremely amusing. While we were having coffee back at the Flore again, in walked Jean-Pierre and a friend of his. (I will not formulate the thought that passed through my mind on seeing him.) Talked to him for a while, and recognized in him again that unanalyzable *tense* quality I noticed when I first met him a fortnight ago.

Spent the rest of the night in Montmartre with the Ryans: at the Liégois, Bricktop's and the Swing Club, trying to find distraction from my unrequited amour, I suppose. Ended up at the Select at 7 this morning, alone with Desmond, who says he wants me to spend a week with him soon at Monte Carlo . . . Went to bed at 8 and slept until shortly after noon. Feel etherialized today.

27.XI.38

Sad, wandering, lonely, absent. Worn-out with wanting what I haven't got (before, it was *money* I wanted: now it's *love:* always either one or the other, generally both), what a relief it would be to have something to rest on. But nothing is firm, there is nothing to prevent one falling. The only unfailing relief is sleep, the humiliating abdication of one's consciousness. (Regarded in that sense, sleep becomes a minor form of suicide.)

Must now try to begin to work really hard and to forget everything else for a while.

Saw Jean-Pierre again last night and am going to meet him again during the coming week.

5.XII.38

Have spent a hectic week Seem now to be in one of those periods when I don't write my journal regularly because there is too much to say and never any time to say it, as happened last year at about this date. I know what kind of risk one runs in leading this sort of life, — seeing dozens of people, going out to places all the time, not sleeping enough, etc. — but after all, it is a risk I am glad enough to take, when I think of the terrible dead state I was in two months ago. I feel *alive* again at last, clear-headed, energetic, not unduly pessimistic about the future, which is becoming increasingly interesting. Also, it is no longer for me a question of a wild, Icarus-like attempt to leave the ground behind ('illusion of flight and speed', as I wrote in a previous entry); I have not lost contact with the 'basis' I reached recently, I have not blotted out the awareness of my difficulties; I'm beginning to have a fairly firm hold on things now. In spite of a tiresome chesty cough, I feel in unusually good health. And I *am* working (not very much, perhaps, but at any rate fairly regularly; am finishing *Oliver Middleton's Confession*, which suddenly interests me again). Analysis continues to be difficult, but one must not be impatient; I am confident that we are gradually getting at something, piecing things together; the business will probably have to go on until next spring.

Had an interesting short extra-analytical talk with Mme. Jouve this evening, about my plans: marriage with Ingrid after Christmas, return to England to get a theatrical job after Easter. (I also keep thinking about the possibility of going to America next year, but don't yet quite see how it could be managed.)

I feel there is a great deal of truth in what Antonia wrote in her last letter:

It would be all right if you were a person to whom the agreeable physical things of life (by which I include everything from amusing food to the books one wants) meant very little, but I know, though you can bravely endure poverty in patches — even destitution — it gets you down. And you are too kind and sensitive to be able to live without turning a hair on credit and friends. To live like that without being oppressed and guilty one has to be either ruthless or innocent. You have neither Miller's temperament nor Barker's (his wants are very few, though he'd *like* a burst now and then) and until you know what standard of living really suits you and face the necessity of getting it, I think you will continue to be wretchedly unhappy and to stick at a certain point in work and development too.

227

Had a long first letter from Ingrid:

> In the last weeks which are gone, you became a friend of mine, even
> if I did not know you, don't know how you look, how you think and
> feel.
>
> It is difficult for me to tell you what that what you will do for me
> means to me. Perhaps I could explain it to you if I could show you
> my life, all that what's gone until today . . .
>
> I don't wish only a paper, it is much more what I look for.
>
> You give me the urge to build new what I lose — encouragement,
> strength, hopes.
>
> I love the world and earth, I drink the wind and the smell of the
> night, I love people, their weaknesses and strength; I believe in all
> that is life and in my stuttering heart; and above all, I believe in the
> future of our present youth.

10.XII.38

(*Hôtel de l'Etoile, Noyers-sur-Serein. Saturday noon.*)

Two days ago I hadn't the least idea that within 40 hours I
should find myself in a hotel in this charming little town
somewhere in Bourgogne, en route for Megève, with Melcarth
and Denham Fouts. The car has broken down and will not be
ready till 3. We left Paris at noon yesterday, and arrived here
at seven last night.

On Wednesday morning, received a *pneu* from Monsieur
C., to say that Auden was in Paris and to ask me to go round
to see him. Went to his hotel to tea in the afternoon, with
Buffie; met Auden, who was staying there, and found him
much pleasanter and easier to meet than I had expected. On
Thursday, after having dinner with Etienne, went to hear his
lecture at the Sorbonne (on the poetic drama: he didn't say

anything startling, but was sympathetic to listen to, and spoke much better than the last time I heard him, about three years ago). Afterwards, met Brian Howard and Tony, the Sterns, Peter Watson and Denham in the hall, and then with Auden, we all went off to the Brasserie Univers. Just as I had got into the car with Denham and Peter Watson, Denham suddenly said: 'You're just the person to come with us on my trip tomorrow,' and later in the evening, he asked me definitely if I'd like to accompany him and Melcarth on a fortnight's trip to the Alps. I naturally accepted at once, in spite of the possibility of being asked to join Desmond at Monte Carlo in a week or so's time. There were just about twelve hours in which to take a little sleep and get everything ready before starting.

After several days of rain, yesterday was dazzlingly fine. A sudden and unexpected departure, the open road, the cold air and sharp sunlight of December! I'm a little dazed by it all. Tomorrow we shall see snow and mountains, and breathe the fine air of the heights; I've always longed for mountains, and Megève is a place I've always particularly wanted to go to. — How strange is chance, and how I love to be *dépaysé* every now and then!

* * *

Auden: Even at the age of 40, he will carry the head of an undergraduate on his shoulders. At 31, he still has an air of disguising only with a difficultly acquired social manner the petulance and embarrassment of an adolescent.

When delivering an opinion, he throws back his head, contracts the brows above his sloping, close-set eyes, and looks at you down his nose, holding a smile in reserve at the corners of his mouth.

Observed in profile, the left side of his face reveals a gentleness contradicted by the right, which is spoilt moreover by a slight protruberence just above the upper lip.

He sat at the end of the café table, dressed in a rather incongruous *frac,* silhouetted against the dark window, through which, on the other side of the rainy street, one could just distinguish the colonnade of the Comédie Française.

19.XII.38
(Annemasse, nr. Geneva. 10 a.m.)
We left Megève, alas, at 8 o'clock this morning, and are on our way back to Paris. Denham and Edward have gone on into Switzerland; I am taking the train to rejoin them at Bellegarde after lunch.

A thick, dull-coloured mist hangs in the valleys; it is impossible to see more, dimly, than the lowest crags of the mountains. The temperature has fallen suddenly all over France; it has been snowing all night long and this morning a few flakes are still falling, here and there, from time to time. The trees are all embalmed in frost, as white and delicate as though carved, not of ivory, but of ash. In the car we pass through villages with white roofs which seem to belong to the scenery of Breughel's *Winter.*

I have been distracted and taken out of myself during our stay at Rochebrune, — decentralized for a while, as though I had left the brooding, restless, struggling part of me behind in Paris. After a week of almost purely physical life, I have no particular desire to find it again, but I suppose I shall very soon.

I should love to spend the whole winter up there at the châlet, in the sun and snow, surrounded by the mountains and the marvellous Alpine sky, — eating well, sleeping well, skiing or walking in the daytime, talking and reading or writing a little at night. Ideal creative 'climate': outside, height and depth, clear invigorating air, sky, space; inside, intimacy, warmth and peace.

After ten days of being with them all the time, I have become genuinely fond of Denham and Edward; and when I say 'genuinely', I mean not merely with an immediate and uncritical liking, but with a 'tested', slowly developed affection, in spite of qualities and characteristics which I usually find unsympathetic and which would separate them from me if I hadn't had the opportunity of knowing them both as well as I do now.

Perhaps the only moment at Rochebrune when I was fully myself was the night when they both stayed down in the valley because of having to go to the bank at Anneçy and, being alone, I read Jouhandeau's *L'Amateur d'Imprudence,* and could not sleep afterwards, because disturbed, exalted, charged with *stimmung.*

(23.XII.38)

While we were at Rochebrune, I went down into Megève one day to see the Laurence Vails. They live in a large châlet called 'Les Cinq Enfants'; (this quintuple progeny was not visible when I called, but Kay Boyle, who received me, wearing a blue maternity gown, was visibly preparing for a sixth). Middle-aged, quiet, gently reserved, she did not enable me to perceive any connection between her personality and her high-flown, ardent prose.

I called again on the day before we left, but did not see her a second time, as she was unwell and in bed. Spent an hour talking to her husband and to Djuna Barnes, who was staying with them. Djuna, glummer than ever, ironically derogatory about everything, imparted an atmosphere of defeat and gloom to the household, I felt. It was twilight and misty and bitterly cold outside. She sat huddled in a corner of the sofa, unable to keep warm, although the heating of the châlet seemed quite adequate. We talked about Antonia and Emily Holmes Coleman. She seemed detached from everybody. Did I know Henry Miller, she asked me, and what was he like? Wasn't he a shit? Look at his picture, she said indignantly, he surely must be a Jew? — His name is really Müller, I told her, and he rather tends to think he's a modern Goethe. He always talks as though he hates the Jews. — All the more reason to suppose he is one, she said. In spite of all this, she seemed ready to admit there was 'something' in *Tropic of Cancer*. 'Three hundred pages of bickering, bitching and buggering: but yes, it has a sort of strength.'

About Henry James: 'Three hundred pages, and absolutely nothing happens. But the suspense is wonderful. Right at the end, Lady Adelaide tears a button off the villain's coat, and the effect is far more shattering than if she'd murdered him.'

About Jane Austen: 'Oh, she's the girl whose heroines have the vapours if they get three flakes of snow on their hair! I can't stand her. Imagine Jane Austen coming to tea! I'd leave the room.'

* * *

Received a strangely cagey second letter from Ingrid:

In your letter I found so many plans and hopes, and I'm not able to say 'yes' to all what you expect. Of course I found phrases too, which say: 'Possible that can't be . . . possible that will not be . . .' but these words and hopes I found in the shadow, and it should be the contrary.

I'm a woman who had a very coloured life. In some ways I'm still a girl, in some ways a woman, in some ways nearly a man, what belongs how I take life in certain situations. I've had enough adventures with men, and enough difficult relationships not to be any more curious. In contrary, I'm a little tired of romantic adventures because I know what happens, I'm a little careful and a little afraid of new disappointings.

I would be foolish if I wouldn't know that there are possibilities between us, and of course a marriage brings those ideas nearer. But please see our marriage as this 'purely a matter of convenience' which I ask from you, as an act of friendship, or the willing to help persons in difficult quarrels. I only can start in this marriage if I can stay for you with quite free feelings and the security that you will be free of plans, or not expect them realized, otherwise it would be too difficult, perhaps impossible.

And please, David, don't believe that I am a beautiful woman and that it must be wonderful to live with me. You must believe me when I tell you that it is not so wonderful as awfully difficult.

God knows I don't imagine that it is anything but difficult to live with anybody! It seems impossible for us to get any further by correspondence. We must wait until we can meet.

31.XII.38
(At the rue du Bac)
It's the last day of the year. I've spent a rather mad Christmas, at No. 44 the entire time, where Denham, Buffie and Michel d'A. are all ill and confined to their apartments. I run up and down the staircase, dropping in to say *bonjour* to Michel, to read aloud from Firbank to Buffie, and every now and then I have to go out to get medicines or magazines or food. Most of the time I spent at Denham's, or rather Peter Watson's (Peter is away at present), where I have had all my meals for the last week and where I have even been sleeping for the

last three nights. The Connollys came over to stay with Denham for Christmas; poor Jean caught the *grippe*, and is still here, confined to the apartment, where she spends the days in a dressing-gown, lying beside the fire on a couch opposite the one on which Denham reclines. Everything that goes on here is crazy. The big central salon has the air of a stage-set. The most extraordinary collection of people wander in and out all day long: dubious friends of Denham's, English pansy or sub-society friends of the Connollys, the actor Jean Marais, Melcarth, servants, detectives and police-inspectors (on account of the theft here at the party on Xmas Eve, when my new beige overcoat, among other more valuable things, was stolen, to be recovered, fortunately, a few days later), and odd, unidentifiable individuals with beards and hats, carrying ladders or portfolios or pieces of furniture about. I flit around giving people drinks or lights for cigarettes, playing backgammon, putting records on the gramophone, ferreting about for books on the shelves, searching for lost objects, pencils, lipsticks, etc., reading aloud from Whitman, and so on: acting as a sort of companion or general aide-de-camp to the invalids. Am taking full advantage of the lavish comfort available, at the same time; which may not perhaps be very wise, as it will probably make me miss it later, when I shall not be able to spend so much of my time here, and chafe at the insufficiency of my usual mode of existence.

There has been a lot of snow, but now it has all melted away. Have written a new poem called: 'Snow in Europe'.

Buffie's mother has arrived from America. I went with her to St. Lazare, to help her get her luggage from the customs, on Boxing Day.

Having been reading rather a lot recently: among other things the horrifying life of Hart Crane (about whom I have rather the same feeling as I have about René Crevel — apart from the fact that they both committed suicide); Elizabeth Bowen's new novel, which I enjoyed a lot; Auden's and Isherwood's new play *On the Frontier*, which is not very good, but has some excellent choruses; also a book on *Character and Physique* by some Viennese psychiatrist, from which I deduced the fact that I belong to the 'cyclothymic schizoid' group. I wonder whether Mme. Jouve can ever really cure this? I suppose not. She can probably only diminish the worst effects.

(Later)

On the evening of Boxing Day, I had a strange adventure. Anne Goossens dropped in to see Buffie while I was there, and later on I took her downstairs to have dinner with Denham. Afterwards I walked up to Montparnasse with her, in the snow. On the way, she suddenly asked me if I knew someone called Nigel Henderson, whom I of course very well remembered having met at Antonia's when I was in England last April. (She also took me to his flat in Charlotte Street for a party he gave on his 21st birthday. As far as I could gather, Antonia White was at that time carrying on a complicated affair with him and with his elder brother both at once.) I had taken to him immediately, and regretted not having had the opportunity of getting to know him better.

When Anne and I reached the Select, there he was, sitting alone in a corner, rather tight. We all went in a taxi, with Ralph B. and Mark Kerr Seymour, to the Flore. Nigel and I began a long conversation, ignoring the others, during which he sobered up considerably. It soon became obvious to both of us that a strong spontaneous sympathy existed between us. At about half-past one, when the others had said good-night and had gone home, we found ourselves wandering aimlessly along the Blvd. St. Germain. I pointed out that we were not going in the direction of his hotel. He then took my hand and said he was going back with me to my room. He behaved strangely all the way, at one moment fell on the pavement and rolled deliberately in the snow; he had been drinking heavily ever since his arrival just before Christmas, and seemed to be in a distraught state of mind. When we got back to my room, the gas-fire lighted and one lamp burning by the bed, the way he fell into my arms, his mouth on mine, was full of abandon and despair. (I was already quite aware of all the darkness behind that mask — strugglings, evasions, contradictions, guilt and impulse of self-destruction. Tragic impenetrable labyrinth of the lost soul, whose contorted recesses I so instinctively understand.) We undressed blindly, fell into bed, terribly alone together in the night.

It would be impossible ever to know with any certainty what was going on in the shadow of his mind. After we had been lying there, locked together, or staring mysteriously, almost with hostility, into one another's faces, for about half-an-hour, he was seized with what seemed a sudden panic, and started up, saying 'I must go now', without any other explanation. I cannot tell what prompted him: delusion, inhibition, fear? Some unpredictable psychic reaction, I suppose. I argued with him, tried to calm him, reassure him, but in vain. He dressed, embraced me a last time, and went out. Leaving me with such a confusion of feelings that I no longer knew what was uppermost in my mind. But I do not really believe that this is the end of the story.

2.I.39

Spent New Year's Eve with a party of five friends. We went to the Boeuf sur le Toit, Graff's, Melody's, the Swing Club and the Binocle. Saw Bettina at the Boeuf, with her American young man, looking very grown-up and beautiful in one of those new strapless evening-gowns. Went to bed at 8 yesterday morning and got up at 7 in the evening.

Had another fantastic adventure last night, with Denham this time. Jean and Brian went out to dinner, leaving me there alone with him. He got restless and rather tight as the evening wore on, and began trying to telephone to Jean Marais, who should have come to see him during the day but hadn't. Suddenly he had the mad idea of going to the Ambassadeurs to see the last act of *Les Parents Terribles*. He is not supposed to move from his couch because of his bad foot, but he was not in a mood in which it was possible to dissuade him from doing anything he had made up his mind about. He telephoned the theatre and asked for a *loge*, sent me out to get a taxi, and appeared a few moments later wearing simply a fur-coat over his pyjamas and clutching a decanter of brandy, two glasses and a large silver cigarette-box. He staggered into the taxi and we drove off to the theatre at top speed.

When we got there, we made a dramatic entrance into a (rather naturally) shocked vestibule. The *ouvreuses* clustered round us immediately, goggling with consternation. We demanded our *loge*, everyone went away to consult someone else, and nothing happened. An absurd person, apparently a friend of Bernstein, the owner of the theatre, came up and insulted us (*'Je sais que vous êtes des anglais, mais tout de même! On ne peut pas faire cela ici.'* — 'On ne vous a pas demandé des leçons d'étiquette, monsieur, merci.'*); until finally, Denham exasperated, said *'Je voudrais voir M. Cocteau, s'il vous plaît'*, whereupon everyone became rather more polite, as though everything had suddenly been explained. We were taken round behind the stage and up a back staircase to Jean Marais' dressing-room, where Cocteau received us with, at first, puzzled surprise, and then, after a moment, with the most charming understanding. *'Mais naturellement'*, he assured us, *'la pièce était écrite pour être vue en pyjama!'* He was extremely nice, drank brandy with us, and did his best to calm down Denham, who was by this time in rather a state. Jean Marais came in to change at the end of the second act; Cocteau told us all the *histoire* about Bernstein and the municipal councillers and the scandal, and said how glad he was the play was being transferred to the Bouffes Parisiens and how much he disliked the Ambassadeurs; Alice Cocéa looked in for a moment; and finally Roger Lannes, who happened to be there, took us down into the theatre and gave us seats in a *loge*, and we saw the whole of the last act very comfortably.

When we returned to the apartment afterwards, we found that Brian and Jean had got back already. Jean went to bed, and Brian and Denham began a discussion about mutual friends of theirs, which became more and more acrimonious until Denham inadvertently let out the fact (which I knew already) that he had belonged to a Nazi Youth Movement when he was in Germany at the age of seventeen; whereupon Brian went off the deep end. It was absolutely inexcusable, he was deeply shocked, he couldn't think what Wystan and Stephen would say when he told them, etc. Denham abruptly left the room. Brian and I, left alone, went on talking for a while. Suddenly, there was a shot in the next room. We looked at each other a moment, then hurried in to Denham, who was lying with his head buried in the pillow and with a smoking revolver beside him on the table by the bed. The window was open; mist was rising in the moonlight among the trees in the garden outside; the long white muslin curtains were faintly moving. Denham lay there sobbing, did not speak. I took the revolver into the sitting-room, turned the light out, and when Brian had gone away, went back and sat on the bed for a while. It was difficult to find anything to say.

13.I.39

Have had another 'bad' period, but seem to have gotten over the worst of it now. Peter Watson came back, so that I couldn't keep going to the rue du Bac; analysis began again, and was very difficult; the usual money situation rearose; I had a bad cold. I slept all day and went out only at night, getting drunk as much as possible. Spent one or two crazy, Dostoievskian nights with Brian Howard: at the Binocle, the Select and elsewhere. Last Saturday I didn't go to see Mme. Jouve at all. This week she told me that I have to go to her every day now, instead of every two days. It's going better at present, and we seem to have started discovering things again; I have innumerable dreams.

22.I.39

The interval since the last entry in this book has been pretty full, but I have been 'discouraged' recently and have not felt like writing. Now that I have finished with analysis, and have decided to return to England, — to work, — and shall in fact probably be leaving Paris in a few days' time, I had better put down what has been happening during the last difficult, complicated, painful week or two.

Everything still seems confused, fragmentary, unfinished, contradictory. Where am I, where are we? I hate this muddle of a world, my muddled life in it. There is always the same wall and constriction: analysis does not yet seem to have been able to break it down, though the real effects will probably not begin to show themselves till later: in any case, it will not have 'changed my destiny' (its fundamental elements) but only 'alleviated' it, as Mme. Jouve says. *'La realité est* aride *pour vous à présent, n'est-ce-pas?'* she said, the other day; and it certainly is.

I know of nothing worse than the kind of reaction I always suffer from when I have an impulse and it is frustrated, as most of my impulses are. It is then that I 'go dead', lose interest in everything, have no strength, no energy; it seems to be always happening; it is what seems to be happening now. Bitter experience of my life: frustration and despair: disruption of the world, sterile agony of the generation of my contemporaries. We all seem to be struggling with shadows in a desert . . .

I want to leave Paris, change my life, lead another, more active, sort of existence, make new friends in other sort of milieux than the ones I know. This is a genuine, strong impulse, born of exasperation, and I *must* go through with it.

23.I.39

The Spenders have been staying with Peter Watson, but have gone back to England now. Stephen was quite friendly this time; I don't think he's really antagonistic, only a little difficult to tɘlk to because so awkwardly sincere. He was appreciative about 'Snow in Europe' which he recommended to *New Writing* and which is now going to appear in the next issue. He also said, when I told him how little verse I've been able to write during the last two years or so: 'I do hope you'll go on writing poetry, though: of your generation there's only you and Dylan Thomas and George Barker.' (John Lehmann, whom I saw yesterday, said the same thing; so I feel rather encouraged.) Inez Spender, whom I hadn't met before, is obviously nice, but belongs, exteriorly, to a rather chilly type of intellectual; one feels she is a young woman of 'very strict integrity'. Brian Howard predicts that she and Christopher Isherwood are going to become the dictators of the British intelligentsia in a few years time . . .

One day about a week and a half ago, I arrived at the rue du Bac just after lunch to find an argument going on over the dessert between Denham and the Spenders and Gertrude Stein; Alice B. Toklas was quietly chatting to Peter Watson. The discussion seemed vaguely all-embracing: the future of humanity, etc. Miss Stein, redoubtably herself, was holding her own quite unscrupulously, making preposterous statements and simply barking 'What? . . . what?' when anyone asked her questions about them, just as she does to people who ask her questions after her lectures. She seemed to have a fixed idea that Spender, whom she'd probably never read, was attacking her from the point of view of 'proletarian literature'. When she went boldly on into politics, the whole conversation, — Gertrude Stein being downright and nonsensical, the Spenders being quietly earnest and conscientious ('But don't you think, Miss Stein . . .?' 'When you say that . . . surely you must see . . .') — became more than faintly comic. Presently Spender had the sense to ask her what she was writing at the moment and whether she'd finished her 'Faust' opera, and they got back to safer ground. 'I've been writing a children's story recently', she said; 'it's about a little girl who discovers that everything is round because the earth is round. I'm also trying to write the Great American Novel. A book I've been at work on for the last four years. It's about Saints.' After a while she got on to her favourite topics: American literature (its 'disembodied' quality), Henry James and Ernest Hemingway. As I sat there listening and watching her, I began to feel there was something 'really rather wonderful', to use her own expression, about the strength of her personality and the ruggedness of her hard square head. I talked to Miss Toklas, who remained very much in the background, for a while; she has a sort of faded, old-world gentility and charm which is rather touching. She was wearing an oddly-perched grey hat which she kept pushing down on to her head as though to reassure herself that it was still there. In her youth, she told me, she had thought of dramatizing James's *Awkward Age*; James wrote her a 'kind and charming' letter, but then she lost courage and gave up the idea. 'I was just a green girl,' she explained, 'straight from the Middle West.' Later, when they were saying goodbye, Gertrude Stein began giving Denham advice about his foot and talking about her medical-student days; she remembered the Klondike, she said, and how people used to get their feet frozen and have to have them cut right off. Everyone relaxed when she had gone; one felt that a natural force had left the room.

* * *

Pierre Jean Jouve has sent me the *N.R.F.* edition of *Kyrie*, which has just appeared. There is something miraculous in his being able to continue to create poetry so intense and pure at a time like this. The first of the two new sections, *Les Quatre Cavaliers*, is magnificent:

Nous avons étonné par nos grandes souffrances
L'inclinaison des astres indifférents . . .

Few writers' work could at first sight appear so remote from the world of politics, yet few poets have so profoundly suffered the events of current history, Czechoslovakia, Austria, Spain; and I know of no one who has so fully expressed the *apocalyptic* atmosphere of our time or with so strong an accent of the 'sublime'.

Nico Calamaris[*] also has sent me a copy of his *Foyers d'Incendie,* which has an enthusiastic preface by Breton and is undoubtedly very brilliant, but is perhaps one of the most rash and imprudent books I have ever read. His head is packed with information and with theories and he rushes from one to the other, without a moment's pause for consideration until one is quite exhausted.

Have been reading Isherwood's *Lions and Shadows,* which I enjoyed very much, it is so fluent and entertaining. But does it anything like justify Isherwood's booming reputation? What is it that makes people imagine he is going to be a great novelist? The most serious criticism one can make of him seems to me to be that he has evaded a certain very important plane of reality (difficult to define, — perhaps I mean the plane of 'intensity' — the plane dealt with by Julian Green, for instance, or by Jouhandeau, — the plane of the sombre and the strange), and that he 'dishonestly' excuses this evasion to himself on the grounds that he is 'grown-up now'.

---

better known as Calas

243

To a certain extent, writers like Isherwood succeed in making one feel pretentious, portentous, absurdly immature and unsophisticated; but only to a certain extent; after that one begins to feel there is a trick somewhere and that the values one most secretly believes in are worth holding on to after all. One cannot properly deal with existence simply by being continually bland and matter-of-fact; if one is to face life unreservedly one needs more than common-sense and a dry sense-of-humour (to face life with) to stand one's stead.

* * *

I went a few nights ago, with Brian Howard, Anne Goossens and a young American, to an enormous *Front Populaire* meeting about Spain at the Vel'd'Hiver. There were about 14,000 people. We stood up for two hours, in the middle of that vast floor, closely packed together, beneath the hanging arc-lamps and the dark roof above them, listening to the passionate and dramatic speeches of Thorez, Jouhaux, Blum and others — small gesticulating figures on the distant platform.

The crowd was wonderful. It was impossible not to be moved, almost to tears at times, by the singing of the 'Internationale', the raising of clenched fists, the thunderous applause and stamping of feet, the long cheering when Thorez rose to speak, the cries of *'Ouvrez les Frontières!'* and *'Unité! Unité!'*. Spain is a terrible tragedy in which we are all implicated, the speakers said; our position is tragic and intolerable; we have suffered to the utmost, we have been harrowed by appalling events; we must decide what to do; we must act. A kind of anguish went through the whole audience; one felt the imminence of an only too real shadow of horror and menace hanging in the air. What was so dreadful was to feel at the same time almost certain that nothing will be done, that in spite of everything the French Government will not open the frontier, because England will not let her . . .

* * *

One day, the week before last, I went to lunch alone at a restaurant in the Place des Victoires, where I hadn't been before. The weather was mild, the sky a gentle Parisian grey with occasional splashes of pale blue. Took a taxi to the end of the Avenue Foch after lunch, and went for a brisk walk through the Bois, along the lakes. Bewintered trees and water, wet leaves and gravel, mufflered children with their nurses. As I was reaching the Longchamps corner, it began to rain, and at the same time the sun began to shine. A strange melodramatic green light struck through the dripping branches, and a magnificent rainbow began to take form over Paris, stretching from the Eiffel Tower to about the middle of the Bois.

The following evening, went to the Boeuf, which wasn't much fun, and afterwards went with Una Mae Carlyle and an American girl called Jerry, to a bar somewhere in Montmartre, where we ran into Henry Miller, whom I hadn't seen for months and who was very friendly and agreeable. He had just been to England and, rather surprisingly, had much enjoyed the trip. After that, Jerry and I went on to the Swing Club, which was dreary because the gramophone had broken down, and there I saw, sitting at the bar, a tall, sensitive-looking and fair-haired young man I had noticed there once before and had wanted to talk to. As there was no music to dance to, people were volunteering to play the piano, which on the whole was worse than nothing at all; and presently the sad-looking young man, egged on from behind by a kindly Negress, staggered forward from the bar, sat down and started playing a horribly difficult, highly abstruse piano-study in the Schönbergian atonal manner, the most advanced music I've ever heard in a night-club! People tittered, but were patient, and applauded politely when he had finished. He rushed shyly back to the bar; and, as Jerry had gone home by then, I went over and spoke to him. The piece he had played turned out to be his own composition; he was an Englishman, and his name was George Measures. We talked for quite a long while, and when we left the place to have breakfast together, found it was already getting light outside. After breakfast, we went for a long walk all over the Butte, and later, took a bus back to my room, where I made tea, and we went on talking all the rest of the morning and most of the afternoon. He turned out to be a lonely, melancholy, almost morbidly sensitive chap, very much tied-up in himself; he earns his keep by teaching English at a *lycée* in Passy, and studies composition with Nadia Boulanger in his spare time. I have run into him several times since then, and have got involved in a clumsy, muddled, impossible sort of relationship with him which is just a pity.

Then there was, or should I say is, Derek Neame, who arrived *chez moi* with an introduction from Roger one morning, just as I was going to bed after having been out all night; whom I have since seen several times, and with whom, also, I have become involved in a relationship which is just another pity, I suppose — *plutôt pour lui* . . .

24.I.39

Roland Cailleux turned up again, back from his annual visit to England, looking very dapper. *'Je viens de faire des ruptures avec tous mes amis — je suis seul, seul, seul,'* he announced. He, George, Derek and I all dined together one evening. It was an unfortunate occasion; Roland behaved just as I might have expected him to (at one time, I should have qualified his behaviour as 'diabolic', but now I can only say he is a *cochon* — though rather an amusing one). Everything became rather too complicatedly futile to be described here. I'm so tired of these kind of scenes.

* * *

A letter, at last, from Bent: —

Non, je n'ai pas oublié ton existence. Mais comme je me dégoûte depuis des mois, je trouve que j'ai très peu de positive à te donner comme ça dans une lettre. En général, je l'avoue, ces mois à Paris me paraissent un rêve, — une assez beau rêve, mais avant tout un rêve très mouvementé et très plein. Mais souvent je vois distinctement tes beaux yeux, aussi tes mains, bonnes et sensibles, que je sens encore sur mon corps. Et je pense aux nuits de notre amitié amoureuse que moi aussi je croyais impossible. — Encore je suis très faible pour qu'une vie comme ça me demande toutes mes forces, alors tu comprends que c'est presque impossible pour moi de travailler dans une telle atmosphère furioso. Néanmoins j'ai grande envie de revenir à Paris, mais peut-être pas avant l'automne, Septembre-Octobre, ça je voudrais bien, si une guerre n'empêche pas un tel séjour. — Ecris-moi si ça va bien chez Mme. Jouve. Suivant ton example je vais commençer à me faire psychanalysé dans deux jours, c'est maintenant mon grand espoir. Je me sens trop disharmonique depuis longtemps —

— Have heard no more from Ingrid, and no longer know what will come of that affair. She was supposed to be coming to Paris, but she hasn't come yet and I don't know when she will.

25.I.39

Have decided to postpone my return to England for a week or so, for at least three reasons: for one thing, I have no money for the fare. Not less important, I've suddenly become involved in a rather strange and quite unexpected love-affair. Also, Antonia has just written to say she's coming over for a long week-end. I was annoyed at first to find myself once more unable to do what I wanted to immediately, but I feel now that a week or so can't make so much difference.

1939 End of January to beginning of March:

March
Last month in Paris: hectic period of physical experiences, sudden and brief intimate relationships, fruitless superficial activity, agitations and distractions, ending in a state of complete emotional exhaustion.

March
Returned to live with family in England. Period of interior relaxation and repose. Digestion of Paris experiences. Peaceful inactivity. The results of analysis taking effect.

April to the end of June
Period of creative activity: poetry. Collection of poems completed and revised. Visit to George Barker in Sussex. First part of *Come Dungeon Dark*. Other poems: poetic technique and personality developed.

   Continued, dynamically forward-moving consciousness leading in gradual stages to a state of acute interior crisis, roughly corresponding to the contemporary world situation. State of more intense self-awareness than ever before.

28.VI.39

All the agony of the past few years of my life, — I see it particularly clearly tonight: all that long anguish at the end of my adolescence: perhaps it was only a struggle towards this final acceptance of a burden whose full weight I now fully realize at last. The sort of desolate clarity with which I can now see who and what I am and what my destiny is to be: that in itself is part of the gift and burden. I have made the choice. I could perhaps, earlier on, have decided to put out the fire, shut my eyes to the vision; to compromise and come to terms with the mediocrity of a 'normal' existence. But I cannot turn back now. To have accepted this and to have realized its implications is like knowing irrevocably that one is suffering from a rare disease that once might have been cured but is now ineradicable. The symptoms: nerves, moods, nostalgia, restlessness, periodic exaltation and depression. Its idiosyncrasies: 'insatiability', quasi-schizophrenic duality, an acute instinct for self-dramatization and self-analysis. The toll one has to pay: a terrible unsharable solitude, a continual knowledge of the chasm which separates one from 'ordinary people' (i.e. 99.9% of the rest of mankind), their way of living and thinking; the impossibility of articulating this knowledge without being treated as a lunatic or a buffoon or a bore; an endless agony of impotence, frustration and despair produced in one by the conflict between one's imaginative, idealistic sense of how the world *might be* and one's realistic, critical sense of how it *is* and always will be, both in general and in relation to oneself; a complete incapacity for dealing with the practical, an inadaptability to society, a continual warfare with the outer world. And the compensation for all this? A not very valuable conviction that one belongs to a kind of spiritual aristocracy; the 'desolate clarity' of one's vision of one's life and *la condition humaine*; a (sometimes) rather exhilarating sense of pioneering on the limits, of nearing the poles of life; *enfin*, the possibility of being able to embody one's experience in some form of written communication; or rather, of having an experience to embody thus; the possibility of being able to write poetry, or whatever it may be, that will have at any rate the value of being the product of a real contact with spiritual truth, — its intensity, its depths, its exaltation, its naked certitude.

3.VII.39
'One is Also a Powet'
'Unfortunately I have to add that one is also what the literati term a powet. This is so bloody embarrassing and inconvenient', as Barker says in one of his letters.

One is impelled by a kind of pretentiousness so incredible that it simply has to be taken seriously.

One is 'a powet'. But this may not mean that one's existence is wholly centred round the mere writing of poems. I would rather say: I am dominated by a voracious imagination, a turbulent creature which inhabits me; whose continual demand, allowing me no rest, is to be fed. The writing of poetry corresponds only to the digestive process of this monster. My life is dedicated to its nourishment.

The imagination is possessed by a force which is not only hunger. It suffers also from a sort of continual claustrophobia, a will to objectivization, a desire to break bounds and thus change the world (sadism). If it were possible, I would sooner give expression to this force *in my life* than in my work.

(Jouhandeau: *'Une passion est seulement morte, quand elle ne nourrit plus son maître: l'imagination, dont l'éclat justifie seul toutes nos erreurs.'*)

7.VII.39

For the first time in my life I am beginning to realize that there is a definite (though fortunately still fairly remote) possibility of my going 'out of my mind . . .' I used always to think that no matter how far my imagination led me, I had a strong enough sense of reality to be able without fail to retain a secure foothold in it. But if one plays with fire one cannot, I suppose, expect to escape indefinitely from burning . . .

Earlier this year, I came to see that my only way of dealing with 'depressions', 'inadaptability', etc., was to *accept* them, as being to a certain degree necessary. This meant that they were to become 'harnessed' in some obscure way; to become a driving-force instead of merely a barrier. Possibly the *only* solution left me, now, to the problem of living, is *to write;* and the only way I can write is, to let writing become *neurotic symptom.* I suppose that to know and to accept this solution is more satisfactory in the long run than to continue in the miserable state of deadlock that I was in previously; but I begin to see how it may at the same time be more *dangerous* than ever I realized until now.

My subjective nature, the private romantic self that one hides from the world because of social conventions, becomes increasingly more turbulent. Yesterday, going out and meeting people after having been at home for some while, *I felt the mask slip:* I couldn't keep up the exterior appearance in the way I always used to be able to; it was like being a fish out of water; and I was able to foresee what it would be like to lose control altogether. . .

It is all very well to be an 'imaginative' writer; but suppose for instance that the only way to be a genuine one was to let all the *other* side of one's work (intellectual argument, criticism, 'philosophy', etc.) become as it were the crazily ingenious, feverishly-spun fabrications of an uncontrollable 'not-self'?

I begin to wonder, with a half-fascinated, vague anxiety, whether it is possible that a schizophrenic *split* is going gradually to carry me further and further away from the outer world, — whether being able to write as I want to, entails a further-outlook of ever-increasing inner ups and downs, fugues, swinging from extreme to extreme, — an intensity of solitude immuring one beyond all human contact? — Painful lucidity.

* * *

(I think the above may mean chiefly that I have been at home for too long a time.)

Some weeks later:
No, I shall never go out of my mind: my critical intelligence is far too detached and is infinitely adaptable. (The 'third person', operator of the sought-for synthesis.)

The kind of struggle that I have noted above, belongs to that long, complex preliminary struggle which it has been necessary for me to go through before being able to reach, and subsequently to deal with, the precious basic material of *my work*.

16.VIII.39
In the middle of a severe *spiritual crisis*.

— *White Nights*. Meditation: my work: poetry and predication (prose — contradiction once again).

— Reread Baudelaire. Had never quite realized, before, how much 'in line' he is. He never covers up the fundamental worst. He records an intensely intimate experience of the metaphysical problems which are most important to me at the

252

moment (tho' he does not fully *exteriorize* them, as I am trying to do).

Reread Nietzsche's 'January' (from *The Wanderer and his Shadow)*. How slow is the development of that which I can no longer avoid accepting to spend my life defining and making clear! It seems that the preliminary working-out process is not yet over, since I am still unable to decide what is the most satisfactory form for saying what I am going to have to say. O the long strain of maintaining a certain balance at the core of chaos! The impatient desire to get 'the message' finally launched!

Want to write a poem about the symbolic significance (as ritual) of the recent A.R.P. 'black-out'. Difficult to write poetry when in the middle of working-out systematic thought, though.

Have been reconsidering the idea of writing *A Man Exists*. If it ever materialized, it is difficult to imagine anyone daring to produce it: it would be so inconceivably brutal to the audience. . .

(Periodic spasms of furious lubricity. Tiresome; but I suppose the only thing to do is to give them free rein, and thus to let the state exhaust itself. No good bottling them up with asceticism. I cannot believe that the sex-act will ever be more for me than an occasional distraction. The satisfying of the flesh's itch is hardly more important to me than smoking, for instance. Best to gratify it as immediately as possible, so that one's real preoccupations may remain undisturbed until continued later.)

Last Friday, met Frederick B. for the first time; a Dostoievskian-underworld sort of figure. He immediately understood what I meant when I started talking about 'the

Void', 'the end of History', 'the open tomb', 'the coming spiritual revolution,' etc.

I believe ever more positively that my own inner struggles represent only an unusually acute consciousness of an experience almost exactly similar to that which an ever-increasing number of people all over the world are becoming vaguely, inarticulately conscious of going through. This experience has to be given a coherent expression, objectivized, universalized. It provides a fundamental significance to this otherwise meaninglessly incoherent moment of human history.

Last Saturday morning, in London (after spending the night with Nigel Henderson). As I walked through the streets, the brilliant unfamiliar sunshine falling on the faces of the crowd, became the hallucinating light of a despair so extreme as to appear *gay* in its nihilism. Sat on a bench in Leicester Square gardens, realizing that I have definitely 'been called' to be one of those who are to announce the true underlying event taking place during this century; aware of being perhaps the only human being there, in the middle of London, with any idea of what is really happening at this time upon this planet, — perhaps the only human being in the middle of London that morning consciously to wonder about what is happening or to care. Was possessed, as I sat there, by a sombre, strange excitement, as though acting the final, unwritten act of *Hamlet*; as though in the pangs of giving birth to a new spiritual reality. *It's a Wonderful World!* announced a huge cinema-poster to the sunny square.

Went to the National Gallery, spent an hour and a half there, feeling acutely sensitive to the pictures, as though the people and places behind all the different frames formed a single world, the visionary interior world of the Western man of the past, from which we are now shut off.

22.VIII.39

For the world, a week of severe crisis has begun.

For me, the interior crisis continues, more intense than ever. Labyrinthine. Incoherent. Inarticulate. At the core of contradiction, of all contradictions. Terrible strain, terrible exhaustion. I have reached certain unshakeable certainties about the present crisis in the development of mankind. But I still do not know how to express them. Poetry impossible, as yet. Too close to the experience and the certainty. What will emerge from it all? Some unquenchable spark drives me on, in spite of the appalling confusion, the aridity and darkness. Am I to become a sort of Prophet after these days in the Wilderness? I have not yet sufficient courage or self-confidence. I am still a little afraid of ending by going mad.

Is it possible that during this crisis I have advanced a little nearer to the possibility of getting *beyond despair* without illusion or dishonesty?

To be able to get Beyond, and to be able to express what I more than half *know* already, it is necessary to *find a centre* (*point de repère*). Suppose this centre were to appear later as 'God' (creation of a new projection of the essential self: Religion of the Future: solitary individual process of creating an objective (superstructure) out of the subjective. *Creatio ex Nihilo*. Rilke's idea of the purpose of mankind on earth being slowly to *create* 'God' (His transcendentally objective existence)).

I am sometimes rather frightened to realize that my so-called normal, 'social', flippant, reasonable self has become almost entirely silent, as though banished. Am strongly aware, at times, of being 'possessed', of being only the mouthpiece, instrument or reflection, of a higher power . . .

Later:
(N.B.: *Frenzied sincerity cancels the possibility of being able to write poetry.*)

Later:
Have been trying practically all day long to produce some sort of poem. Nothing but unsatisfactory scraps and fragments. Exasperating frustration. The touble is that I am right *in the midst* of this spiritual experience, so that poetry (which, on account of its form, is the most objective of all modes of expression, really) is the last medium in which I might hope to get anything said for the moment. Absurd desire to try and write a poem which would be *strictly* true to my present intuitions.

Absence of images. The essential nature of the experience being *Negation. The Void, das Nichts, Nada, le Néant.* Practically the only image that presents itself at all strongly to me is *a black vacuum in (or through) which two eyes are fixedly staring.* Can find no simile strong enough to convey the utter *blindness of desperation* at the core of all this. Oh, *Anguish!* It goes on multiplying itself indefinitely because it is by nature inarticulate: impossible to express.

As for the vision of man's present spiritual crisis and of the future, I have as yet been quite unable to find the right *tone,* the adequate *style,* for conveying this 'message'. I have not yet been able to find the right attitude to adopt towards an audience. It is a terribly difficult problem. Perhaps it simply is not possible to say this particular thing, except in prose. The poem 'Elsewhere' was moderately successful, but I do not want to go on writing endless variations on a single poem. A *prophetic* tone seems clearly indicated, but how direct can one be, how straightforward, etc.? To allow the thing to appear too cranky, too pompous or naive, would be to defeat its purpose from the start. (What more than a fraction of what the poet intended did anyone ever get from Blake's prophetic books, for instance?) In modern English poetry it is 'not done' for the poet seriously *to believe* what he is saying; it is understood that his fingers must permanently be crossed. (Barker an exception; perhaps also the later Eliot.)

Alas! I cannot help being seriously worried by the flagrantly *schizophrenic* aspect of the whole business — an aspect of which I am only too well aware. Should like to consult Mme. Jouve about this (or possibly Dr. Howe?). The only thing that at all reassures me, is my completely detached and objective conviction to the effect that *'schizophrenia'* is one of the fundamental hallmarks of everything important that is happening in the modern exterior world, so that one ought surely not to avoid *insisting* on it. (Being definitely a schizo type, though, perhaps I am more inclined than I realized to exaggerate this?)

* * *

Was rather upset yesterday by reading Duhamel's *Journal de Salavin*.

Am reading Nietzsche's *Dawn of Day*, which also disturbs me.

Altogether, what with all this inward turmoil, and the 'nerve-war' crisis that the newspapers are full of, and the thundery weather, I shall probably be left quite prostrate soon.

* * *

Listened to Mahler's *Kindertotenlieder* on the radio tonight.

24.VIII.39

Beastly, bloody nightmare of a world, Another crisis. We're in for it now. What's the use? We might as well all be struck off the register. I feel almost calm about the situation: resigned. It's the endless waiting about and hanging on that's so wretched.

Like this wretched season of the year. It's always the same. Will always be my annual purgatory, I suppose.

Something's *got* to happen. I don't mean only the war. I've got to get away soon, somewhere. Must write to Blanche Jouve. Make a lot of effort, I'm becoming gradually more and more dotty, fanatical, otherworldly. Lucid today. Must reinstate myself. Make a break; then I can start this 'spiritual' business again. I'm not strong enough to go on indefinitely without interruption.

What I need most of all at the moment is *people*. Far too much solitude. If only there were some woman capable of dealing with me, to take me in hand for a while . . .

28.VIII.39

Either war within a week, or a miracle. Worse situation than last year. The world seems hypnotized — *Zero hour*.

In spite of the petrifying nature of the situation outside I can accept the worst with more calm now than I found possible a week or two ago; because I seem at last to have won through to at least sufficient interior understanding to stand on amidst the increasing chaos of these *last days*. To emerge from the mental turmoil I have been going through this summer with some sense of certainty, terrible though I know this certainty to be, may give me new strength and determination with which to face the utterly black Future.

I believe that tonight must represent a turning-point in my life. I have accepted the path of *predication*. I have at last left *literature* behind.

Nothing will ever be the same again.

31.VIII.39

The tension continues unabated, and one begins to grow almost accustomed to it. More mobilization. Evacuation tomorrow. To-night, Germany's 'peace' proposals were announced, but one cannot yet tell how much they may contribute to easing the situation.

Meanwhile, my private crisis also continues. Having accepted the idea of myself as a kind of 'prophet', I find the weight of this rôle increasingly overwhelming . . . The day before yesterday I had a strange sort of inspiration — an understanding of the contemporary human situation by which I am being, since then, alternately crushed and exalted. If I can grasp it and make something of it, if it really does correspond, as I am at present forced to believe it must, to that explanation of the situation which all thinking people so desperately need, if what I see now is more than a bizarre and practically incommunicable delusion, then I must face a far greater responsibility than I ever expected to have to reckon with.

How terribly intense one's solitude becomes as soon as one finds oneself alone with a new idea. And when it is an idea as horrifying as *this* . . . Everything except the possibility of making people hear what I've got to say seems to me unimportant and beside the point from now on. Whether my interpretation of things is 'true' or not, whether my sanity is deteriorating, whether my ideas are only reflections of the nerve-strain of the crisis — all these possibilities seem unimportant: all that matters is to have enough self-confidence and force to be able to *create* my own truth and to impose it on the outside world, even if I cannot *altogether believe* in it myself.

1.IX.39
Such a task is super-human: how can any solitary individual possibly hope to transcend the utter confusion of thought now raging deafeningly around every individual's solitude? A single truthful expression of man's situation in terms which could be understood by more than an insignificant minority seems impossible: the last glimmer of light has disappeared: there is nothing left now but this struggling, chaotic, fateful obscurity formed of half-truths, fragmentary truths, subjective truths, — opportunist, compromising, deceptive, superficial, *negative* truths, — under which reality lies buried.

All but completely physical types of people must be suffering unconsciously or inarticulately from *this* truth (that the present smoke-screen of relative and approximate truths has completely blacked-out the immediate knowledge of reality upon which the individual's sense of security and fellowship with his kind depends); and the conscious seeker-after-truth suffers from it unbearably. When reality is as painful as it is at this hour, how can the disillusioned few who are capable of seeing it hope to be able to make other men open their eyes to what they see. Is the 'ordinary man' even capable of a moral suffering great enough to force itself inescapably upon his consciousness and to make him admit its existence openly? If not, it would seem that the conscious few have no choice but to witness the irredeemably tragic spectable of mankind rushing blindly and incoherently like the Gadarene swine, into a sea of horror and obliteration.

Pascal speaks of 'that ignorance which is the wisdom of mankind'. Oh, why have I had to lose that wisdom! Perhaps it is really a fearful thing to see even an inch further than the end of one's nose . . .

What am I — what can any individual be, if he can see that reality which I now see — other than *a voice crying in the Wilderness: Prepare ye . . .* '?

3.IX.39

Today, which is the day on which the outbreak of the *Last War* has occurred, is a day of such immeasurable historical significance, that it seems that to write anything more than 'Today is the 3rd of September, 1939, — the day Great Britain and France declared war on Hitler', would only be irrelevant and unnecessary. Today, the individual is transcended . . .

* * *

And yet, although our way of living and thinking has suddenly undergone a profound change, although the dimensions of common reality itself seem to have altered, somehow, yet we have to go on living as human beings. Though my self and my reactions are of such infinitesimally small importance that they are as nothing by the scale of what is happening, they have not ceased to exist. Though human beings are united now in a way in which they were not united a week ago, each one continues to be separate. Overwhelmingly conscious of the communal drama, I have not, I cannot, lose consciousness of 'my' individual drama. I intend to go on keeping this journal.

* * *

261

Gradually recovering from the stunning blow struck by the horror of actuality. The first full shock came last Friday morning, with the news of the German invasion of Poland. Then everyone knew that the war was coming, had already come.

At the same moment the mental and spiritual war which had been going on inside me for weeks and months — perhaps years? — beforehand, suddenly reached its final cataclysm, and I knew that it had to come to an end, had in fact already ended.

Zero is over. Now I have some sort of assurance and strength which I never had before. Though it may seem strange and perhaps unmoral of me to say so, in face of the long horror which lies ahead for everyone, I feel today that midnight has struck and, although the worst of the night is still to come, from now on we move forward towards the distant morning light which until this happened it was not really possible to *believe* in. As the result of what I went through last week, I *know,* at last, what is going to happen, with a certainty I never had before. What is going to emerge is still absolutely vague and shrouded with obscurity, but one can no longer help knowing that *it is there* and that the moment has at last come for it to begin gradually to emerge into an ever more complete clarity. . .

As far as I am concerned personally, what it amounts to, I suppose, is that I now believe in myself, ultimately, and in my right to claim to be nothing more nor less than a kind of apparatus capable of receiving and giving expression to human beings' most profound and inarticulate intuition of their common destiny . . . Badly expressed; but I mean that I believe I am sensitive enough to pick up certain vibrations from the atmosphere of time, to formulate the knowledge of that which others only know without yet knowing it . . .

My best and strongest reason for hoping I shall not be killed before this war is over, is that I want so much to be able to see how my intuitions will be fulfilled; and because I have believed that the only way in which I might be of some use to society was by helping to bring about the fulfilment of these intuitions. *Peut-être que ce serait trop beau* . . .

It is as though the hard-core of my long frustration had dissolved. In the struggle to accept the stark fact of the war, I have overcome 'the Void'. (This also means, on another plane — the plane of common experience — that the agony of uncertainty and suspense has been followed by the relief of irrevocable decision: the crisis is over . . .)

The sudden vivid realization which came to me during the crisis — what I call my 'revelation' — is not much good to anyone but

       — (interruption by an air-raid warning) —

to anyone but myself, at present. What I must do now, if possible, is 'humanize' it, make it communicate, reduce it to its simplest terms.

* * *

Everyday life has suddenly become incredibly dramatic and fantastic and spectacular. The most extraordinary Sunday I have ever known. Last night, the second night of black-out, a terrific thunderstorm broke out at about 12; I had gone over to Richmond and was with some friends in a café there, listening to the late news on the radio, when it started. The most brilliant lightning I have seen for many years, an uncanny violet colour, more intense than daylight, not followed by very much thunder. Rapid flashes; short, sharp detonations. It seemed inevitably a part of the general situation, — just a feature in the 'war of nerves'. — Weird drive home through the storm in the Shaw-Lawrence's car.

The official announcement of the beginning of the war came through on the radio at 11.15 this morning; one accepted it as a matter of course, without the least surprise. Immediately afterwards came the first air-raid warning (which later turned out to be a false alarm). Slept heavily all the afternoon, from sheer nervous and emotional exhaustion. At 6 in the evening, the King delivered a singularly unimpressive and uninspired wireless message to the Empire, in a slow, expressionless voice; but this did not seem to matter very much, — the occasion being such as to make even Kings appear irrelevant.

9.IX.39

The nervous exhaustion brought about by 'the crisis', the terrible shock and strain of the first week of the war, made it necessary for me to deaden my inner consciousness for a few days, to sleep a great deal, to preoccupy myself entirely with physical, mechanical forms of activity. I dared not risk allowing myself to meditate fully and deeply on what is happening to the world; not, at any rate, for more than a few moments at a time. But such is my task; and now, by degree, I must begin to open my faculty of awareness again to its fullest capacity. Apart from its being essential to my subsequent 'work', this resumption of continual, daily 'awareness' is necessary if I am to continue to make some sort of record of my feelings and reactions during these incredible times, as I want to be able to do.

12.IX.39

I want, then, to try to make some sort of intimate record in these pages, of my experience of the War. I have calmed down quite a lot during the last few days, and am now therefore better able to begin to do so than during the first week.

It has occurred to me that, before continuing, a little self-criticism about the journal itself might be useful.

So universal and emotion-fraught an experience as that of War would seem to necessitate as calm and restrained a tone as possible in the recording of it. But such a tone would hardly be in keeping with that of the rest of this journal . . . ? Because my aim in this journal has been to write in the tone and language that is most material to me in my private soliloquies with myself, in my thoughts; and in my most personal thoughts, I am at present neither calm nor restrained . . . Is my interior life, then, entirely undisciplined? If I admit that this is so, I must add that it is at least disciplined by a continual concern to be completely *myself,* even to the limit of my 'worst' idiosyncrasies. Very well; but as I have already implied, this is not a discipline suited to the making of a record of the experience of War, since any *record* requires a strong leavening of objectivity . . .

The truth is, I suppose, that this journal from now on will constitute only a record of my usual 'interior-life' continued during — and in spite of — War-time.

What are the other present possibilities for a journal-writer? Generalizations about the meaning and the purpose of the war (the making of such generalizations takes up a very large part of my 'interior-life', in any case, — too much?). Completely detached accounts of typical observed incidents, perhaps: Camera-Eye pieces (I might try this from time to time). Attempts to define general atmosphere and other people's unexpressed feelings. Criticisms of policy, private comments on the actions of the various governments and on significant facts and events reported in the press (not quite my line nowadays: the people on the *N S & N*[*] for instance, should be doing this well enough). Objectifications of my own essential inner reactions to the development of the war, with the intention of 'providing useful material for the future historian' of individual life during this crazy period. (But I should never be 'useful' to anyone in this latter sense, I imagine, now that I have individualized myself to such an extent that I am sometimes even afraid of becoming considered a queer, cranky fellow (of a kind such as no-one can have any real sympathy with). — Perhaps my not having been through the smoothing-out process of going to a University has something to do with this . . .)

The question arises: ought I not to try now to become a calmer, more detached and less impulsively emotional person (or rather, not *ought* I, but *shall* I)? And the answer to that is, that in being completely myself, as I set out to be, I achieve a *discontinuous* personality; my truest nature is a many-sided, contradictory one; for I am quite capable of being intensely serious and emotional — sincerely elevated, prophetic, anguished, — at one moment, and of being critically cool and detached, normally conversational and *terre-à-terre,* the next. My 'interior-life' conforms entirely to this sort of pattern of quick changes and ups-and-downs. Lamentably unstable temperament, — neurotic, of course. (But fundamentally I think I always know how 'to keep my head' through it all; I even sometimes think that what I really want is to be able to

---

New Statesman and Nation.

lose it altogether for once.) (I ascribe this mercurial many-sidedness of my character to my stage ancestry on my mother's side of the family.)

* * *

All these considerations, however, are somewhat irrelevant at the moment, and seem to have led me into an intellectual evasion of the brute fact of what I really intended to write about. — The War, and its deepest impact on my own life. (It is with just this sort of evasion that I am rather inclined to reproach the contemporary British intelligentsia, for instance.)

I have long held the opinion that the intelligentsia to which I belong — particularly the writers' — is suffering from a deadly spiritual sickness; and this malady has seemed to me to express itself chiefly in the form of that intellectual sophistication and detachment which betrays a latent *fundamental indifference to everything* (of the writers, etc., to their most personal selves and subsequently to all exterior forms of activity, physical as well as mental), since it refuses to admit the relevance of personal 'passion' in any sort of discussion. To express this criticism of contemporary intellectuals in more banal terms: they have sacrificed the heart to the head, they have 'hardened their hearts', they can talk about anything under the sun, but they never allow what they say to express the least *genuine feeling* (by which I mean, deeply caring about the things one says). 'It does not do to lose one's sense of humour and of proportion: *il faut garder son sang-froid*', etc. Realizing this to be a sick attitude, I reacted against it by making it my ambition to become a 'subjective' thinker, in the Kierkegaardian sense: an 'existential' thinker (to become which first entails becoming a real *person* with an unique *existence*). It has seemed to me that this malady of my contemporaries is most likely to be

267

cured by their having to undergo some immediate experience of what I call *Anguish* (sense of the Void; of being personally implicated in imminent human disaster and in tragic human futility, etc.). During the crisis just before the War broke out, I became more convinced than ever that this experience of Anguish was becoming universal (and I do not mean merely the obvious universal anxiety as to the issue: peace or war). It seemed — as it still seems — to me, that this is a necessary and salutary experience, through which the thinking minority on whom the whole future of society depends may become purged of their false and sterile intellectual *detachment* — a detachment from those vital problems which nevertheless involve them and their deepest feelings as immediately as they involve everyone else.

Everyone — even the Conservative statesman — is now saying that when the War is over we must build up a new and better order of things. It has always been obvious to me, of course, that this is what *has got to* happen soon. As I see it, this new order will inevitably involve the necessity of a deep *inner* change, a change in our very habits of thought. I believe that this inner change will have to be, for thinking people, a change in our very habits of thought. I believe that this inner change will have to be, for thinking people, a change from the present (perhaps already changing) habit of divorcing the intelligence from the feelings. I believe that we must learn to *think with our hearts* and to *feel with our minds;* and that we shall be forced to learn this lesson by the ultimately inescapable Anguish brought by the War.

(I have stated this idea and am developing other, similar reflections on the inner meaning and function of the War considered as a moment in the history of human development, in my *Blind Man's Buff* note-book.)

Not until we have learnt this lesson shall we be free of the destructive and inhuman tyranny of abstractions.

Abstractions, when used by an intelligence divorced from feeling, constitute an evasion of reality. (I have already expressed these ideas, in more or less embryonic form, in certain entries in this journal written two or three years ago; but now I understand them more fully, and can truly feel their implications.)

I began this exposition by mentioning the present danger of an intellectual evasion of reality which is more immediate but which really belongs to very much the same sort of category. I meant the possibility that the 'intellectuals', faced by the War, may take advantage of the 'national duty' of 'preserving one's sense of proportion', of avoiding brooding, of keeping calm, carrying on as usual, etc. etc., by using it as an excuse for evading the true experience of Anguish. One can still think with the old, false detachment even about the fact that we are once again involved in the hated toils of War. To do so seems to me little better than fiddling while Rome burns. If 'duty' is to be mentioned then it is the *duty* of all thinking people to *feel* the horror of what is happening, to *suffer* from their knowledge and understanding of the present human situation, right to the end.

Of course, I would not dream of maintaining that people should think and feel deeply about the War every day and at every hour of the day. For self-preservation's sake, one cannot allow oneself to be continually conscious of it and its terrible implications. (Not even the toughest mind could stand complete awareness of it for too long at a time.) I mean simply that one should not allow this *necessary self-preservation* to become a camouflage for an *unnecessary evasion* of reality, of the feelings which are our truest reaction to it.

One of the most fundamental causes of modern Man's predicament is surely his inability to face up to and so overcome certain secret fears. He is afraid to face reality with a completely *undetached* gaze, because he is also afraid of his own emotions, and these emotions are most alarmingly aroused in him as soon as he faces undisguised reality . . . If we can go through this War without altogether evading the reality of our feelings, then when it is over we ought to be prepared to build up a new common attitude to life: one which will be able to face and overcome our fear of our emotions (without thereby losing our control over them — which would only be to repeat the sacrifice of feeling to intelligence in the other direction) and which will no longer have any use for that intellectual detachment which so many modern thinking people have until now regarded as a cardinal virtue.

(The contradiction between feeling and intelligence corresponds fundamentally to the contradiction between the subjective and the objective. See *Blind Man's Buff*. — The resolution of this contradiction is what Breton and the surrealists used to clamour for; but one would search vainly through their writings for any clear understanding and extensive explanation of its real nature.)

But *still* I have written nothing about my personal everyday experience of the War! Actually, there has not been anything really sensational to record. There have been no more air-raid warnings since the first day or two. One spends a lot of time reading the newspapers and listening to the radio news-bulletins, but the news we get still seems to be rigorously sifted, and so far, apart from the sinking of the

Athenia, nothing outstanding has taken place except the German advance in Poland, the Polish resistance, the defence of Warsaw, the French advance across the Siegfried Line, the arrival of the first British troops on the Western front, the admirable RAF distribution of 12,000,000 leaflets in Germany, one or two speeches . . . (Must really write a paragraph or two about Chamberlain some time; he seems to me now to be a much more curiously interesting figure than I would have given him credit for being a few months ago.) Both sides appear to be waiting for the moment when Hitler will consider Poland to be 'finished off'. Impossible to foresee quite what will happen then.

Every night at about a quarter-past seven, we have to start putting up brown-paper screens over the windows for the black-out, as we have not yet got thick enough curtains. I have not been out very much yet. In the evening, in the pitch darkness, I usually feel my way to the Shaw-Lawrence's house round the corner, simply in order to see and talk to human beings other than my family. Of course, no-one ever talks about anything but *the situation*. I do not approve of the Shaw-Lawrence's war-time *morale* and they rather get on my nerves sometimes. Once or twice we have been down to the local riverside pub after supper: fuggy, twilight atmosphere, everyone very calm and philosophical, no rowdy jingoist chanting or anything like that. Went over to Richmond in the Shaw-Lawrence's car one evening to see a mutual friend; met his cousin, a volatile, wistful young woman who reminded me of Joan S. (who is in America at present); we drank a lot of Cinzano, and I had to walk most of the way home in my house-slippers.

Philip Marsh is getting married on Saturday. I am supposed to be going over to Sutton for the reception.

Went over to Richmond in the daytime also one day last week to see Aunt Kate. Glorious weather made a sinister paradox of the gas-mask box slung round one's neck. Had lunch there, and afterwards went up into the Park, where I fell asleep lying in the sunshine in one of the enclosures, and had mad dreams about the War all the afternoon.

A half-daft old man sitting on a bench outside the Star and Garter Home beckoned me over to him, and then said, pointing with a horrified finger to the huge red building: 'You don't belong in there, do you? You haven't let them put you in there?' I managed to blurt out: 'Not yet!' before hurrying away. The view from Richmond Terrace looked as beautifully peaceful as ever.

We are digging a shelter-trench in the garden; but my Father is at the same time putting up a new greenhouse . . .

Three poems of mine were published in *The Nineteenth Century and After* on Sept. 1st: one of them was 'The Open Tomb'. *New Writing*'s next issue is still supposed to be coming out this Winter, and if it does, will contain part of 'Come Dungeon Dark'. Have written one or two 'crisis' poems: 'Three Stars' and 'Prophetic Mouth'; also, yesterday, wrote 'Artist' (the title and general shape and feeling of which came to me in a dream: I dreamt a book of my poems had been published, and this was supposed to be one of the best poems in it; but I'm afraid the subsequent reconstruction's not nearly so remarkable as the oneiric original!) Am sending these poems (also 'Elsewhere') to Eliot, and trying to make him come to a final decision about the collection which he is supposed to be considering for Fabers. The War seems to me to make what poetry I have written even *more* relevant than before, I feel, and I very much want to see it published this winter; (I also feel that there's a much greater chance for it of being appreciated now . . .).

Am trying hard to get some sort of a job. Can't write much; and it's too much of a strain simply to hang around waiting for conscription. Ought to be able to get something to do with French translation.

Have recently destroyed practically all my old MSS and papers. Am affixing instructions to the cover of this book, to the effect that it should be published in the event of my being killed during the War. There is nothing else that I should wish to be preserved, in such a case; except the few poems of which I have kept copies, and the *Blind Man's Buff* notebook (which does already contain, I think, the living germ of a philosophy corresponding to the needs of our time, — in spite of all the present incoherence of this unrevised rough material).

13.IX.39

The Alien Reality of War

It is a soft, fine, early autumn day. Except for the papers, and the gas-mask boxes which are carried by everyone outdoors, one might never have known there was a War on. This morning, before breakfast, I walked over to the gravel-pits on the other side of the river, and sat there on a solitary weed-grown mound, in the middle of the moist early grey-ness, gazing around at the wide Thames-valley landscape, trying to feel the full weight of the great shadow that is hanging across the world. But the peace of the immediate scene was too strong a contradiction for me, of the wider grim reality in which it lay islanded. 'Now' was still no more than the isolated 'now' of that quiet place . . .

Zero

273

10.X.39

— My 23rd birthday. Sixth week of the War.

— *Vita Nuova.* In spite of the War (probably in fact, *because* of it), I have truly emerged at last from the dark, constricting chrysalis of the last few years of my life and now *I am.* Everything — inner and outer, and the whole relationship between them — is now clear. I have accepted the great fundamental contradiction, and have died of it; and am risen again; and now the old Contradiction is no more. It now remains to me to write down my total vision, if possible, before getting called up for some form or other of national service.

My book will be a sort of philosophically-determined prophecy (The Greater Crisis: the Holy Revolution: the New Christendom).

Glorious walk through autumnal Richmond Park this afternoon. Tomorrow, going up to town to have lunch with Peter Watson (whom I have not seen since last winter, when we were both living in Paris).

* * *

And here (for the time being, at any rate), I close this journal. It has served its purpose. The most profound of the many intuitions I have recorded in it have all come *'true'*. The ploughing and the sowing have borne harvest. My life has passed on to another plane.

I am full of a great wonder and astonishment, and of exaltation. The world is very deep, the War is horrifying; yet the Future of this Century has begun to burn with an extraordinary, unseen and secret radiance, which I feel I can no longer speak of here, since it has become my task to proclaim it to those to whom it has not yet appeared. . .

274

May I be granted the grace not to fail or become discouraged before the purpose and responsibility of a new life.   *(1.XI.39)*

III

On the Eve of the New Year
When I wrote the final page of my Journal, last October (— it seems very much longer than two months ago —) I really did not think it at all likely that I should be starting to write another volume of the kind so soon. But, although at that moment (during which I was experiencing the full immediacy of a state of intellectual and psychological 'illumination' which at the time seemed marked by a definite finality) I felt that I had probably reached a point beyond which journal-writing would no longer fulfil a useful function in my development, — it was not long before I began once more to feel the need of a personal note-book in which to take some sort of stock of my existence, and of my thought in relation to the unfolding of it, from time to time.

(N.B., however: this new volume is to be of a different *type* from the last one. A more consistent tone, this time; the entries less diary-like in character. Existential reflection; notation of transient ideas difficultly classifiable otherwise than as primarily 'intimate'. A journal more of the Kierkegaard type (Appalling ridiculous presumption!) than the one I kept before. Corresponding to a new and radically different phase of my life, with new and peculiar problems of its own.)

8-9.I.40

'A new phase of my life'? There can be little doubt of that; yet at the moment I seem to be living, (at the beginning of this phase), through a sort of *interlude*: one containing a repetition of an experience and of problems which are already even *too* familiar — I did not expect things to take for me just now the sort of turn they are at present taking . . .

But because of my immediate personal past (period of intense solitary psycho-philosophical experience) and of the quite unknowable but surely unprecedented sinister general future which lies immediately ahead, the element of unwelcome familiarity in my present situation is made *un*familiar (by its context) and bafflingly difficult, except at first sight, to sum up in coherent statement . . .

Tick-tock, tick-tock; cogitation, cerebration: confusion: contradiction; frustration, isolation . . .

And oh! the heart's ineptitude!

On New Year's Eve, just over a week ago, I came up to town, through a particularly dense and adventurous black-out, to go to a party. It was given by some people I hardly knew, but Peter Watson, Stephen Spender and Tony Hyndman were there. And during the evening I met for the first time Michael Redgrave.

Since then I have been staying at Peter Watson's flat in Berkeley Square.

To pass from a long, comparatively uninterrupted and outwardly uneventful period of isolation and independent (existential) thinking, to one of social activity, London life, distraction, etc., is difficult and confusing enough as it is; and added to that there is the daily strain of the War and the continually nearer possibility of my whole life being interrupted and completely changed by my having to go into the Army (the proclamation calling-up the age-group to which I belong has already been signed); and then, on top of that, the fact that for the first time (or pretty well) in more than eighteen months, I am in love . . . (Only with the greatest effort have I written the last two words.)

My whole critical intelligence revolts, though impatiently, against the absurdity, the perversity, the hopelessness and ridiculous ineptitude of falling in love with Michael R. But there it is; and all I can do is try to be patient and to endure.

There is so much to be said about the situation that I could not fully analyse and explain it if I wrote even twenty pages on the subject; so for the time being I will simply abdicate from all attempt to do so until I can see it in a clearer and more calm perspective. At present it really seems fundamentally not only incomprehensible but incommunicable, — *Chanson sans paroles*, — (*sans auditeur*).

I am the thrall of a daimon (to use an expression of Stefan Zweig's). I live always on the edge of the Void.

22-23.I.40
Well, that's all over and done with now, apparently. Michael has gone away, and will be away from London for another five weeks. What he has left behind in me — unknown, unnamed — is no doubt *real* (for me, at least, to be looked back on, an *Event*: of a kind that does not take place in me at all often): but whether it is deep and substantial enough to be able to last so long (time seems quite abnormally long and slow just now, being 'out of joint') and able to flare up again and become actively demonstrative when he has returned, I cannot at present tell. I must admit that it still seems, to the detached part of my self, indescribably silly and unmentionable to be 'in love with' M. at all, — to be unable to

expect him to respond in any way except with embarrassment if ever he were to become aware of my state, — to be solemnly sitting here writing entries in a secret journal about it, like an infatuated schoolgirl . . .

Stayed in Berkeley Square at Peter Watson's for three weeks. Returned home the day before yesterday. Muddled. Dislocated. But am now beginning to settle down again to comparatively normal existence. Feeling that in spite of everything, it's good, after having been intensely concentrated, integrated, in oneself, through 'withdrawal from the world', to be broken up again for a while; — that it's salutary and necessary to be muddled and dislocated, distracted and decentralized by contact with 'the social world' every now and again. It shakes up the sediment; tests one; aids mental digestion; and modifies unnatural extremes.

* * *

But I've said nothing, so far, in this journal, about what is really important; nothing of what I really want to say. But *how* to say it? Do I want to rave or to lament? My attitude and emotions are at once almost too complex and yet too simple to record. The war has had the effect of blotting out all the kinds of perspective which make contemplative reflection possible, and also that of numbing one's central affectivity, retarding one's deepest reactions.

It is probably this that is the matter: I am stultified by a continuous, daily sense of the monstrousness of the outside world, the world of today, and simultaneously, of the monstrousness of my own isolated individual being. A horrifying dual fascination, leaving me practically speechless. There seems to be overwhelmingly too much to say, and at the same time I feel that to say what is most essential demands a brevity and simplicity such as I have never been

279

able to master; being, as I have just said, monstrous, by which I mean ungovernably complex, labyrinthine, contradictory and ultimately, in all probability, both incoherent and incommunicable . . .

Those who persist in living 'on the edge of the Void', end by finding themselves reduced to silence — (I suppose that is that is what is meant by Kierkegaard's 'category of the secret', which until quite recently was among all K.'s conceptions the one which I found the most difficult fully to grasp.)

The most likely fate of those whose desire is to communicate *everything* (romantic fatal desire for the infinite and the unlimited) would be to find themselves finally incapable of communicating anything at all: *to choke*. (Dialectical justice of irony.)

* * *

Cyril Connolly, who was also staying at Peter Watson's for a time while I was there, shocked me by saying that I ought to resign myself to being never anything but what he called a 'literary' writer: 'In fact,' he said 'you are much *worse* than *literary*, really'; adding, however, that he did not use the word in a derogatory sense. — What exactly did he mean, I wondered, anxiously; and why, after all, should I be so upset by this opinion? How much truth was there in it? I tried to be honest with myself.

If I really *am*, fundamentally, in my integral personality, *literary*, in the sense in which Connolly understands the word, then that must be what I really *want* to be, since I have never wanted to be anything more than to be completely *myself*, down to the very last idiosyncrasy. And yet I am sure that I should always have said that to be 'literary' was one of the last things on earth that I wanted to be; I should have said that I conceived literature and life as being in insoluble contradiction one with the other and that I was on the side of life as against literature (distortion, romantic deception -- at best petrification) every time, striving in what I wrote only for the paradox and imperfection of reality, — only to release, communicate and awaken in others that true human *passion* which, it has always seemed to me, is negated and frustrated by what is known as *literature*; at any rate, by those elements of arrangement and style, of systematization, which seem to me to be inseparable from it, in one form or another.

I have always been ready to respect Connolly's critical opinions; I believe him to have as shrewd and perspicacious a mind as that of anyone I know. Is it possible that what he thinks he can distinguish about me is something quite objective but which for some (hidden) reason I am unable or merely unwilling to recognize? To what extent ought I to trust and rely on my assured belief that I 'know myself' without illusions, in and out? And being as scrupulous and unceasing in my self-examination, as genuinely sincere in my desire for self-knowledge, as I believe myself to be, how, if I were to discover this long-standing belief to be deceptive or untrustworthy, should I be able ever to hope to see myself in a more truthful light?

It is true that what I am probably best at writing are critical or expository essays about poetry or philosophy; and I find increasingly that as soon as I start writing this sort of thing I become involved in a long-winded, complicated style altogether unlike that of spontaneous speech (and which might well be accused of being stilted, precious, even pompous; though to call it unnatural would hardly be exact, since it seems to come quite naturally to me to write in that way). And yet, even if it is true that what I write (quite apart from poetry) is 'literary' in form (essays) and style, I still

281

cannot see that its essential content and the attitude to life revealed by it are obviously of the kind that one expects from a writer who has read more than he has lived (and who would like to press 'life', 'experience', 'truth', etc., between the pages of books, as a collector presses flowers, in order to be able to catalogue and annotate them, and then put them away . . .).

Living reality is chaotic and evanescent, and so infinitely complex and contradictory that it can never be wholly communicated in words; and the nearer to reality a writer lives and thinks, the greater must necessarily be the formal discipline and scrupulosity in his expression of it. — (This is an example of the kind of paradox that I have learnt to expect to find everywhere.)

(What Connolly's remark implied, *detachment*, rather. Explain this.)

* * *

Later: I feel that somehow the following quotation from Kierkegaard has considerable relevance to the above (tho' I don't for a moment wish to seem to be daring to compare myself with K. — I have sufficient sense of the limitations of my own powers!):

> The expression 'an author's author' . . . really denotes something which I possess over and above the usual. I am really an author for authors; I have no direct relation to the public; no, as an author I make others productive. Therein lies my suffering, as long as this is not understood, for during that time the something in me which is over and above the usual becomes a minus instead of a plus.
>
> *Journal*

27.II-1.III.40

Influences

Today I received, as a gift from Peter Watson, the English translation of the *Journals* of Kierkegaard (also the *Christian Discourses*). This is a book I have long desired to possess, but perhaps I had not fully realized, before actually looking into it, how tremendously important a book it is, for me particularly. A book that I feel is bound to become a major influence in my life; one among a very few others, such as Pascal's *Pensées* and Rimbaud's *Saison en Enfer*.

* * *

— What have been the other chief influences on my inmost development, so far? — Marx and Freud, of course; but then, who among my generation has escaped their influence? They represent for us what Hegel represented in S.K.'s day. Breton, I think; though that influence has long ceased to be an active one.

— My relationship with Antonia White; though it would be difficult to sum up in a precise statement exactly what that influence — a deep one — constituted: it was that of a spiritual 'mid-wife', but also something much more unique than that. Benjamin Fondane: an incidental yet greatly fortuitous and important influence. Miller, no doubt, even though only indirectly — Jouve, to a great extent, and Blanche Jouve quite as much . . . Marcel Jouhandeau, I wonder? More a strong but not identical affinity, than an influence.

(And much though I appreciate and admire M.J.'s writings, above all the *Algèbre*, I can't help feeling there's a certain flaw somewhere, something that I don't quite trust: perhaps it is a too over-balancing proportion of 'the aesthetic' in his attitude. In any case, compared with Kierkegaard for instance, he is only a minor figure, however extraordinary a

one, and in spite of his own enormous opinion of himself
. . .)*

Myself and the War

A week ago last Saturday, I registered for Military Service, and
am expecting to be called-up in about three weeks time.
Today I have applied to be enrolled in the Special Duties
branch of the Military Police Corps . . . My present attitude
to all this? A fatalistic one of immensely ironic resignation!

Oh, of course I have gone over and over, in my mind, all
the pros and cons of conscientious objection, although I have
written nothing down of that debate. I don't think I have
ever had much doubt about having to reject it (C.O.) as a
solution at present. From the practical point of view, in any
case, I am convinced that no tribunal would have accepted
my objections — which I myself cannot honestly regard as
fundamental ones. If I were really a sincere pacifist, of course
I should glory in being sent to prison, as that sort of sincerity
always does glory in (I mean enjoy) crusading and martyrdom
of such a kind; but as it is, I can't see much to choose
between going to prison and going into the army. The army
will at least be for me a new, active and intense experience,
whereas the solitude, meditation and frustration of prison are
already only too familiar an experience in my life.

It is not so much my lack of 'patriotism' that makes me
resigned instead of enthusiastic about the army; nor my
political views (a conviction that the wrong people are
conducting the present war for wrong but not openly avowed
reasons, and a considerable scepticism as to the kind of

---

* I might perhaps add Martin Heidegger, though I have only read the French
translation of his *Was ist Metaphysik*.

'improvement' in the European situation that the ultimate Peace will bring). Rather I feel that it is ironic that *I*, of all people, should be considered eligible as material out of which to make a soldier, a numbered uniform in a drilled machine! — I feel, well, they can try, if they like, I can appreciate the joke too, — but they'll never succeed in making anything out of me except what I am, i.e., one of the most unmilitary individuals who ever stepped into khaki!

Apart from these considerations (which are not without their core of paradox, as I fully appreciate), my attitude is also largely determined by my sense of the universal human implications of the war-situation, existentially speaking; my feeling that it is a manifestation of that human futility in which, as surely as in original sin, we are all involved, whether we acquiesce in it or not. Everyone living has their share in the responsibility for this general situation of human futility, of which War is an expression; and I cannot see why I should be able to evade the full acceptance of my own particular share. On a lower level, another possible expression of this point of view is implied when I say simply that I cannot see why *I* in particular should be able to get out of an unpleasant necessity when so many others of my age, and with my intellectual and other abilities, are having to go through with it, — however exceptional I may subjectively consider myself to be.

To carry self-detachment a step further: I also realize that behind the apparent calmness of my resignation (and the fact that, in spite of previous resolutions, I have done practically nothing to prevent what is by now inevitable), lies my deep-rooted familiar contradiction: that is to say, my instinct always to correct any extreme in myself by going eventually to its opposite. This was what was really behind my active

Communist Party phase, for instance. What it means is, that one goes to one's opposite extreme in order to *sharpen oneself* against it, as it were, — to reinforce and intensify *what one is* fundamentally. To strengthen oneself through test and strain.

And now, what extreme more contrary, more contradictorily opposed to all that I have until now appeared to be and to represent, would it be possible to imagine, than to be a soldier in a modern War? I cannot help feeling intensely curious, in a way, — in a highly ironical, self-detached way, — to see what this will 'do' to me, see how I shall emerge from this most extreme of contradictions. Above and beyond everything, I trust and believe in *my own identity*, that is to say my own *destiny*, which, though superficially it may appear to do so, nothing that ever happens to me will be able really to alter!

1.III.40

Kierkegaard

Miguel de Unamuno speaks of 'our brother Kierkegaard' — I wish I too could use that expression, make that presumption; only my astonished veneration of K. is such that I hesitate.

I have now been reading about him, and odd texts by him, off and on, for these three years or more, of course, and the main features of his life and thought have long been more or less familiar to me (all the thought and study I devoted to existential philosophy last year, when working on *The Last Judgement*). But his living personality, and the full sense of the huge living importance of his life and work, never struck me, I think, with so forcible an impact as that with which I have been struck on looking for the first time through the

Journals (of which I had a foretaste before Christmas in the extracts in French translation included in Jean Wahl's *Etudes*).

What a figure! Tremendous, even terrifying in complexity: a sombre palace full of mirrors, traps and winding corridors — I can see hardly any other figure so outstandingly remarkable in the whole of the 19th century. Marx, perhaps; but how poor is Marx, beside him, in human and 'dramatic' qualities. — He makes even Rimbaud — my passionate interest in whom probably depends on almost the same reasons as those on account of which K. attracts me so powerfully — seem altogether immature, fragmentary, 'ethically' uncertain.

About K. I now feel as though an integral part of myself had always been waiting to understand him perfectly; as though that part of me were somehow inseparably bound up with his character. — *I understand him through myself, I understand myself through him*! (And at the same time, I wonder: is not this the effect that he must have on almost every sensitive, intuitively understanding reader, and is not this due to the extraordinary objectivity of his psychological genius, which enabled him to perceive and hence record, his own most personal intricacies of mind and soul, in as impersonal and widely-relevant a light as possible?)

He is a mine so rich that it can never be exhausted by analysis or commentary. Sufficient material for many lifetimes' work. How true, when he speaks of himself as 'an author's author': 'I make others productive'! I already realize how very much I shall have received from him by the time my own work shall be finished — which will not be for a very long while yet, D.V.!

I can hardly doubt that in my own case there are certain marked affinities between my own mind and nature and that of K. I have always been naturally apt to understand more immediately than most people his complex dialectic of inner contradiction. Irony, melancholy, anguish, — the mask of secrecy, — demoniac multiplicity, — the conflict between the 'aesthetic' and the 'ethical', the poet and the philosopher, between the individually particular and the Absolute, — all are concepts which I can at once grasp through my most intimate personal experience. They have never been merely intellectual abstractions or generalizations for me.

The categories, concepts and terminology employed by Kierkegaard are wonderful intellectual instruments bequeathed by him to those who are capable of grasping and making use of them; instruments by means of which the individual, the 'subjective thinker', can obtain the most penetrating and authentic insight into the human situation, and become fit to deal effectively with what is perhaps the fundamental existential problem: How to integrate one's 'speculative' thinking about existence (in general) with one's own (personal, private) existence? to integrate one's own particular, immediate existence with *absolute existence*?

Of the greatest spiritual aid and inspiration: yes, emphatically. But while it is obvious that K. is that, one should nevertheless attempt to calculate, fully to realize, the extent to which he *may* represent for one a snare, even a serious *danger*.

As an influence upon a certain type of mind, the danger of K.'s thought is this: that in certain ways it may tend to encourage and thus aggravate the auto-destructive, i.e. *demoniac* element that forms one of the principal distinguishing features of this type; may encourage and aggravate its innate psychic complexity, inter-division, indefinitely repeatable 'sub-detachment', etc.

Up to a point, to be able to become aware of, and consequently to admit, all the contradictoriness, confusion and uncertainty within oneself (that chaos which is generally concealed under the quite arbitrary disguise known nowadays as 'personality') implies possession of a courageous intellectual honesty and sincerity, and yet, just beyond that point may be the danger of falling a prey to subtle but violent forces of disintegration; of becoming horribly, vulnerably exposed to the deadly temptation that leads one to abandon oneself to self-deception, duplicity, *wilful* incoherences, empty theatricalism, vain pursuit of mere 'interestingness', voluntary hysterics, voluptuously exhibitionistic suicide, etc., etc.

* * *

Today, Myself . . .

After a gloomily gusty, rattling night, today has turned out to be a day of cold, crisp, ice-clear radiance; perfect example of the austere beauty of early March weather at its best. Oh, that *blue*! The heavenly azure (which has by now a margin of pure palest gold) is still extraordinarily intense in hue at half-past three this afternoon.

After having been as though buried beneath a suffocating weight, during the last ten days or so (fit of the old black-out and paralysis worse than any that I've had for quite a year) today I am able once again to emerge into the light. The grave-stone seems to have been rolled away.

* * *

Heard over the radio, from Basle, this evening the first performance of the new Honegger-Claudel cantata, *Danse des morts*. Grim, hard, dramatically very effective, and at moments deeply moving.

* * *

Eluard

Am trying hard to finish my essay on Eluard, but seem somehow to be finding it very difficult to get on with. E.'s poetry is one of the most *evasive* subject imaginable; at the touch of the probing finger of analysis, it seems to crumble or evaporate away. An exercise in the unravelling and exposition of paradoxical complexity.

2.III.40
Another sunlit, windy, azure day.

This morning I received papers summoning me to the army medical exam. on the 6th.

4.III.40

> *Sans contact aujourd'hui je suis, sinon*
> *Avec le sein de Dieu*
> *Sans amour aujourd'hui de suis, sinon*
> *Dans les vallées de Dieu*
> *Et le soleil emprisonné par les forêts*
> *Le coeur, emprisonné par le ciel de la guerre . . .*
>
> P. J. Jouve: *Kyrie*

4.III.40 *(continued)*
On the Confines of Consciousness
Suspended, as it were, between *analytical* and *lyrical* utterance, one ends in silence.

Emotion and cerebration struggle with one another within me for speech.

Sometimes I lose all sense of Time's proportions. Oscillating breathlessly — and with what a deep ache buried in the breast! — between the clearest peak of this all-seeing and all- understanding Consciousness, and the most obscure, womb-like regions of abandonment and sleep, in which the Will is quite obliterated, and the Ego all unknown, and where all become enveloped in an unquestioned (an *unquestionable*) Mystery . . .

At both the outmost and the innermost limits of awareness, one begins to lose hold of one's identity. (The meaning I want to convey here is *inexpressible*, perhaps . . .)

Continuously wandering for years on end, between brief intervals of stupefied repose — or of 'normality' as most people would call it — across the most desolate and bewildering uplands of existence, or through the tenebrous uncertainty of its underworld . . . To these strange, solitary wanderings, no end seems possible. Upon the edge of these introspective confines which are my most constant territory (I have sometimes wondered whether it might not be said that my task in life was that of 'experimental introspection'), one's combined sense of 'everyday' time, of proportion, of objective relationships, of self, of personal identity and hence of *distinction*, becomes fluid, hazy, evanescent; sense (or 'statement') seems to become exactly balanced by what can only be defined as an ubiquitous, expressionless, all-embracing *namelessness*, so that the two cancel one another out, as it were; and yet, in spite of the apprehension of the immanence of a limitless and overwhelming *flux* (perpetual dissolution of the centreless universe?) a certain conscious awareness is always maintained, though it would seem to lie beyond the power of language to define *by what*, or by whom: where, or by what means . . .

— And then comes always the return, in the end, to the immediate, personal circumstances of the present moment of one's life! Today, tomorrow, the familiar continuity of habit, and the making of decisions, distractions of hope and fear, the endurance of small discomforts and the satisfaction of small daily desires . . . (Yet all this is only the mere surface of experience.)

* * *

Jamais durant toute ma vie, je ne me suis senti identique à ma personne. Jamais je n'ai éprouvé que l'individu eût une valeur essentielle, que mon moi subit les états, de mes actes successifs, de ce que j'éprouvais et de ce qui m'arrivait.

Keyserling

5.III.40 *(2.30 a.m.)*
Tenebrae

— Night. 'The stars look down . . . '

— At midnight I went out of the lighted, blacked-out house, the room in which I had been writing beneath a lamp; and it was like entering another dimension, to step into the great motionless sea of darkness which lay outside. Like entering an exteriorization of that unwalled intimate dark space with which I am so familiar *within* myself. I looked up; and slowly the absolute blackness of the sky revealed itself, and the immensely stoic scintillation of the stars by which it was made manifest; and irresistibly I felt the outer and the inner night exchange themselves, so that the minute but intensely hard stars became as though one with all these tiny fires of painful joy — or of exultant pain? — innumerably nailed across that inner firmament of which the centre is my heart.

— To stand alone and silent in the dark, and to look up into the sky's incomprehensible black wastes, is to realize the abandonment of one's situation *at the bottom of the universe*: in *ces bas-fonds du monde*:

O ma soeur misère accablée qui me révèle a moi-même,
Le monde est-il si bas? nous sommes au plus bas du monde sans
pouvoir jamais remonter,
Et les accordéons des bas-fonds soupirent dans les conques,
Nous sommes plus bas encore —

Jean Wahl: Connaître sans Connaître

Peut-être ceux-là seuls qui savent cet abandon au fond de l'univers,
une inquiétude sauvage les libère et les équilibre.   P. B.

Flammantia moenia:
inquiétude, sauvage en moi
je n'ai plus besoin de soutien
Car mon inquiétude est si grande,
Elle me brûle, elle m'agrandit
Je sens sa flamme
elle me libère et inéquilibre
Dans ce monde brûlant et vibrant . . .

Jean Wahl: Connaître sans Connaître

The X Position of the Artist

Nobody can drown in the ocean of reality who voluntarily gives himself up to the experience. Whatever there be of progress in life comes not through adaptation but through daring, through obeying the blind urge. 'No daring is fatal', said René Crevel, a phrase which I shall never forget. The whole logic of the universe is contained in daring, i.e., in creating from the flimsiest, slenderest support. In the beginning this daring is mistaken for will, but with time will drops away and the automatic process takes its place, which again has to be broken or dropped and a new certitude established which has nothing to do with knowledge, skill, technique or faith. By daring one arrives at this mysterious X position of the artist, and it is this anchorage which no one can describe in words but yet subsists and exudes from every line that is written.

Henry Miller: Reflections on Writing

Netherworld

— And then, from beneath the underlying crust of Sleep, there may burst upwards, every now and then, into the waking consciousness, tumultuous waves of memory, nostalgia, poetry, exasperation and revolt.

— Oh, that anarchic netherworld, whose violent and strange-coloured suns illuminate the upturned faces of those distant beings whom an unknown heart in me still loves, though I had long forgotten them. — Oh, wanderings and journeys through the dusk, among extinct volcanoes, quicksands, prehistoric rocks, ever towards the fatal conflagrations of a dying sky! There I have lived unnumbered lives, lives outside time, — an emperor, a criminal, a child, without sex and without a face; there I have murdered, sung, flown like a bird, devoured forbidden flesh, worn jewelled robes, and danced on fire to terrifying drums . . . How can I know I shall not finally awaken in that world, to find all memory of *this* world lost beyond recall?

* * *

(*Sans date*)

Je m'égare — en marge de tout.

Silence du vent immobile, et l'accalmie des nerfs.
Soleil de minuit. Il n'y a presque plus de temps.

Et pourtant, le printemps . . .

* * *

14.III.40

Grade III

On March the 6th (a week ago yesterday), I went into Kingston to be medically examined for the army. After having been kept waiting all the morning, I was told to come back two days later, as I had not got my glasses with me (the oculist had been unable to finish my new pair in time). I went back on the 8th, with my glasses, and to my great surprise, found the doctors quite kindly and sympathetic. They ended by classing me in Grade III. The chairman of the board told me 'If you're in a job, don't leave it. Grade III are not being called up. If they are ever called, it won't be for a long time yet; most probably *never*. In any case, you are only fit for work of a sedentary nature.'

And so, after having worked myself up into an 'exalted' state of resignation and acceptance, after having been quite convinced that I should be in uniform by Easter, here I am now, — new irony! — faced with the very future which I had thought it no longer possible to expect, with a freedom such as I had not even attempted to plan for, and having to readapt myself to circumstances all over again!

Of course I am really very relieved. Yet at the same time, there is a certain feeling of *anti-climax* — or very nearly — about my present situation; which is one of considerable uncertainty and indecision, though I expect I shall soon get accustomed to it.

I must begin trying to make up my mind as to what I am going to do now. I don't much care for the idea of staying on at home here in Teddington 'for the duration', that is to say indefinitely; though I feel that I should very much like to get down to a lot of writing now, and staying at home seems at present the only way in which it would be possible to do this.

* * *

15.III.40

Writing Projects.

Essays begun and still unfinished:

    The Poetry of Paul Eluard.

    A Philosophy of Life (reviews of Graham Howe's *The Open Way*).

    Logical Positivism and the Void.

    Notes on an Engraving by Picasso.

    Des Oeuvres Récentes de Henry Moore.

* * *

On making a list of titles of the various books I want to write, I found the other day that I have got altogether *fourteen* works planned out, in rough notes and synopses, and in my head. If only I could get *one* of them actually finished and published this year!

David Archer's scheme to publish *The Open Tomb* seems to have collapsed, so I am now submitting the MS to the Oxford University Press. I shall soon be so sick of bothering about this collection that I shall put it away in a drawer and forget its existence entirely.

Have also decided to approach the Oxford University Press with regard to an anthological *Introduction to Existential Philosophy*, and the possibility of translating Chestov's *Kierkegaard* and/or perhaps Fondane's *Conscience Malheureuse*. For the last week or so, I have been thinking continually about the story which I originally thought of calling *The City of Night* (new title: *Benighted in Babylon*), a theme which first occurred to me more than two years ago. It has suddenly become quite clear in my mind, and my imagination is in a state of unusual excitement about it. If I could once get really started on it, it ought not to be difficult

296

to finish it within, say, three months. Curious that all of a sudden I should find myself wanting to write something that is almost entirely 'aesthetic', (imaginative, poetical), just when my attention was so preoccupied with critical theory and systematic speculation. The creative mechanism would appear to work through unpredictable reactions. Perhaps it is irrelevant and unnecessary to try to arrive at a conscious intellectual determination as to what type of writer one is 'meant' to be (poet or philosopher, novelist or critic, aesthete or moralist, etc., etc.); one simply writes whatever happens most forcibly *to demand* to be written, and only afterwards can one decide to what classification and *genre* one's work belongs.

How should I describe *Benighted in Babylon*, beyond saying that it's an *allegorical fantasia*? The allegorical element, which perhaps has affinities with (derives from) Kafka, is really only incidental; it simply happens to provide a convenient structure of development upon which to hang the series of more or less inconsequential scenes and incidents, descriptions, characters and atmosphere, which make up the real substance of the book. Combination of fantasy and realism, of sober reminiscence (Paris, etc.) and spontaneous imaginative invention. Attempt to invest everything that is described in the book with a *multiple* significance; constant suggestion, by indirect means, of the unseen and the unanalysable; unconsciously apprehended symbolism, not to be elucidated. Evocation of the essential underlying mysteriousness of Reality, and of the ever-disturbing, irreducible *strangeness of human existence*.

19.III.40 *(2 a.m.)*

The other morning, received from Fabers an advance copy of Barker's *Lament and Triumph*. It is by far his best work up till now, and contains some of the finest poetry that has been written in English during recent years. I am so proud of the dedication to me of the last poem in the book!

I am sad when I think of his being so far away. He was almost the only person in England with whom I had any really valuable communication. I seem to have no intimate friends, now. I hardly ever see Antonia White, who writes me only occasional pernickety postcards about borrowed books, etc. Durrell is in Athens and I have had only one brief card from him since the beginning of the War. I can think of no-one else? Peter Watson, perhaps, but he is not yet quite an *intimate* friend ... René C., whom I met recently, is someone who may in time become one of my closest friends. Depressing topic.

Saw Denham Fouts one evening last week. He is growing a moustache, and is beginning to look extraordinarily like Errol Flynn.

I am thinking of going to Bristol to stay with J.H. for a few days. I might get a job there with the BBC?

Le Monde Désert

— A frightful interior aridity.

— I slept almost all day long yesterday, all night and most of today as well. Out of sheer boredom, chiefly. *Spleen*.

— I accomplish nothing, I don't know where I'm going, I am terribly alone. Shambles and dereliction. The War drags slowly on and on.

— Aimless nostalgia.

20.III.40

— History is being made this week, so the newspapers say; but I can hardly work up the least inner reaction to daily events any longer.

— What I am suffering from at present is sheer spiritual exhaustion, and what I most need is relaxation and a change of scene in order to recuperate. Already I feel better, simply from having realised this.

26.III.40

Went down into Hertfordshire with David Archer last Saturday to spend the Easter week-end at Bill B.'s cottage, and came back this afternoon. The change, short though it was, has done me good.

27.III.40

Beautiful day. Went out without a coat this morning. The almond-trees are in full blossom all down Strawberry Vale.

28.III.40

The essay on Eluard is still unfinished. Worked on it yesterday and today, but do not seem to have got much further. Am beginning to be a little tired of it. The trouble is not so much that the subject is a difficult and subtle one, as that I have much *too much* to say about it, I find, and have to keep compressing my material, of which I have probably almost enough (in note form) to fill a small book.

18.IV.40

A writer develops the muscles of his mind. This training leaves but little leisure for sport, it demands sufferings, falls, idleness, weakness,

299

failures, fatigues, mournings, insomnias — exercises which are the reverse of those which develop the body.

This note of Cocteau's, which I came across while re-reading his *Opium Journal* yesterday, is one that I find very consoling, just now. In the same book, I also discovered the following, so nearly the expression of one of my own most dominating ideas, of the attitude which I am at present trying to embody in the poems of *Conquest of Defeat*.

The only durable aesthetic is that of failure. The man who does not understand failure is lost.

The importance of failure is capital. I am not speaking of what fails. If one has not understood this secret, this aesthetic, this ethic of failure, one has understood nothing, and glory is vain.

* * *

April 1940 — July 1941: Lapse

* * *

12.VII.41

Recapitulation

If there can be said to have been any one principal reason for my failure to keep my journal up-to-date during a period of over a year, it is surely to be found in that new (or renewed) understanding the achievement of which, during the last week or so, has provided me with the impetus to return to the task of filling-up this book.

This new insight has given me the detachment which was necessary to enable me to view clearly and as a whole my inner development since the beginning of the War (actually, since the end of my analysis with Blanche Jouve and my subsequent return to England in the Spring of 1939).

During the last two years, more or less, I have truly been as one who is dead. I foresaw that this would be so (though without foreseeing how this kind of death would actually affect my everyday existence). At the same time, during all this while, a concealed and only very occasionally and very vaguely suspected drama has been taking place in me, deep below the surface of conscious awareness. This drama is of a kind that may be described (though by no means wholly satisfactorily) as: the reorganization (reorientation?) of the personality in relation to the self.

* * *

The initial factor enabling me to reach this new stage of enlightenment has been Jung's book *The Integration of the Personality*, which I have just finished reading, and which has impressed and helped me more than any other book I have come across for a very long time. Through it, I have recovered confidence in what I can only refer to as 'my vocation', and also arrived at a much more definite understanding of its nature.

Jung's explanation of the true inner and spiritual significance of the mediaeval tradition of Alchemy (with its preoccupation with the 'dialectical' reconciliation of contradictions and dichotomies; its dependence on an obscure language of symbolism derived from the Unconscious; its devotion to a mysterious, and practically speaking, useless, task referred to as 'the work'; its demand of the devotee that he should live in spiritual isolation from his fellow-men, without hope of any kind of worldly success, in conditions resembling those of 'the wilderness'; and its belief in the secret importance of its own function as being that of assisting somehow in the development and progressive 'redemption' of humanity in general), and his comparison of it with the most significant aspects of the tradition of modern psychology, and with certain of the profound teachings of Eastern metaphysics (the Tao), have helped me to realize more clearly than hitherto the peculiar character of my own most deep-rooted aspirations, and to see the latter in relation to their real context.

As I see it now, the Surrealist movement represented nothing less than an instinctive Twentieth-century attempt to fulfill an equivalent social and historical function to that fulfilled by the Alchemists during the Middle Ages and early Renaissance. The fundamental similarity of purpose between the alchemical 'Magnum Opus' and the surrealists' major proposition: 'to reduce and finally to dispose altogether of the flagrant contradition existing between . . . the subjective and the objective,' is particularly striking, for instance — I say, above, 'an instinctive attempt'; but although I do not think they were anything like adequately conscious of the deep underlying significance of the similarity I have mentioned, they were not, however, wholly unaware of the existence of the connection, as is shown by certain remarks of Breton's, for example in his *Second Manifeste du S.*, such as:

L'admirable XIVe siècle est-il moins grand dans le sens d'espoir (. . .) humain, parce qu'un homme du génie de Flamel reçut d'une puissance mystérieuse le manuscrit, qui existait déjà, du livre d'Abraham Juif, ou parce que les secrets d'Hermès n'avaient pas été complètement perdus? Je n'en crois rien . . .

. . . Je demande qu'on veuille bien observer que les recherches surréalistes présentent, avec les recherches alchimiques, une remarquable analogie de but: la pierre philosophale n'est rien autre que ce qui devait permettre à l'imagination de l'homme de prendre sur toutes choses une revanche éclatant et nous voici de nouveau, après des siècles de domestication de l'esprit et de

resignation folle, à tenter d'affranchir definitivement cette imagination par le 'long, immense, raisonné derèglement de tous les sens' *et le reste.*

He goes on to quote, from an alchemical text of Flamel's, a description of a symbolical 'Magic' figure, concluding: *'Ne dira-t-on* le *tableau surréaliste?'*

For reasons not unconnected, no doubt, with those which now lead me to consider the passage I have just quoted to be inadequate and misleading (even though illuminating in certain respects), I have long held the surrealist movement as a whole to have been necessarily a failure as regards what were, or should have been, its fundamental philosophical (or 'Metaphysical') aims. — At the same time, on the other hand, I can now see what was the real latent significance of, and reason for, my own early association with the surrealist group. ('. . . *il est clair que [la vérité]* prend possession de nous. *Dieu sait si, en vous engageant sur le sentier du surréalisme, vous en étiez loin!'* — Letter from B. Fondane)

I can also see, at present, a necessary connection between alchemical ideas, the ideas which originally attracted me in surrealism, and the system of thought I have attempted to develop experimentally under the name of 'super-materialist dialectics', 'dialectical super-materialism', etc.

* * *

As I understand it now, the aim and *raison d'être* of the *Tao* (in its sense of 'the *True Way*') is roughly this: To bring about the identification of the Self with neither the Conscious nor the Unconscious, neither the intellect nor the emotions, neither objectivity nor subjectivity, but with the nameless and Unknown, something not of this world, (— in a certain sense,

303

with Nothing). This identification once established, the Self is able to become the 'diamond body' (spoken of in *The Secret of the Golden Flower*); that is to say, something extraordinarily hard and concentrated, pure, clear, precious and enduring.

This is what is meant by 'the process of individuation'. In a sense, it is a *creatio ex nihilo*.

* * *

The intention of the philosophers was to transform imperfect matter chemically into gold, the panacea, or the elixir vitae, but philosophically or mystically into the divine hermaphroditus, the second Adam, the glorified incorruptible body of the resurrection, or the lumen luminum, the illumination of the human mind or the sapients. As I have shown, Chinese alchemy produced the same idea, that the goal of the opus magnum is the creation of the 'diamond body'.
Jung: Psychology & Religion

14.VII.41

It is obvious to me, now, that the fundamental 'subject' of this journal, the central theme, giving it continuity and cohesion, providing its real *raison d'être*, is the kind of process referred to in the preceding entry. The phrase 'integration of the personality' occurs in a previous *cahier* as long ago as *25.VI.37*, — three years before Jung's book, which I have just been reading, was even published. Subsequent references to the same thing, though not all of them are so explicit, occur over and over again ('To make a diamond out of dust', for instance, *23.XI.38*). The evidence is so strong that I cannot hesitate to regard the fulfillment of this mysterious 'process' as being my 'vocation'.

One of my earliest important intuitions was the idea of what I used to refer to then (without any real understanding of what I meant by the expression) as '*the Third Person*'.

Another early intuition, which has especial meaning for me again just now, was: '*On ne se repose jamais*'. That is to say, as long as life lasts, the 'process' can have no absolute conclusion, though possibly one reaches the end of various greater and lesser successive *phases* of it, as would appear to be happening at present.

If I have reached, or am reaching, just now, the end of such a phase, the latter must be one roughly corresponding to the period during which this journal was left unwritten, and its essential 'meaning' probably corresponds to the 'statement' I have been trying, during the last eighteen months or so, to embody in *The Conquest of Defeat*. The theme of *The Anchorite*, one of the longest poems in this collection (still unfinished), which occurred to me quite spontaneously, without my fully realizing, at the time, its significance in relation to myself, appears more or less to sum up the main spiritual problem of this recent phase.

Characteristics of this phase: sense of spiritual death, of sterility, of non-progression, lack of interest in my own problems, a disillusioned indifference to 'fate', — sense of separation (severance) from unconscious sources of inspiration, — vision of the utter barrenness of contemporary spiritual reality . . .

The month I spent at Yarmouth, in the Examination Service, last Spring, seems to have had some sort of significance in relation to the development of this phase; symbolizing, apparently, a descent into the womb of the Unconscious (a ship, the sea, — mental attention entirely devoted to, diverted by, exterior and practical affairs, — each night, a flood of extraordinarily vivid and cogent dreams); and perhaps representing, in some way, a turning point . . .

* * *

Every morning the sun rises on millions of men, but where among those millions is one heart that responds to it in pure music like the pillar of Memnon? — but my heart was separated from theirs. When has the morning sun ever really illuminated me? Once, perhaps, in that brief dream. But I shall go to where a virgin light shall meet me on virgin shores.

Every beginning is serene. Hail to him who can always begin again.

* * *

Fate is fulfilled in what is most individual — in what is most individual lies power. Nothing that is to work magically is in any way vague or general, but most particular, most momentary. Love — illuminated by a sudden ridiculous fancy, an awkwardness, a hesitation, or by a gesture of courage, of freedom. — The ordinary 'I' an insignificant construction, a scarecrow.   Hugo von Hofmannsthal: *Andreas*

* * *

Friends

This summer : two new friends, — David Carr, Robert le Masle (and the L's). Have also had the pleasure of recently making the acquaintance of Alphonse Kahn, one of the most charming, cultivated, gracious old men I have ever met — Mrs. L., Robert and I went with him one evening to Hampton Court, where we dined at The Mitre. Exceptionally interesting conversation about painting, French writers, painters; A.K. reminiscing about Renoir, Proust (with whom he used to play in the Champs Elysées as a child) etc.

— With David, almost a romantic friendship. Sunday afternoon walks, visits to Hampton Court and Kew, dinner at his father's beautiful house in Petersham, evenings together in town, etc. — A definite but by no means yet complete development towards intimacy. A self-sufficient, evasive nature, *au fond*; divided not altogether unconsciously, by curious conflict between hereditary influence of commonplace

306

bourgeois background, and devotion to an unusually strong sense of artistic vocation. — A relationship, *enfin*, not altogether devoid, perhaps, of latent possibilities; (but it would be unwise to attempt to gauge its significance, if any, at the present stage).

* * *

Note on Benighted in Babylon

Since writing the brief description of *B. in B.* on page 297, I have progressed with the actual writing of this book hardly any further than I was then; but my general conception of it has developed considerably, and I am still far from abandoning the hope that some day I shall really be able to settle down to producing it. I have worked out the outline of the first two parts (three altogether, twelve chapters each) in detail, and have by now accumulated a considerable quantity of notes.

What I originally thought of as allegorical *framework* merely, has now acquired a much greater importance in my general conception of the book. As I see it at present, the underlying theme of the whole is 'the Quest for the Self'.

Kierkegaard once suggested: 'One ought to be able to write a whole novel in which the present conjunctive was the invisible soul, the light and shade in painting.' (*Journal*, 157). And if by the present conjunctive one understands: might, could, would or should be, — that is to say, the implication of *possibility*, — the kind of novel imagined by K. is more or less what *B. in B.* will amount to. Simon goes to 'Babylon' to search for his lost twin brother, Peter (his real, or latent, self). Everywhere he goes, in his nocturnal wanderings through the city, he discovers traces of Peter — people who claim to have known him and can describe what he is like — hints as to the true nature of this mysterious brother and of his life. But all this information which Simon manages to collect is totally contradictory and confusing; every new piece of evidence reveals a quite different sort of character; each successive person he meets gives him a different account of Peter's way of living. Thus, Simon is confronted with one after another of a whole series of hypothetical personages, each of whom *might be* his 'lost brother', i.e., he examines one by one all the various possibilities of character and 'destiny' that are latent within him, seeking to discover which one represents his very own truest and most complete Self.

The various women Simon encounters in the course of his peripatations, — 'Madame Sosostris', Helen (*chez la Générale*), Carmen, the woman who helps him escape from the *bal masqué*, the young anarchist, laundress, etc., — all represent different aspects of his *anima* . . .

The figure of the Philosopher, who keeps reappearing throughout the story, symbolizes the objective intellect, the interpretative, critical faculty, — and in a sense, the Super-ego. He is also the 'wise old man' of collective dream-symbolism. He acts as Virgil to Simon's Dante in the young man's wanderings through the Babylonian underworld. Also, he serves as Chorus. As a character, his portrait is based to a certain extent on Henry Miller . . .

The various alter-egos, other existences, that Simon discovers in his search for the mysterious Peter, his twin, include: a poor student, a 'libertine' (Aragon), a homosexual, a *noctambule*, a wealthy man of fashion and dilettante, a member of a fascist type of secret society (Cagoulards), an unsuccessful poet and literary failure, an anarchist conspirator, a drug-addict, a 'hermit' or mystical fanatic, etc., etc.

In the final episode of the book, Simon is kidnapped (by order of the head of a certain secret 'masonic' type of organization) in mistake for P.; by chance, this incident puts him in possession of the actual address where P. is living, to find which until now he has sought in vain. He makes a dramatic escape from his kidnappers' headquarters, and hurries through the deserted streets to the newly-discovered address of P.'s room. It is just before dawn. P.'s attic is at the top of an old dark house, the street-door of which Simon has no difficulty in opening. He climbs the stairs, opens the unlocked door of his brother's room, — and in the dim first light of dawn sees a lifeless figure dangling by a noose from a beam supporting the ceiling. Its back is hanging turned towards the door; Simon cannot see its face. Horrified, he strikes a match, lights a candle standing on a table by the window, and catches sight of a document lying there which is addressed to himself, and on which the ink appears scarcely dry. In this letter (the full sense of which cannot be summarized here), P. makes Simon solely responsible for their mutual inheritance, explains the enigma of his life and of its relationship to Simon's, and imparts to him the invaluable lessons that his experience of Babylon have taught him; ending by telling S. that he must realize he is 'only at the beginning of a perhaps endless voyage . . .' When S. has finished perusing this last letter from his brother, he turns to cast his gaze once more upon the tragic body, — and to his utter amazement finds that it has vanished without leaving any trace! And at the same moment, a sudden gust of wind through the open window lifts P.'s letter into the air and bears it fluttering away out of the room into the space above the narrow street, away across the opposite roofs and out of sight. Simon is alone in the little room. He has found himself.

— *Finis*

20.VII.41

— Have just finished reading, with rapturous enthusiasm and scarcely a pause from first page to last, Stendhal's *Chartreuse de Parme* (in Scott-Moncrieff's translation).

Also read, last week, Rebecca West's little book on Saint Augustine.

Have begun to read, for the first time, Amiel's *Journal*. Insidiously depressing. Fruitful material for analysis, however (with regard to my own intimate problems, etc.). Don't feel in the mood to make any comments on him today.

— Last Wednesday, went with David Carr to a concert at the Albert Hall, and heard Mozart's 'Haffner' and G minor (K.183) Symphonies, Brahms' 2nd Piano Concerto (magnificent work, to which I grow more attached each time I hear it) and 4th Symphony. — Profound emotion.

— Start rehearsing in London tomorrow in four plays in which I shall be appearing during August in Welwyn and St. Albans.

(Memo: Shortly, endeavour to record a quite short, regular sequence of dreams — say over a period of three weeks or a month.)

. . . birds build — but not I build; no, but strain,
Time's eunuch, and not breed one work that wakes.
Mine, O thou lord of life, send my roots rain.

Gerard Manley Hopkins.

25.VIII.41

— Returned home yesterday from Welwyn Garden City, after acting for three weeks — three plays — in 'repertory' there; the fourth week — St. John Ervine's dreary, dated, unreal *First Mrs. Frazer* — having fortunately been cancelled on account of impossibility of casting *Mr*. Frazer.

Exhausting work, but on the whole have enjoyed the experience, which I'm sure has been valuable. Just *beginning* to learn how to act, only; but feel I have made a genuine start. — Dorothea Alexander says that having made an apparently promising start at *any*thing, it's a bad thing not to go on with it, somehow, until one feels one's at least reasonably proficient at it. But of course, I don't at present feel I'll *ever* come to think of myself as being an *actor* in the same way as I've always thought of myself as being a *writer*.

Have laid the foundations of a clear theoretical and practical approach to the problems of dramatic technique and of acting psychology (introspective habit and training useful while actually on a stage performing, in this respect), etc.

— During the last few weeks, have by degrees grown really very fond of Joan Greenwood — Intuition of 'specialness'.

— Immediate future as usual vague. Somewhat cloudily still, the prospect of being called upon, fairly soon, to do 'work of national importance' — fire-watching? — looms ahead.

Am at present engaged most of the time in studying the role of *Ford*, in *The Merry Wives of Windsor*, which I shall be performing, in Dorothea Alexanders's production of the play, at Windsor, on September 16th.

4.IX.41

While travelling back from Windsor after a rehearsal yesterday evening, received the initial impetus for a new poem (the first for some months), the subject of which being a meditation: *On France in her Darkness*. — The impulse, strong and unmistakable, to produce this poem, which for the most part remains as yet hazy and undefined in my mind, arose from the insignificant chance of my eye's happening to fall on the following small and banal enough paragraph in one corner of the centre page of an evening-newspaper lying crumpled on the opposite seat of the railway carriage.

> *In Darkest France*: A Wellington bomber pilot, flying low over a French town at night, flashed the 'V' signal. At once, from motor-car lamps, windows and skylights, a succession of Morse Vs twinkled in reply.

I am quite unable to account for the unusually forceful poignancy with which, spontaneously, this tiny, simple *fait-divers* penetrated, struck through, to the buried level of the source of emotional genesis within me.

* * *

4.IX.41 *(continued)*
N.B. — The all-importance of maintaining *continuity*.
(*Mem*: conversation with Joan G. and Anne Goossens at Welwyn.)

* * *

Am reading at present:
Baudelaire:	*Le Fanfarlo*
Stanislavski:	*An Actor Prepares*.
Thomas Mann:	*Lotte in Weimar*.
" "	*The Transposed Heads*.
T. S. Eliot:	*Elizabethan Essays*
Edward Thomas:	Poems.
Thomas Hardy:	Poems.

* * *

Very recently, read Ronald Firbank's *Vainglory*, and his *Princess Zoubaroff*, with keen delight. F. unequalled for relaxation and refreshment. (Alphonse Kahn, by the way, told me F. was one of his favourite modern English authors.) How strange it is to reflect that the kind of society 'set' (or set of 'sets' rather) most typical of 1920-40 — the kind of curriculum-vitae, costumes, décors, mannerisms, glamour-ideals, etc., described and depicted, for example, by Cecil Beaton in his *Scrap Book, New York* and, most recently, *Time-Exposure* — were to a very considerable extent *invented* by Firbank alone. What is so incredible now about *Vainglory* is that it was first published in 1915. — (A propos, *viz.*, Madame Helena Rubinstein, the face-pack queen, *chez elle*, in the current issue of the American *Life* magazine, — a living masterpiece of sheer Firbankery . . .)

No matter what critically-objective theories I may happen to expound to myself concerning the direction in which the poetry I write ought 'dialectically', etc., to develop, it seems none the less to stumble onwards blindly towards goals of its own of a kind I myself certainly would never at one time have suspected. (Bareness, sobriety, simplicity, formal discipline, clarity of pattern, — themes drawn from *Nature*, restricted palette of only the more subdued colourings, — a certain blunt, chill, 'pensive' interior music . . .) Altogether, in fact, my Muse seems to have gone on to a diet of bread and water; — though this, of course, may still be due chiefly to a prolonged indigestion . . .

* * *

15.IX.41

The dress-rehearsal of *The Merry Wives of W.* was the day before yesterday; the performance takes place tomorrow evening. Was not very pleased with myself on Saturday; but then, I'm always rather poor at dress-rehearsals, — shaky, uncertain of my way about the stage, of acoustics, etc. — Think I'm at least pretty near word-perfect in my lines by now. *Ford* is the longest part I've ever had to learn.

If I go on acting, it will be with the aim of becoming eventually a *producer*. Have been thinking a lot lately about methods, possibilities, etc. — Want to build myself a model stage, for planning and designing experimental sets, and for working-out groupings, movement, etc.

One of my most cherished theatrical ambitions would be to put on a production of Beddoes' *Death's Jest-Book* (which I have been re-reading during the last few days). With a good deal of judicious cutting, and so on, I believe it really could be done, and even that it would prove dramatically effective. — Ideal material for a production in the manner of Antonin Artaud. Plenty of music (a specially commissioned score? Lambert?); decor by Edward Burra; highly stylized movement and diction . . .

* * *

Commentaire sans Commentaire . . .

> *Quant au bonheur établi, domestique ou non* . . . *Non, je ne peux pas. Je suis trop dissipé, trop faible. La vie fleurit par le travail, vielle vérité; moi, ma vie n'est pas assez pesante, elle s'envole et flotte loin au-dessus de l'action, ce cher point du monde.*
>
> * * *
>
> *Farce continuelle? Mon innocence me ferait pleurer. La vie est la farce à moner par tous.* Rimbaud: *Une Saison en Enfer.*

4.X.41.

Glasgow: 8a Sandyford Place

After a lot of rather tiresome waiting-about, postponement and indecisive muddle, which went on during more than a week, I finally arrived here, to stay with David Archer for a short period, at an early hour this morning, having left Euston by the night-train yesterday. Rather a pleasing *dépaysement*; and I've certainly been needing one lately. Curious, how things invariably start happening in more or less unexpected ways round about this time of year (this is my birth-month). War or no war.

Think I may just now be entering a new period of being able to write. Dangerous thing to say! — Very keen to get on now with the 'Babylon' thing (n.b.: write more concerning this presently). And it might be a good thing if while I'm in Scotland I wrote plenty of entries in this journal; in the style, perhaps, of a *journal de voyage*. (Which reminds me: Was fortunate enough, the other day, to pick up, in a little semi-pornographic bookseller's shop in the Charing X Rd., a copy of Henri Michaux's fascinating *Ecuador*; also a copy of *Flaques de Verre*, prose-poems by Reverdy — the last thing I should have expected to come across just there.)

On the train last night, read the entire volume of Vollard's *Recollections* — an enchanting book; cannot think how I can have missed reading it for so long.

During the last few months, have found myself developing an increasing interest in (curiosity about) Cézanne; who never before really made any particular *personal* appeal to me. Never, that is to say, until recently, has C. been for me the subject of an authentic inner *affective experience*, in the way that El Greco, the Flemish masters, Georges de La Tour,

Grünewald, Daumier, Van Gogh, Picasso, perhaps Klee, have been to me at various times.

Took the opportunity, before leaving London, of visiting the big retrospective Sickert show now on at the National Gallery; and was glad not to have missed it. Must say I can't agree with the quite numerous people who are maintaining that the G.O.M.'s gift has been deteriorating during the last fifteen years. One of the canvases I liked best out of the whole exhibition was, as it happens, a reclining woman's head — with raven hair against olive and plum-coloured cushions — dated 1941; such splendid assurance in every slightest brush-stroke! — (Oh! and how nice it would have been, it occurred to me as I stood there looking at it, if some perspicacious Maecenas, before James Joyce's recent death, had acquired S.'s delightfully fresh-tinted panorama of Dublin, city and bay, and made an anonymous presentation of it, in token of esteem, to the great exiled Irish master.)

28.X.41
(*Teddington*)
Went today to Drury Lane Theatre, was interviewed by Henry Oscar, and succeeded in getting an acting job, in ENSA, at £6 p.w. Touring in the Coventry Repertory Co.'s production of *It's a Wise Child*, for an indefinite period, possibly for 'the duration'. — Travelling up to Darlington, to join the company for rehearsals, next Monday.

27.XI.41
(*Darlington, Co. Durham. Extract from a letter home*:
. . . Time seems to have rushed by during this last week or two. As you see, we are still in Darlington; but we leave here

on Sunday to go to Bridlington (Yorks) for a week. As far as I know, we shall all be staying at the same hotel there . . .

My first week of actual acting was really rather agonising and I was very glad when it was over. I don't think I've ever had such bad stage-nerves in my life as I had on the first night; and what made it worse, I didn't fully realize this until I actually got onto the stage. I gave a frightful performance. Somehow it was so much more intimidating than any ordinary first night, — everyone else in the company being highly experienced and efficient and, of course, all knowing their lines backwards, many of them having been acting in this same play for a whole year now.

It wasn't until the end of the week that I began to be able to do my part at all competently; the first two or three nights I was so bad that I really was quite afraid of getting sacked! — though I must say, everyone in the company was as nice about it as they could be.

By this time, of course, I have quite settled down, and on the whole am getting on pretty well. There is a good deal to be learnt from a long run in the same play (even if it's a bad play) — which is something I've never had the opportunity of doing before now.

The others are all *very* 'professional' and hardly ever talk anything else than shop, but they're a pleasant, friendly lot, and I manage to get along on good terms with all of them . . .

I've already told you, I believe, about our 'week-out'? It's Dec. 7th-14th, so I'll probably be arriving home late on the Sunday after next. Will let you know more definitely as soon as I've found out particulars about trains, times, luggage, etc. . . .

16-17.XII.41.

(*Northampton*)

Our 'week-out' wasn't really a very great success, — speaking for myself. Spent more than half the time out at Teddington, at home, doing nothing, feeling frankly flat, sleeping to excess. Was genuinely glad, in fact, to get back to 'the boards' again on Monday night.

Went out one evening to dinner with John Lehmann; which was quite pleasant but ended tiresomely early, leaving me stranded with nothing to do . . . Went to Peter W. on Friday, but wasn't feeling very bright. Listened to the new recording of the Shostakovitch Piano Concerto (soloist Eileen Joyce).

Went with Peter on the Saturday afternoon to a concert of Soviet chamber music: a very restrained and *sotto voce* quartet by Shostakovitch, and a severe, concentrated, rather colourless ditto by Shebalin. A charming, large-sized middle-aged Russian lady[*] with very dark locks, earrings, and a billowy-sleeved coatee, sang a setting by Prokovieff of Hans Andersen's *Ugly Duckling*, in a tremendously expressive, indeed portentous 'bedtime-story' manner, manipulating her huge, heavily-bound copy of the music, held-out at arm's length in front of her, with superb, apparently unconscious deftness — (If only Peter Ustinov could have seen — or should I say heard — this number!).

On Saturday evening, went to see a somewhat trying play called *Jupiter Laughs*, concerning an unpleasant set of doctors, matrons and so on, in a private nursing-home, but with a solemn 'message' as squib in the tail. Some undoubtedly clever performances by the cast. Was under the

---

[*] Olga Slobodskaya

impression until afterwards that the piece was by Bridie, while actually it was by A. J. Cronin; *mais qu'est-ce que ça pouvait faire?*

Went on Sunday afternoon with Kathleen Raine and Sonia Brownell to a concert at the Cambridge Theatre, at which Cyril Smith was the soloist in the Brahms Concerto No. 2 — by no means an ideal performance, but thoroughly enjoyed it, I adore the music.

* * *

Early Enthusiasm of a Lapsed Cineaste: entry for December 19th, 1941, in a Wartime Journal (revised)

Having just seen *High Sierra*, have come to the conclusion that it is probably a masterpiece of its kind, — the kind being the tragic gangster film (of which *You Only Live Once* and *Le Dernier Tournant*, as the French version of *The Postman Always Rings Twice* was called, are two other examples which most immediately come to mind). Remember reading good notices of this picture, but do not think that when it first appeared it received its full due of discriminating appraisal.

The chief thing I liked about it is that quality of 'tension' or 'resonance' which almost invariably, I find, distinguishes those works I most admire, whether in literature, music or the drama. First, the artist lays his wires (of theme, plot, situation, characters, etc.), making sure that only a single consummate conclusion can result from these preparations; so that as the work develops, these wires are gradually and inevitably drawn into an increasingly great tension, ever more rigidly outlining its essential features; until, at the moment of the final climax, they become as though charged with an electric current of transfiguration (i.e., catharsis).

High Sierra illustrates this process perfectly. Its concluding scenes are charged with a plangent implacability, a violent exaltation and a deep, tragic beauty which give it a place among the very small number of 'classic' works the cinema has so far produced in this genre. It may well claim to represent the *apotheosis* of the Gangster Film (of which by now the day most probably is done). I was unusually moved by it, though it would probably be thought absurd if I were to say that there is something about it which suggested both Aeschylus and Webster to me.

This sort of film is the authentic dramatic product of its time, the equivalent, on an inevitably much lower plane, of the high poetic tragedy of the past, standing in very much the same relation to the present age as, for instance, *The Duchess of Malfi* to the Jacobean decadence.

This is how *High Sierra* ends: After a breakneck car-chase, along hairpin-bending mountain roads, set amidst superb Californian scenery, — pines and precipices, rugged tors and massed, majestic clouds against a sky of darkest blue, — the hunted Gangster (Humphrey Bogart) is at last forced to take refuge in a perilous rocky eyrie from which no further escape seems possible. He holds back with his machine-gun the ring of cops finally closing in round the foot of the rocky wall on which he's perched. From under the cover of boulders, the chiefs of police, their voices resoundingly echoed by the mountain crags about him, shout up to him demanding his surrender; but he shouts back in defiance; peppering them with machine-gun bullets, each of which irretrievably diminishes the length of his last belt of ammunition. Night falls; the stalemate continues. Fresh reinforcements of police keep arriving from below; and their ranks are now being constantly augmented by swarms of craning sensation-hunters, avid for the kill. Press-photographers' bulbs have started to flash amongst the blackness of the pines, reporters stand waiting in tense groups, all eyes are upturned towards the Gangster on his ledge, and above the mingled sounds of the commotion is heard the voice of the radio-commentator, pouring an ecstatic eyewitness account of the situation into his microphone, keeping the nation's eager, vengeful masses informed as to the approach of the sacrificial victim's certain death. Tense vigil. Marie, the Gangster's anguished Moll (played by Ida Lupino), who, having been drawn irresistibly to the scene of the drama on which nation-wide attention is now focused, and has by this time been recognized and seized by the besieging police, gazes up from among her captors with fearful, sleepless eyes.

Dawn breaks at last, a fan of rays behind the sombre peaks. Her lover's hunters unsuccessfully endeavour to get Marie to shout up to him and persuade him to give himself up, as he hasn't a chance. Once again he hurls down shouts of defiance, and this time his voice is heard by his dog, which Marie has brought with her in a basket. Thrilled to hear his master, the dog dashes off up the mountainside, scaling the dangerous slope by leaps and bounds, soon reaching the fugitive's ledge. As soon as he sees the dog, the Gangster knows that Marie must be present in the crowd below. He staggers out of ambush into full view of the armed men waiting for his appearance, calling her name, and is at once shot dead; Marie screams; his body topples over a cliff, falls precipitously, tumbles, rolls down to where the now silent crowd is waiting. Marie rushes forward, kneels sobbing beside the broken body; the devoted dog runs up to lick his slain master's hand.

'There lies Clarke. Not much to look at now,' comments the radio-reporter. Marie looks up at him and asks: 'Mister, what does it mean when a man says he's smashed out?' —

'Why, that means that he's free, sister.' — 'Free!' she repeats to herself as the cops drag her away, a wild and agonized triumph gradually burning through her tears, 'free . . . *free!*' — The End.

Among the other things I liked about this film were some of the early sequences, reminiscent in their atmosphere of passages in Faulkner's *Sanctuary*, for instance, and as carefully detailed in their naturalism as the work of a French director such as Renoir. Ida Lupino's face framed in an open doorway, her lower features haggard in the moonlight, the eyes above them smouldering, deadly, inscrutable behind a veil of shadow. The episode involving two crime-infatuated youths, their clumsy confusion, loucheness, stealth and abrupt brutality. The scene in which Bogart and the young girl with the club-foot stand gazing at the stars blazing above the Sierra: 'That one's Jupiter . . . and there's Venus . . . I often watch the stars. Sometimes it makes you feel how the earth's just a spinning ball with us all clinging on to it in the darkness . . .' And then the scene in which Bogart talks incoherently in his sleep, twisting to and fro, foreseeing his own death in a dream, while Marie stands there in her nightgown, motionless, peering down at him through the curtains, her pale face tranquil with a brooding sadness. Ida Lupino, incidentally, proves herself a fine actress, difficult to categorize and insufficiently recognized.

An important part of the appeal of films of this type depends on *la poésie du mal*, the dark romantic pathos of the damned. — Exploitation of the sado-masochistic romanticism inherent in the conflict between the criminal and society. ('*Encore tout enfant, j'admirais le forçat intraitable sur qui se referme toujours le bagne. Je voyais l'univers de ses yeux . . .*': Rimbaud.) Glorification of the singlehanded enemy of a callous, hidebound collectivity; of the misfit, the underdog, the scapegoat, the lone wolf; *l'héros du malheur*, pre-destined to defeat ... *'Je suis celui qui souffre et s'est revolté.'* This is related by a fundamental similarity of inspiration to Dreiser's *An American Tragedy* (not a great masterpiece, but deeply symptomatic of its period and its underlying myths), James Cain's *Postman* (even less of a masterpiece but significantly celebrated) and, in a slightly different field, the ballads of Brecht and Prévert, all of which are recognizably marked by the same sign of convention, a constant undercurrent of irrational violence, brutality and hysteria, against which they no doubt protest, but which can be detected in them too.

Christmas Eve 1941
(*Aylesbury*)

> Shall we come out of it all, some day, as one does from a tunnel?
> Will it be all at once, without our doing or asking,
> We shall behold clear day, the trees and meadows about us,
> And the faces of friends, and the eyes we loved looking at us?
> Who knows? Who can say? It will not do to suppose it.
>
> A. H. Clough: *Amours de Voyage*

30.XII.41
(*Colchester*)
Today started reading Søren Kierkegaard's *Stages on Life's Way* (Lowrie trans.)

* * *

Multiplicity is my daimonia

* * *

4.I.42

(*On Tour, Colchester*)

Found a certain consolation the other day in the following passage from an article ('Genesis of *Swann*' by Robert Vigneron) in the latest issue of *Partisan Review*:

> There [in Cabourg] he [Proust] discovered that his strength had appreciably decreased in the course of one year. In the summer of 1907, he had been able to lead a relatively active life, drive all over the countryside with A. (his chauffeur), and explore most of Normandy. Now, while he still could venture out on the beach, motoring had become impossible. Towards the end of September, he left Cabourg and drove to Versailles, where he put up at the Hôtel des Reservoirs. There he immediately suffered such terrific attacks that he had to remain in seclusion in his apartment for several weeks, with scarcely any other company than his valet and A., with whom he played dominoes. But in spite of his miseries, so eager was he to express himself though a work of art before a death he believed imminent, that he made a supreme effort to resume his writing and twice, in his 'less bad hours', managed to set to work, twenty minutes each time.
>
> These were brave but unavailing attempts: days, weeks, and months went by, and Proust seemed to have forsaken his project. In the first days of November he had returned to his boulevard Haussmann apartment; but about the end of 1908 or the beginning of 1909 his condition became such that he could not even try to write a few lines without suffering terrible headaches. In desperation, he then resigned himself to reverting to a genre which the year before he had deemed stupid: he corrected a few left-over pastiches and in March 1909 published in the *Figaro* one more instalment of his *Affaire Lemoine*. After which he relapsed into his pathetic inaction; but he had not yet given up all hope. — As a matter of fact, toward the end of the spring of 1909, he suddenly came back to life. On May 23 . . .

— It is sometimes cheering to remember, after months and months, and years, of apparent sterility, — in the midst of a seemingly endless, weary, uncreative existence, — that such resurrections *have*, in fact, occurred, and are therefore not beyond the pale of possibility.

6.II.42

(*King's Lynn*)

Since joining ENSA, I have rapidly developed an absolute passion for *book-collecting*; an appetite for new books and for the sheer material acquisition of them, of an intensity greater than I have ever felt, in that connection, before. And during the same time, I have likewise become more and more intimately and enthusiastically interested in Henry James.

What was my excitement, therefore, last week, in Ipswich, to find myself able to pick-up H. J.'s collected correspondence — a couple of hefty out-of-print tomes, — for a mere 8/6! Also last week, found a copy of the autobiographical fragment entitled *The Middle Years* (at an old dealers called Greene & Hatfield).

Yesterday, Philip Ingram (a fellow-member of the company I'm touring in) very kindly presented me, being cognizant of my current H. J. passion, with a copy of *The Ivory Tower*, together with a copy of Rebecca West's sharply intelligent brief essay on J. (written just after his death in 1916; just 9 months, as it oddly happens, — James' death, I mean — before I was born), on the fly-leaf of which he (P.I.) had been kind enough to write: 'Please write a book one day, about H. J.' I do, in fact, ask myself whether some day, ever, I shall? At any rate, I shall presently have plenty enough to say about him, his mind and work. (Almost as much, I should think, as I have, by this time, to say about old S.K., — to whom, incidentally, who *could* have borne less resemblance, superficially, than J.?)

Another of my Ipswich 'finds' was what I believed to be a copy of the 1st edn. of Whitman's *Leaves of Grass*; anyway, a most attractively got-up old copy, valuable or not.

Today I bought a miscellaneous selection from Whitman's prose writings. Also Gilchrist's *Life of Blake* . . .

Oh, how all too heavy-laden have my suitcases become! I find myself having to send home a heavy parcel of books almost every week-end, now.

* * *

N. B. re Henry James

Write a note, soon, about H. J.'s 'later-manner' tales (so unanimously disapproved of and on the whole, still generally misunderstood), and the light possibly to be shed on them by a comparison with certain of Mallarmé's *Divigations*. Meeting of a certain essential *poetry* and a certain essential *prose*, at their extremes? — Compare, too, the initial triviality of H. J.'s 'props' and 'themes', with the triviality (necessary and deliberate) of the 'objects' (articles of domestic furniture, *bibelots* — probably 'Nouveau-Art' in style!) employed by Mallarmé as initial images in so many of his sonnets — towards an ideal 'algebra' of the psyche?

7.II.42

(*King's Lynn*)

The long-neglected muddle of my 'inner life' — if I can still lay claim to such a thing, after the seemingly interminable series of exhaustions and confusions comprising my present 'outward' mode of existence! Oh, the ironical the pities (*sotto voce*)! *The sheer horror* — as dear, far-distant Denham F. would say — *of it all* !

But really what a muzzy, fuddled tangle it all is! It seems hardly possible to set down, any more, to anything like saying 'where I am'.

— As I have already written, I see, *Multiplicity is my daimonia*.

— And (or But), as I find I have noted, what is *important* is above all *continuity* (secret *unity* of selfhood).

25.II.42

(The Bell Hotel, Norwich)

In the latest issue of *Partisan Review*, which reached me from America last week (while we were at Cambridge), an unusually thought-provoking essay on Stendhal ('In Quest of Henri Beyle') by Wm. Troy of Bennington College; its dominant thesis being that the hidden key to the true interpretation of both Stendhal's novels and of his character and life, is to be found in *a secret obsession with impotence*. This struck me; as it was precisely the same conclusion that I reached some time ago (most definitely, perhaps, upon reading the extraordinary *Beast in the Jungle* last autumn) in connection with Henry James. Pondering this, I am still further struck by the undeniable fact that one might, with varying degrees of certainty, come to the same sort of conclusion concerning practically all the writers of, say, the last two hundred years, in whom I happened to be most interested: Beckford, Beddoes, Coleridge, Kierkegaard, Baudelaire, probably Rimbaud, certainly Mallarmé (*M'introduire dans ton histoire* and *Herodïade* alone are sufficient to convince me in the latter case). Proust, Kafka, Roussel, quite possibly Sartre, to name by no means all. Yet it seems to me, at the same time, that by putting down to a fundamentally *sexual* impotence, or *sterility alone*, (inability, on account of ineradicable

327

inhibitions of unconscious origin, to achieve satisfactory 'integration with' the Objective, i.e. the Reality of everything outside the subjective world of the Self) one precludes a possibility that may be waiting in this direction of attaining to a quite new understanding of a specifically modern type of genius, and also of the as yet quite unrecognised insight into *la condition humaine*, — concerning the true nature of which mankind is still so largely (and so alarmingly) unconscious — that might be found to have provided the essential subject matter of the works of all those writers of genius who can be said to belong psychologically to this particular type.

* * *

N.B. — Enlarge on the above later: clarify and develop possible alternative thesis.

26.II.42

In the Stendhal article aforementioned, the passage which for me stands out particularly, as being richest in latent implications, is the following:

Because his heroes are incapable of action in the classic sense, Stendhal is forced to rely almost exclusively upon analysis. [This seems to me somewhat debatable, but does not I think compromise the validity of the general conclusions to be drawn from the rest of the passage.] Of course one admits that the analytical is the modern habit of mind; *Hamlet*, as Monseignor Kalbe has pointed out, is fundamentally a play *about* analysis. But in Stendhal the analysis is a vast and endless improvisation without center and without limits — a medley of conflicting themes and motifs that can never be resolved because they are never really grasped. Distinctions, comparisons, and qualifications of the most tenuous sort must be made for every movement of the mind or sensibility. It would not be hard to

328

discover in this *mania* for analysis a symptom of what today we call paranoia . . .

This criticism admirably brings out the daemonic element in the analytical tendency of mind, relating it unmistakably to the *daimonia of multiplicity* frequently referred to in earlier notes of mine.

15.III.42
(Tunbridge Wells, Sunday evening)
Had a thrilling afternoon the other day in a little bookshop here (C. Howes), discovering, among other things, an almost new-condition copy of *The Life and Letters of Saml. Palmer* (1892, never re-printed), for which I paid a mere 6/-. I discovered a copy of this in Chelmsford last January, priced 12/6, which was more than I could afford that week, and subsequently much regretted having missed the opportunity of picking it up. — Grigson's new study of Palmer should be being brought out by Fabers some time quite soon, by the way. The chief deficiency in the *Life* is the poverty of the illustrations; only works not originally in colour are reproduced and of these, but half-a-dozen at most are representative of Palmer's true genius (*Ruth Returning from the Gleaning* and *The Bright Cloud*, for instance). The *Letters*, which take up about half the volume, I find extremely good examples of epistolatory style, — vivid, quivering with personality, abounding in verbal felicities and graphic thumbnail sketches of *choses vues* — etc. I can't think why they are so much less widely known than they deserve to be.

I transcribe the following extract as an example of the essential Palmer, and also a piece of admonition of a kind I myself need more than ever, perhaps, just now:

And all this is only one little corner of Art [he writes, after enumerating in note-form the technical aims of his work]. The conclusion of the whole matter is this, that it is almost impossible to do rightly or wrongly. That conceit, self-complacency, and indolence, should be incessantly hunted out of the inner man. That everything we do should be done with all our might, and that rest and recreation should be proportionately separated and entire. What a blessed thing is sleep to a mind always on the rack for improvement!

Another sample excerpt from Samuel Palmer's Writings:

FLASHES OF LIGHT or BLOW OF DARK.

To get vast space, what a world of power does serial perspective open! From the dockleaf at our feet, far, far away to the isles of the ocean. And thence — far thence, into the abyss of boundless light. O! what heavenly greys does this suggest!'

Another:

The bask of beautiful landscape in glorious sunlight is in nature perfectly delicious and congenial with the mind and heart of man, but the imitative power is so limited — particularly so as to the lowness of the light pigments with which we imitate — that the above, when upon paper or canvas, should perhaps only be considered as the corpse which is to be ANIMATED.

The ANIMATOR is CHIAROSCURO. HOLES OF DARK, BOLD CAST SHADOWS — the same PLAYFUL and INTRICATE sometimes, when cast from trees like (blueish) soft, coal gray, blotting or dazzling over the finished matter (figures most beautiful under this effect). When figures or sheep come in nearly front light against holes of shade under trees they are like plates or bassi-relievi of wrought gold.

29.III.42
(Fleur de Lys Hotel, Canterbury)
The work I still carry about in my head and which hitherto I
have referred to, first as *The City of Night* then as *Babylonian
Nights*, etc., I have finally decided to baptize: *The Journey to
Byzantium*. The immediate reference is, of course, to Yeats'
poem, which refers symbolically, as far as I understand it, to
the soul's progress towards the accomplishment of its final
'integration'/'consummation', and this, as I have explained in
a previous note, is the basic underlying theme of my fantasy:
i.e. the Quest for the Self; (or at least, if this and the Yeats
theme are not perhaps quite identical, they are closely related
and co-dependent). Byzantium is also really a much more
satisfactory name for my mythical city, which is meant to
symbolize XXth Century urban civilization, with particular
stress on the aspect of its *decadence*; which Byzantium sums
up far better than Babylon (viz. Georges Duthuit's fascinating
essay: *Byzantines Décadents*).

I am beginning to be able to visualize a number of
wonderful little scenes with which to embellish this work.
Intense chiaroscuros, hallucinatory perspectives; momentarily
glimpsed and minutely observed mask-like faces; vivid specks
of supernatural colour, of occasional costumes, of decors, of
certain significant objects, of the night-sky . . .

28.IV.42
(At Ipswich)
And so the tour is coming to an end at the end of the present
week: 6 months exactly, after the date of my first joining the
company! We first received this news a week ago last
Saturday, while we were at Chatham; and I had had a strong

331

premonition, about the show discontinuing before long, only a day or two previously . . . I am more relieved, I think, than anything else, though it is of course in many ways a pity.

What I need now for a while is rest, seclusion, quiet, freedom from the tyranny of the clock; an opportunity, in fact, to give complete attention to my most serious preoccupations, and to get down at last to some sustained creative writing.

30.IV.42

Ha-ha! (slightly bitter laughter) — No sooner have I written the above, of course, than we receive word, yesterday evening, from Drury Lane, that the tour is to continue after all ! So much for 'strong premonitions'; and as to 'sustained creative writing', I'm afraid that will have to go on waiting till some indefinite date in the future after all. A week's holiday, starting Monday next, another week's rehearsal at Drury Lane, — and then we set out on the road once more.

* * *

This journal has been very much neglected, I'm afraid, during recent weeks. I have kept meaning to make a note of this and that, — *choses vues*, landscapes, books read, and so on — but travelling and time have been tyrannical, and here we are, with Spring already well advanced and Summer soon to be at hand, and nothing has got written after all.

While I was staying at Tunbridge Wells, for instance, six weeks ago, I had to go up to London one day, and went up by bus; and one of the things I very much wanted to record a short description of here, was the exhilarating beauty of the Kentish landscape, between Tunbridge and Sevenoaks, as I saw it then, on one of the earliest days in Spring, this year. (I had just been reading the Samuel Palmer book I mentioned a few pages back, and I think this must have had a certain influence on the way I saw the scenery of Kent that morning: everything painted itself on my sight with the vivid intensity of a rare vision; and the countryside before my eyes happened to be the very same as that in which Palmer lived in his youth and where he produced the best and most personal of his early work.)

I do not remember ever having seen the English countryside transfigured by such perfect loveliness as this year's Spring has brought with it.

1.V.42

Books.

The book-collecting mania aforementioned has not as yet by any means abated. I must have acquired several hundred volumes during the past six months; and during next week's holiday, when I shall probably be at Teddington most of the time, I hope to be able to devote myself to cataloguing and arranging them in at least some semblance of order, as at present they are lying about the floor of my room in haphazard heaps . . .

This collection has not been assembled entirely without system. The books that I have bought can in fact be divided into a certain number of main groups, more or less as follows:

(a) *The English Poets*, from Langland to the End of the XIXth Century (Surrey, Wyatt, Drayton, Campion, Waller, Marvell, Crashaw, Vaughan, Traherne, Smart, Blair, Chatterton, Emily Brontë, (Poe, Emily Dickinson,) Beddoes, Landor, Arnold, Clough, Patmore, Christina Rossetti, Meredith, James Thompson, Edward Dowden, Ernest Dowson, etc.)   (All these being in addition, of course, to the more obvious 'classics' already in my possession.)

(b) *Letters, Journals and Autobiographies* (St. Augustine, Swift, Amiel, Bashkirtseff, Rutherford, Rimbaud, Baudelaire, Cézanne, Fanny Kemble, Mrs. Carlyle, Henry James, Lady Welby, Baron von Hügel, Kierkegaard, Flaubert, Tchehov, etc., etc.)

(c) The Complete Works of Henry James.

(d) Books on Acting, the Drama, Stagecraft, Theatrical History, and Playwriting.

(e) 19th Century French Works of the Imagination.

8.V.42

At home (*Teddington*)

This evening, suddenly, — *gratuitously*, as it were, — was re-visited once more, after how long and weary an absence! by (I will not say 'the ghost of') my deeper — my 'true'? — Self.

Serenity,   confidence,   richness,   resilience,   control! (Control, i.e., over the daimoniae of disintegrating multiplicity, of melancholia, of weary and sick-hearted lubricity, of suicidally precipitous febrility, etc., etc.) — A sense of reawakened strength, uprising, like a dear strangely, touchingly familiar Angel, from the seldom-stirring, ageless obscure depths of latency within me. Oh! like a wonderfully fresh, invigorating upland wind!

How can I hope that this vitality will outlast the first few brief hours of its re-emergence? Yet even if I should wake tomorrow or the next day to find the Moving Spirit vanished beyond recall, I shall still nevertheless have been granted a most precious signal, a message of profound re-assurance, enduring the constant validity of that hope which alone enables me to persevere through the present seemingly endless 'bad lands' of barrenness and postponement . . .

Manifestations of spirit which even the human entity is plainly susceptible of.   S.A.: *The Science of Alchemy* — 1893

* * *

— Religion is Man's greatest communal act of creative self-consciousness.

* * *

AFTERWORD

The International Surrealist Exhibition of 1936 at London's New Burlington Galleries, of which I had been one of the organizers, came to an end on July the 4th, having attracted large crowds during nearly two months. About two and a half months later I made the first entry in a journal that I continued to keep intermittently for the next six years. During that period I lived in my family's home in a S.W. London suburb, in a Paris attic, and back in Teddington again; then, after the outbreak of war, having been found unfit for military service, I eventually became an actor, touring the country for a year with the Coventry Repertory Company in a farce for ENSA. In conversations with a fellow member of the cast, I must have reminisced occasionally about my connection with surrealism and my days in pre-war Paris, and told her of having kept a journal, as before the tour was over she had the curiosity to ask to be allowed to read it. It had been written in one of a couple of thick exercise books with marbled board covers and unlined pages of a kind once obtainable from branches of Straker the stationers. When asked a year later to return this manuscript, my young actress friend replied with embarrassment that she had mislaid it; someone else had asked to read it and it could no longer be found. When the ENSA tour ended, I continued to find work as an actor for a while, but by the end of the War had left the stage and lost touch with the friends I had made in the theatre. The emigration of my parents to British Columbia following my father's retirement in 1946 led to the loss of a tallboy, containing a great many papers, letters and manuscripts, that had been part of the furniture of our Teddington home.

Before long I had become resigned to the loss of the written records of my life in the Thirties, and gradually forgot their existence. Though I continued to write and publish poetry, my output was disappointingly small. After a year spent in the States and Canada I returned to write *Night Thoughts* for radio, first broadcast in 1955. During most of the ten following years, I lived in France, the summers at Aix-en-Provence, the winters in Paris, returning from time to time to visit my parents, who by now were resettled in England. At this time my ability to write had completely deserted me. Even postcards home became difficult to pen. This period of sterility and lost self-confidence culminated in 1964 in a mental breakdown which resulted in my being interned in a psychiatric hospital run by the prefecture in a Parisian banlieue. After some months, the directors of this establishment ordained that I should be sent back to England: 'and on no account should you live alone', I was told. I could not envisage imposing myself on anyone in England other than my ageing parents, who had just moved by then to the Isle of Wight. A year after coming to share their last home in the house I still occupy, my *Collected Poems* were published by the Oxford University Press. I had signed the contract for this book during my last winter in Paris. Now I hoped its appearance might help to persuade my parents, who when I was young had never insisted on my getting a steady job, that my life had not after all been completely wasted. But in the late Sixties, after the death of my father, I once more went out of my mind, while on a visit to London, and found myself incarcerated for a seemingly endless period in a huge psychiatric hospital on the outskirts of Epsom. I have since then succeeded in giving some account of this experience in a monologue called *Self-Discharged*, broadcast a few years ago by Radio 3. In 1970, Alan Clodd of the Enitharmon Press published in a limited edition under the title *The Sun at Midnight* a series of aphorisms and two poems symptomatic of the disturbed state of my mind at that time if not of its illumination. About two years later, the death of my mother soon led to the onset of a long bout of acute clinical depression.

These pages are not intended to constitute a fragment of autobiography but rather to specify and explain how the preceding journals came to be written, lost, recovered and finally published. Before they eventually achieved print I had passed through and begun to emerge from the nadir of apathetic hopelessness. Before meeting my future wife in the local asylum where she was a visitor and I a patient undergoing treatment, the possibility of my ever being able to write again could never have occurred to me. The discrepancy between precocious promise and minimal published work was still a factor hindering the recovery of my self-assurance at the moment when, about a year after my marriage, an undreamed-of surprise packet arrived by one morning's post. It contained the old exercise-book in which my pre-war Paris journal was written. My actress friend of ENSA days had been astonished after so many years to find it after all still in her possession and had taken the trouble to find out my address and return it.

This unexpected restoration of the written record of what now seemed a previous existence soon prompted me to think of publishing it, thereby adding an item to my all too brief bibliography. Alan Clodd, who had already shown unusual interest in my work, decided to add it to his Enitharmon Press list. It appeared in 1978, with a Preface by Lawrence Durrell, received a mainly favourable press, sold out and was not reprinted. It had only just been published when one morning the postman delivered another wholly unexpected package: it contained the exercise book in which I had written the first part of the Journal, starting soon after the International Surrealist Exhibition of 1936 and ending not long before my departure to live in Paris in 1937. This manuscript had been discovered among the papers of the recently deceased French wife of a doctor friend I had known since my country childhood. She had worked for a while in the same wartime ministerial office as Sonia Brownell, who later married George Orwell, and at that time shared a flat with her. I had often seen Sonia early in the War when she was still Cyril Connolly's secretary at *Horizon*. I have no recollection of having lent her my journal to read, but have no other explanation of how it came into the possession of her flat-mate, whom I did not know she knew.

The *Paris Journal 1937-1939* was selling well enough to persuade Alan Clodd to follow it up by publishing these other lost and recovered pages as a second instalment, though it should have been the first. As when printed they only amounted to 82, it was decided that this volume should also contain two unrelated reprinted texts in order to make it the same length as its predecessor. So the book that appeared in 1980 as *Journal 1936-1937* also included 'Death of an Explorer', a short story first published in a 1937 anthology, and an essay on Léon Chestov that had originally appeared in *Horizon* soon after the end of the War. It was prefaced by a dozen introductory pages of information that I shall attempt to abridge hereafter.

Soon after this I had the good fortune to meet Christine Jordis of the British Council in Paris, where I had been invited to give a poetry reading. Having read the two volumes of the Journal, she generously undertook the risk of translating them into French. The October issues of the *Nouvelle Revue Française* for 1982 and 1983 contained extracts from her translation. While she was still at work on it, yet another old exercise-book of mine turned up mysteriously. It contained material written intermittently during the first three years of the War. These pages are published here in English for the first time. Mme. Jordis was able to incorporate them in the *Journal de Paris et d'ailleurs — 1936-42* which she eventually published in Flammarion's *Domaine anglaise* series in 1984. Flammarion is one of the larger old *maisons d'édition*; its publicity department is expertly organized. The book achieved an instant *succès d'estime*: for a week I was interviewed on radio and TV, and by journalists representing all the best-known dailies and current affairs weeklies. Articles continued to appear in monthly *revues*, and in provincial and Belgian papers, during the following six months. No doubt the amount of interest the book aroused in France was due in part to its recording a young Englishman's unusual experience of pre-war Parisian milieux, and in part to the remarkable excellence of the translation. But ever since then I have had the feeling that my journal might have achieved more recognition and wider circulation had it originally appeared in its natural chronological order and in one volume. I still owe a debt of gratitude, however, to Alan Clodd, who has now relinquished responsibility for Enitharmon Press, for his faith in the intrinsic interest of these annals of early struggles and aspirations; as I do now to Skoob Books for being willing to make them once more available to English readers.

When an editor recently asked permission to print one of my earliest letters to him in a memorial collection, saying I was at liberty to alter or suppress anything in it I now disliked, I told him in my reply that I tended to adhere to 'the warts-and-all principle'. This tendency may well seem all too evident in the present reprint. There are enough embarrassing passages to make my not having deleted them seem to amount to a perverse form of self-exposure. My account of visiting Barcelona in October 1936 was interrupted at the start by lack of time to write it contemporaneously, so the passage summarizing it was interpolated from memory in 1979: forty years had not diminished the vividness to me of the incidents evoked in it. Rereading them in preparation for the present edition, what strikes me most about these annals of fifty years ago is the number of opportunities missed on account of my inability to keep entries regularly up to date.

The BBC recently began broadcasting a series of readings from diaries and journals during concert intervals on Radio 3. It happened that the entry for April 8, 1937, in my Journal, in which casual reference is made to having lunch with Enid Starkie in a Soho restaurant on that day, was broadcast just at the moment when I was belatedly reading *Flaubert's Parrot*, already a contemporary classic. In it Dr. Starkie makes an appearance in the memoir of Julian Barnes' fictional narrator as a character perpetrating unjust inaccuracies about Flaubert and quoting French in her lectures with a noticeably bad accent. If only, I thought, I had bothered to write up the off-duty professor I once knew as a mercurially mischievous woman with an unmistakably Irish gift of the gab, formidably scathing when roused, and given to a flamboyance of attire not limited to her well-known *matelot* get-up. My own accent in those days was still so *onglay* that I could scarcely have presumed to judge hers disparagingly. After I had moved to Paris, later in 1937, I might well have recorded the day when Enid Starkie accompanied me to the little shop, at the southern end of the rue de Seine, of Henri Matarasso, to whom I was able to introduce her having already met him through surrealist Georges Hugnet: the result of this encounter was that Matarasso provided all the photo-documentation illustrating Enid Starkie's *Arthur Rimbaud* of 1938, for long the definitive English biography. Incidentally, I can only be grateful in retrospect to the author for having succeeded in dissuading me from pursuing my intention at that time to write my own study of Rimbaud (provisionally entitled, I wince to confess, *Diabolic Angel*).

Similarly, it would have been amusing if I had thought it worth while, at much the same date, to devote a paragraph to registering an encounter with Herbert Read and his son, then a schoolboy, in the grounds of that year's great *Exposition Internationale*, stretching on both banks of the Seine, from Concorde to Trocadero. Read and I had often met during the preparations for and period of the International Surrealist Exhibition, and occasionally since, but I never felt I had got to know him well; I suspected his mild and diffident demeanour of concealing a disapproval of untrained precocity as far as I was concerned. He was amiable enough on this occasion to invite me to accompany him and his son to the amusement park that occupied one end of the Champ de Mars. I believe it can but have been Piers Paul Read who, tired of trying to appreciate *Guernica* in the Spanish pavilion, the giant Dufy mural of Electricity, the Le Corbusier exhibit and other cultural attractions, had managed to persuade his father to indulge in a ride on the giant swing-boats rising high above the crowds. My most enduring and endearing memory of Herbert Read is that of his pale forced smile as we hung for a moment almost upside down before gradually subsiding to the ground-level of Les Invalides.

I had arrived in Paris equipped with Herbert Read's then just published *Art Now* when I first crossed the Channel in the autumn of 1933. When I started this Journal three years later I already regretted not having begun it then. It must have been largely through George Reavey, whom I'd encountered at David Archer's Parton Street Bookshop, that I first made the acquaintance of many people who continued to play a role in my life for some time to come. George belonged to the illustrious Cambridge generation that also contained William Empson, Malcolm Lowry, Kathleen Raine, Charles Madge, Humphrey Jennings and Michael Redgrave, to name but a few; he was a poet, but best remembered as an expert on early XXth century Russian literature and pioneer translator of Blok, Mayakovsky, Essenine and Pasternak, as of Berdyaev. It was through him that I first met the painter Julian Trevelyan, who many years later designed three striking book-jackets for me; through Julian in turn I met S.W. Hayter, with whom he was studying engraving at Atelier 17; and Kay Hime, a girl little older than myself whom he knew because like him she had been a Bedalian. It was also during this first stay in Paris that I first met Cyril Connolly: I was 17, Cobden-Sanderson had just published my novel *Opening Day*, and he was intrigued by my early 'promise'. George introduced me to Walter Lowenfels, an American avant-garde poet of the expatriate generation, who insisted that I really ought to meet his friend Henry Miller (this did not happen till some years later): Cyril Connolly and Miller were both first published by J. Kahane's Obelisk Press. Apart from these social contacts, I regularly frequented Sylvia Beach's Shakespeare & Co. shop and her friend Adrianne Monnier's *Maison des amis du livre*, and succeeded in visiting the ateliers of Zadkine, Jean Hélion, Max Ernst, Pavel Tchelitchev and Veira da Silva. . .

A propos of Kay Hime: in 1983, Collins published David Pryce-Jones' *Cyril Connolly: Journal and Memoir*. An undated entry in the Journal reads: 'Sunday — picnic — Hindhead, Liphook, Midhurst, Goodwood, Chichester, Selsey. Dylan Thomas, Kay, David Gascoyne. At lunch on beach threw stones at bottles representing Edith Sitwell, Virginia Woolf, John Lehmann, Michael Roberts, Engels. Back by Arundel, Amberley, Pulborough, Leith Hill. Dylan stays night.' David Pryce-Jones' footnote to Kay's name refers to the Introduction to my *Journal 1936-37*, not reprinted here, in which I explain that Julian Trevelyan had first introduced her to me at a party in Montparnasse in 1933, when she had just left school and was supposed to be studying French, and goes on to quote from my reply to his query regarding her: 'She was a radiantly healthy blonde with a style of dress and coiffure that now appears to me peculiarly typical of the Thirties, and it was not long before I "fell in love" with her.' The excursion referred to by Connolly must have occurred in 1935, I think; I wish I could now remember whether before or after my visit to Paris that year to survey Surrealism for Cobden-Sanderson. When my short history of the movement was published, Cyril Connolly's review of it in *The New Statesman* was the most cordial it received. Though Connolly was intensely irritated by Kay's adoption of a broad colleen brogue when relating an Irish anecdote during our excursion, and told her so, I believe he was in fact as charmed as I was by her air of being a home counties Riabouchinska, whose probable 'role model', as they say now, had been Gertrude Lawrence in *Nymph Errant*, a show she'd been to see three times.

Shortly after I had returned during the winter of 1933/4 from my first visit to Paris, David Archer of the Parton Street Bookshop already referred to introduced me to Roger Roughton, one of his most recent regulars. Our first meeting took place in the Hampstead apartment where he was then living with his mother and younger half-sister. Roger and I were almost exact contemporaries. His father, an RAF pilot during the first years of the Great War, had been killed before the birth of his only child, but having foreseen his own probable death had made a will ensuring that his future offspring should inherit a considerable amount of his wealth on attaining maturity. Roger and I immediately established a sympathetic rapport. He had just left Uppingham, a school at which he had been bullied, wretched and refractory — I could sense his mother's tacit anxiety and disapproval on account of this — and seemed to have no friends of his own age with whom to share his special interests, which were very similar to my own. He too aspired to write poetry; he was exploring with excitement the current manifestations of 'modernity' in literature and the arts, then flourishing in a state of ferment unparalleled since the immediate post-Armistice period. There was a piano in his mother's flat, and I dimly remember impressing him by being able to perform on it one of Erik Satie's simpler pieces (probably a *Pièce froide* or a *Gymnopédie*) that I had been trying to teach myself since leaving my first school, where I had had weekly piano lessons since the age of eight.

The eventual outcome of our initial encounters was an agreement to share together a small flat that I discovered early in 1934 in a then still wholly unfashionable part of London: Southwark, on the south side of London Bridge. The name of its address compensated considerably for the undeniably dingy nature of the building of which the flat constituted the top floor: Great Maze Pond, a short narrow lane running alongside the then still dilapidated Guy's Hospital. My choice of this out-of-the-way corner of the south bank was largely determined by the vague project I was entertaining at the time of following up my novel *Opening Day* (which though far from creating a sensation, had been favourably reviewed by at least Harold Nicolson and Mary Butts) with a quite different, more ambitious second, provisionally entitled *London Bridge*. The idea was certainly inspired, not only by the fact that my father was by now working at the head-office of the Midland Bank facing the Stock Exchange just across the Thames, but above all by this passage in Eliot's *The Waste Land*:

> Unreal City,
> Under the brown fog of a winter dawn,
> A crowd flowed over London Bridge, so many,
> I had not thought death had undone so many.

When I say 'share together a small flat', this is not intended as a euphemism for 'live together in'. I was by now fully aware that my sexual preferences were fundamentally ambiguous, but could distinguish nothing about my new friend suggestive of his being homosexual. If he had been typically so, he would not have attracted me at all.

At the end of the week during which we moved into Great Maze Pond with our few bits and pieces of furniture, crockery and other indispensable domestic items, and hung the Ernst gouache of a *Oiseau en forêt* that I'd brought back with me from Paris over the living-room fire-place, we threw a house-warming party. My mother came up from East Twickenham to bring sandwiches and sausage-rolls, then withdrew. Mrs. Roughton made no appearance. During the evening, enough guests arrived to pack the little flat to overflowing. I think I can claim that for a pair of teenage hosts in the Thirties, we gave quite a distinguished party. Arthur Bliss the composer, a family friend of Roger's, had been invited, but perhaps got lost on the way. Cyril and Jeannie Connolly were there, and they brought with them Peter Quennell and his current adored one, the most beautiful woman present (he spent most of the evening on his knees gazing at her beseechingly, unless my memory deceives me). Julian Trevelyan was undoubtedly there: at a climactic moment his abundant hair caught fire from the gas-bracket which provided picturesquely primitive illumination, and blazed alarmingly for a hilarious moment. David Archer of Parton Street must have been there, as were David Abercrombie, one of the two sons of Lascelles Abercrombie, the Georgian poet, and George Reavey, both frequenters of his bookshop. Dylan Thomas, whom I'd met the previous summer at one of Victor Neuburg's *Sunday Referee* Poets' Corner weekends at Steyning, would have been an obvious guest, but must have been in Swansea at the time. (In April 1941, Dylan was to write to our friend John Davenport, after learning of Roger's suicide in Dublin: 'Deeply, really distressed to hear about poor, dear, old Roger. Although I hadn't seen him for more than two years . . . I find that, straightaway after your letter, I miss him an awful lot.')

There was no lack of drink at the party; most guests brought bottles. When it was all over and everyone had gone home, Roger and I certainly did not go sober to bed. After the gas was extinguished, I was surprised to find Roger slipping between my sheets. This was not at all what I had expected of him, nor had I given him reason to suppose otherwise. I believe that the party had generated a certain atmosphere of inebriate randiness which made him feel it would be better to go to bed with me than with no-one at all. It did not take us long to discover that the move had been a disastrous one. A certain coolness prevailed between us for the next day or two, but no grudges were borne and the incident seemed promptly forgotten.

Earlier in these pages, I remarked that I had not intended them to constitute 'a fragment of autobiography'; but I realize that that is what in fact they have by now become. Having gone back to my brief Great Maze Pond period, I might as well relate an incident involving Kay Hime there, as it sheds some light on a whole area of my life regarding which I may seem to have been on the whole over-reticent. Kay was at that time still living with her parents, a retired military man and his wife, in the neighbourhood of Farnham. We had continued to exchange letters since our first daily meetings in Montparnasse, but she had been unable to get up to London to attend our party. One day during the few months that followed it, however, I invited her to tea in the flat where it had been held. Roger, who appreciated her looks but never attempted to cultivate her friendship, was out pursuing his own affairs. Kay and I found ourselves alone in a room together for perhaps the first time, and there was a divan-bed in it. Presently I manoeuvred her towards it, and for a moment succeeded in persuading her to lie down by my side. Had she been a few years older, more experienced, more attracted by my elongated, rather skinny physique than by that of one of Augustus John's sons whom she had just started going out with (a handsome, muscular and laconic type whose ambition was to become a professional boxer), who knows how the rest of my life might have turned out? I ask myself this question somewhat rhetorically now, at the safe distance of some fifty-five years. I had been frank with Kay from the first, and had made the mistake of being unable to resist telling her what had occurred in Paris when I'd left her alone at the Dôme one evening after dinner in order to visit the atelier somewhere near Vaugirard which Pavel Tchelitchev was then sharing with Charles Henri Ford. After that she always rightly regarded my capacities as a prospective lover with tolerant suspicion. Our Great Maze Pond tea-party failed to turn out as I'd planned.

My plan to live in London independently of my family failed to materialize for longer than a few months. My father was never able to provide me with anything like a regular stipend: he was then having to pay for the education of my twin brothers, six years my juniors, as well as the upkeep of the house and garden in Teddington to which we moved at about this time. I succeeded in getting occasional book-review work to do. Geoffrey Grigson, who had already published early poems of mine in *New Verse*, was then literary editor of *The Morning Post*, and would sporadically pass on a new novel for me to write about for his columns. I was pleased to have an article accepted by *Everyman*, the weekly that the English master at my first school had allowed me to read when he'd finished with it. *John O'London's Weekly* printed one or two short notices of mine. I even achieved the distinction of having a review of a new French book about Rimbaud published in Eliot's *The Criterion*. And this was the year when A. R. Orage encouraged me to write regular but after a while only fortnightly, then monthly articles on current West End art shows and new books on painters and painting for *The New English Weekly* which had succeeded his once prestigious *The New Age*. He seemed not to object to my being outrageously brash, but once reminded me that Sickert had observed that there was an element of what he called 'the tea-tray' about all the best pictures. I must have occasionally hit it off by following my intuition, as when about forty years later Rodrigo Moynihan had a grand retrospective put on at Burlington House, an excerpt from what I had once written about some pictures of his 'abstract impressionist' period in a 1934 exhibition at Zwemmer's was included in the text of the catalogue. I should like to think that the decline in regularity and eventual cessation of my contributions to Orage's periodical were due to my increased awareness, through growing exposure to and knowledge of modern and classical art, of my incapacity to make fittingly mature comment on works I admired or disliked; but the cause is more likely to have been an apparently innate inability to 'keep things up'. The last of many minutely calligraphed postcards that I once received from Orage read simply: 'What's become of Waring?'

A. R. Orage did not believe in paying his contributors (who included from time to time Ezra Pound, then an enthusiast for Major Douglas's Social Credit scheme, Orage's own favoured panacea) even a token fee. One was lucky to be paid a maximum of £5 for a review in most of the literary journals of those days. My earnings during six months were scarcely able to cover my share of the cost of the minimal rent at Great Maze Pond, and of bare necessities in the way of food and drink, cigarettes, transport and pocket-money for pubs, incurred during an average week. The delivery of a new novel would at least have brought me £25 in the way of advance royalties from Cobden-Sanderson, but though I still clung to the belief that I had a talent for producing readable fiction, my projected *London Bridge* amounted to no more than a few pale purple pages of atmospheric description, only the vaguest of characters, and a plot devoid of either climax or plausibility. Roger's own financial resources were not yet much more extensive than mine. Though the sum he was to inherit from his father somehow became available to him before his coming-of-age in 1937, he was not yet able to lay claim to any of it. We were probably both glad to have to quit Great Maze Pond before long: I went back to my family a half-hour's commuter-journey away from Waterloo, while Roger found that there was a two-room flat to let on the first floor above Meg's Cafe, which faced David Archer's establishment in Parton Street, and was able to persuade his mother to help him rent it. Perhaps what I now least regret about the period of sharing an address with Roughton is the opportunity it provided us with of exploring at night, sometimes separately, sometimes together, the labyrinth of ill-lit and mysteriously pungent lanes between the warehouses then situated between the Fire Monument and the Prospect of Whitby, or the even less familiar south-bank docklands east of Southwark, now so unrecognizably transformed.

It seems strange to me now that, although David Archer undoubtedly first introduced me to George Barker in 1933, the year when he published the green board-covered *Thirty Preliminary Poems*, I cannot recollect seeing much of him during the time when I was seeing Roger Roughton every day. I was as deeply impressed by the originality of the personal diction of the *Thirty Poems* as I was haunted by the singular prose cadences of *Alannah Autumnal*, published by John Wishart the same year. The age-gap between us, small but then significant — George had like myself been a pupil at the Regent Street Polytechnic Secondary School, but he had left it the year I started attending it in 1930 — somehow made him seem to me a slightly forbidding figure, despite all the charm of his undoubted friendliness. Whatever else they may have had in common, George had nothing of the boisterous Welsh bonhomie of Dylan Thomas. It was not until a couple of years later that I began to feel really at ease with him.

There are two other figures particularly associated for me with Parton Street, that miniature *carrefour* of Thirties intelligentsia on the fringe of Bloomsbury. One was Esmond Romilly, who made his abode above Archer's shop when he defected from Wellington; the other a rather older and entirely different figure: Albert Lancaster (usually known as Bert) Lloyd. Despite Kevin Ingram's *Rebel: The Short Life of Esmond Romilly* (Weidenfeld and Nicolson, 1985), and the fact that as far as I know no-one as yet has chronicled the life and achievement of A. L. Lloyd, the latter is a name better-known today than Esmond's was to the national press in 1934, when his founding, editing and printing of the left-wing magazine *Out of Bounds* for distribution among the country's public schools created a considerable scandal.

Few accounts of David Archer (and there have not been that many) have given a fair impression of this outwardly ineffectual, awkwardly apologetic and absurdly generous man. I have long wanted to make good this deficiency, but my memories of him would fill a separate monograph, and I have space to limn sketches of only one or two of the notable and diverse characters originally attracted to Parton Street during the Thirties on account of the special nature of the small left-wing bookshop to be found in it and its eccentrically benevolent proprietor. Among them, Albert Lancaster Lloyd made his appearance about 1934. Although at least five years our senior, it was not long after our meeting him through Archer that he began to be on specially friendly terms with Roger Roughton and myself. He first came to see us before we had left the Great Maze Pond flat. To the best of my recollection, he had returned to England not long before from a stay in his native Australia, where he had sheared sheep on a station in the vastness of the outback. Stocky and wiry of build, he had vivid, humorous eyes and a voice with an indefinable regional accent and a distinctive timbre that was to become familiar to millions of radio listeners during the post-war decades. He strikes me still as the very paradigm of a self-educated polymath. His left-wing principles were uncompromisingly strict, his loyalty to the CP of GB unswerving, yet his otherwise easy-going nature would never have allowed him to become a fanatic.

Bert Lloyd turned out to be an apparently inexhaustible source of information about modern art and music, the history of cinema, particularly Russian, as well as European and American literature, past and present. He was among the first before the Spanish Civil War to translate Lorca, notably the then still little-known *Lament for the Death of a Bull-fighter*; he was equally enthusiastic about Franz Kafka. He seemed intimately acquainted with the cultural history of the Weimar Republic, and to know everything worth knowing about Brecht and of course Weill. But he was never tediously didactic; his knowledge of contemporary politics, as well as the arts, as it came across in everyday conversation, was always illustrated by entertaining anecdotes. His intimate familiarity with folk-song and popular music in general was already manifest, but it was not yet obvious that a time would come when he would be widely regarded as Britain's leading authority on the folk music and customs of the world. Geoffrey Grigson, whom I was still seeing at this time, did not yet know A. L. Lloyd, as he was later to be best known, but when they met he developed great respect for him, and I believe they became close friends.

It became obvious to me from the time when Roger moved to his Parton Street rooms that he found Bert Lloyd a more captivating and compatible companion than myself. Had he been homosexually attractive to me and I become emotionally involved with him, no doubt this situation would have led to bitterness and jealousy on my part; but nothing of the kind occurred. I continued to see Roger every time I came up to town from Teddington, which was then often at least twice a week. I too admired Bert Lloyd, and enjoyed his company; it would have been difficult to dislike him. But even before the outbreak of the Spanish Civil War it had become patent that he had developed a powerful political ascendancy over Roughton. Roger did not I think find Esmond Romilly, then always diving in and out of Parton Street, especially sympathetic, since Esmond's interest in the arts and writing other than journalism was largely perfunctory. Romilly shared with Grigson the distinction of publishing some of Gavin Ewart's earliest poetry; but this was because he had been at Wellington with him and at once recognized his contemporary's potential for subversion. Both Esmond and Roger were active CP members (though distrusted in at least Esmond's case by the hierarchy) before my own short-lived

354

adherence to the Party. Looking back later on this period, I was amused to recognize that I had probably been teased into joining the Party by Roger's and Bert's tendency to be satirical at my expense, regarding me as too interested in dreams and introspection to concern myself responsibly with the toiling masses or face the necessity for 'the expending of power / On the flat ephemeral pamphlet and the boring meeting'. In the second year of the war in Spain, I moved to Paris and soon began to frequent Henry Miller's Villa Seurat circle; before long I found myself being teased by Miller and Lawrence Durrell for being so naive as to believe that Communism could possibly provide society with a satisfactory solution of its problems.

In the capacious *Dictionnaire Général du Surréalisme et de ses environs* published in 1982, one may find the following paragraph under *Roughton*, Roger (1916-1941 (Dublin)):

Poet and critic. Member of the Communist Party, he lived the double adventure of the English left and of Surrealism, of which he was one of the 'pioneers'. In May 1936, he launched *Contemporary Poetry and Prose*, in which French and English surrealist poetry were immediately revealed, in particular a large number of translations published in the second issue, June 1936. He exhibited a few objects in the International Exhibition of Surrealism in June 1936,* signed the *International Bulletin* in September, and published several short stories and poems in *The Criterion* and *Contemporary Poetry and Prose*. Seeing the failure of his attempts to create a united front in which art and social progress, Surrealism and communism would cease to be mutually antagonistic (see his editorial to no. 4 of *Contemporary Poetry & Prose*), he broke off relations with the group

---

* They are not listed in the Exhibition catalogue. D.G.

and left England for Ireland, where he killed himself (*met fin à ses jours*).

This entry is signed M. R., initials standing for Michel Rémy, the principal French authority on British Surrealism, whom I have now known for many years; he can hardly have been born at the time to which he refers. The entry fails to take account of Roger's visit to the USA, an important episode in his later life. By 1936 he had at last succeeded in gaining access to the considerable sum left him in the will of the father he had never known, although he did not come of age till the following year. I was never, in any case, privy to the details of his financial affairs. A large part of his inheritance went towards the publication of *Contemporary Poetry and Prose*. This little magazine ran to 10 numbers, and may fairly be ranked as the most adventurous and consistently superior in quality of the many small literary magazines of the period. It did not perhaps achieve the prestige of Grigson's *New Verse*, founded three years earlier, which had broken new ground in format and content; nor did it rely on contributions from representatives of the *New Signatures/ New Country* generation that had immediately preceded us. The translations Roughton published were not only from members of the surrealist movement, many of which were versions of mine and included at my suggestion. There was novel material of anthropological interest probably supplied by Lloyd. One issue contained perhaps the most extraordinary of Dylan Thomas's pre-war short stories, 'The Burning Babe', and some of Gavin Ewart's best early poems, another William Empson's 'Just a Smack at Auden' and a story by Isaac Babel. The magazine published a remarkably beautiful short poem by Antonia White, as well as some of

Humphrey Jennings' fascinating collage prose-poems. Roger had an unusually open and receptive mind, together with an instinctive flair for quality. His own story 'The Journey', and the few poems Eliot published in *The Criterion*, show him to have been among the most promising new talents of his time. Among the few pamphlets he published supplementary to *Contemporary Poetry and Prose* were *A Bunch of Carrots* (retitled *Remove Your Hat*), the result of a collaboration between Humphrey Jennings and myself in translating a selection of poems by Benjamin Péret (republished in 1986 by Alastair Brotchie's Atlas Press), and *1/20*, the very first collection of poems by e. e. cummings to appear in England.

America in the Thirties had greater allure for the young than it has today, when it has become so much easier of access that crossing the Atlantic is completely commonplace. The States in those days still had an almost mysterious novelty of a kind unlike anything that Europe had to offer. They appealed to my imagination almost as much as France, while Roger felt their attraction even more than I. What is now referred to as classic jazz — Armstrong, Ellington, Waller — had not yet lost the pristine shiver of its raunchy pulse. Since 1945, innumerable road-trek movies, and Kerouac and Kesey, have made the highways, wide-open spaces, Hopperesque small towns with their drugstores, gas-stations and motels from East to West of America, almost as familiar to us as to urban Americans themselves. Roger set out on a compelling voyage of discovery, his newly acquired legacy enabling him at the same time to indulge his taste for driving fast sports-models. He travelled from New York to California in a series of rented cars, smashing them up and leaving them behind without serious consequences en route. On reaching Hollywood, he succeeded in getting himself engaged as an extra in one of Katherine Hepburn's earliest vehicles, an adaptation of Compton Mackenzie's *Carnival*: I was later able to recognize him in a scene in it for about 15 seconds. He brought back with him a repetitive imitation of Groucho Marx's stagger, the manuscript of a series of poems by e. e. cummings and the poet's permission to publish them as a pamphlet, and the travelling companionship of James Thurber, then making his first visit to England. As soon as Roger had re-established himself in Parton Street, he gave a party in honour of the wry cartoonist, who had not yet quite reached the zenith of his fame; his air of glum reticence suggested that he shrank from publicity. Whether or not he ever felt at home in England, he soon acquired unusually widespread popularity here. Is he still appreciated in Margaret Thatcher's Britain?

My first encounter with Antonia White did not occur until two years after the beginning of my friendship with Roger Roughton. The opening entry of the preceding Journals (22.IX.36) refers to Roger, to D. M. (a young man in charge of the municipal library at Richmond that I used occasionally at that time: I have long since forgotten his name), to Humphrey Jennings and to Antonia White. Roger probably met Antonia at least once, since as already mentioned he published a poem of hers in *Contemporary Poetry and Prose*. According to Antonia's younger daughter, Lyndall P. Hopkinson, it was Humphrey Jennings who persuaded him to publish it. My remembered chronology of the events and meetings of that year, a particularly eventful one for me, is now hopelessly confused prior to my beginning to keep a journal. In her *Nothing to Forgive: A daughter's life of Antonia White* (Chatto & Windus, 1988), Lyndall Hopkinson, after recounting her father Tom's affair with Frances Grigson (something of which I was entirely unaware at the time, though I remember meeting Grigson's wife once in Hampstead, not long before she finally left him), goes on to quote from a notebook that Antonia was keeping that autumn: 'I feel much more at ease and stimulated among the young, Barker, Jennings, Gascoyne, than among the Connollys, Quennells, Mortimers. I seem in a way to have gone back seventeen years'. This omission of his name confirms my belief that though Antonia may have met Roughton, they cannot ever have become friends. I believe Roger had in fact a marked aversion to intimacy with older women; through being on unfortunate terms with his mother, he had if anything an anti-Oedipal complex.

Antonia White died of cancer in St. Raphael's, a Sussex nursing-home, during the early spring of 1980. Among faithful visitors to her bedside were the Austro-Czech-born poet Fred Marnau and his wife Senta, who had been close friends of mine since we first met in the Forties. Kathleen Raine also proved her devotion to Antonia during her final illness. I had been unable to see her again since a visit to London in July 1974 with my future wife Judy Lewis, when she was still sufficiently well to come round from Courtfield Gardens one afternoon to visit us at the Basil Street Hotel in Knightsbridge where we were staying for a week. She seemed perfectly serene in comparison with the Antonia I had known when she was still undergoing a long, painful course of psychoanalysis, unreconciled as yet with the Catholic Church and anxious about what she knew to be her quite inadequate care for her two young daughters. She had by now become rather hard of hearing, which she evidently found trying, but during our long last conversation she gave ample demonstration of her undiminished capacity for affection and wit.   If surprised at the idea of my finally becoming a husband, she did not show it, but seemed happy to meet Judy, with whom she got on well immediately, and to learn of our new decision to marry.   I was at that time only just beginning to recover from a long bout of clinical depression, and had not much hope of ever being able to write again. But by 1980, the year of Antonia's death, I had become an occasional contributor to the *Literary Review*, which Anne Smith had founded in Edinburgh and was then still editing there.   No. 21 of this periodical (July/August) contained two pages of mine headed 'Antonia White: A Personal Appreciation'. Speculating in this article on the possibility of a future biography of Antonia, I wrote that I thought it unlikely that she would have left, like Auden, a testamentary request that no biography of herself should be written after her death, as 'her fundamental modesty' (here I should have written 'lack of self-confidence') 'was such that it would have made the idea of someone wanting to write her life seem surprising and improbable to her'. I went on to say that 'my own contribution to such a biography could be no more than a small one, nor do I see myself as having played more than a minor and all too brief role in Antonia White's life, crucially important though the role she played in mine now seems to me to have been.'

A requiem mass in memory of Antonia White was celebrated in London on May 16th 1980. Judy and I were passing through town that day, and I was glad to be able to attend. The service was at a Catholic church near Smithfields and the Holborn Viaduct, and was followed by a buffet lunch in an adjacent upper room. Many of Antonia's relatives and friends were present, among them some I had often heard Antonia talk about but had never before met.   Tom

Hopkinson, whom to my regret I could scarcely claim to know, was there, as was Dorothy Kingsmill, whom I had often visited at one time, and Malcolm Muggeridge, who had been one of Hugh Kingsmill's closest friends and had later become one of Antonia's. Of most interest to me on this occasion was being able after some forty years to meet Antonia's daughters again, both Susan, Lady Chitty, who had married the novelist known as Thomas Hinde, and her younger sister Lyndall, the wife of an Italian Count. I could hardly expect them to remember me: they were small children I saw for only a few minutes at a time whenever I went to visit their mother in their Cecil Court flat, off the Fulham Road, before the War. I remembered them only as having been shy and perhaps not much disposed to like young men calling on their mother: it certainly never occurred to me at the time that they were scared of her when she used to come home tired in the evenings, usually packing them off to their room when I arrived. Both have declared in their different ways that this was the case, however, in books about Antonia published in the Eighties. Both talked to me after the requiem and seemed to know who I was: had I not known their mother well, after all, I should hardly have been invited to be there. Kathleen Raine and the Marnaus, who had not known Antonia as long as I, were also in the congregation. Carmen Callil, founder of Virago Press, must have been present, but I do not recall being introduced to her. Virago had republished *Frost in May* to some acclaim in 1977, and two later novels had had similar success before Antonia's death. Preparations were already afoot by then for the BBC TV adaptation of her works.

I found Lyndall Passerini unusually sympathetic. She even told me she would gladly have us to stay at her home in

Cortona should we ever happen to be in northern Italy. Greatly to my regret, I failed to keep in touch with her as I ever since then intended to. Envelopes addressed to her lay at the side of my desk waiting to be filled for years. Not long after our encounter at the memorial requiem, her sister Susan wrote to tell me of her intention to refer to my relationship with Antonia in her *Now to my Mother* (Weidenfeld, 1985) which she had begun to write, and later even sent me a few pages of the proofs of the book in case there were anything I might object to in what she had written about me. There seemed to be hardly anything to take objection to. I had the impression that she had not bothered to read the photocopy of the personal tribute in *The Literary Review* that I had sent her until after the book had gone to press. My relationship with her mother had not suddenly ceased after 1937. She came to Paris to visit me during the winter before the War, and I was able to take her to meet Miller and Durrell and their Villa Seurat friends, who greatly admired her *The House of Clouds* and reprinted it in a number of their 'house mag'. *The Booster*. I often had news of her from mutual friends during and after the War, when we had long ceased writing to one another. I saw her more than once after her reception back into the Church, and she had told me that the nuns of the Sacred Heart at Roedean had declared that they had never ceased to pray for her since the disastrous incident recounted in *Frost in May*. But such minor details were of no use to Susan Chitty's memoir, in which I feature simply as one among a series of young poets with whom her mother sought temporary dalliance during the breakup of her marriage to Tom Hopkinson. She seemed to me, and to not a few others, to have made no effort to present an unprejudiced view of her mother's life. When her book was roundly, even passionately, denounced by Germaine Greer on a BBC TV book programme, I could not help feeling sorry for her, but neither could I help feeling that her critic's strictures were not without considerable justification.

Susan Chitty's half-sister's *Nothing to Forgive*, already referred to, is an often distressing but far more rewarding work. Almost as much the author's autobiography as the life of her mother, it is packed with thoroughly researched information concerning the complex, emotionally charged web of relationships that Antonia White spun about her throughout her long life. I discovered from it that I did not in fact know half as much about even her pre-1940 life as I had supposed; yet it does not portray a woman altogether unlike the one I remember. Its chief effect on me was to redouble my regret at not having entered as I had intended into correspondence with Lyndall Passerini while she was still working on it. The passages she quotes from my Journal fit uneasily into the context of her reconstruction of what occurred in Antonia's life at the time when I knew her best, as what I wrote then was not a diary, and had I related all the facts of my relationship with her and my developing reaction to them, I might have ended by devoting an entire notebook to the subject, which I simply had not the time to do, even had I been an effortless writer. I do not believe I have ever had an exaggerated idea of my importance for Antonia, neither have I underestimated hers in my own development. But it is hardly surprising that without certain clarifications that I could have supplied her with, Lyndall found it difficult to make out exactly what part I played in her mother's life in 1936 and the early months of the following year, or that she should have found comments of mine on what occurred at that time 'enigmatic', but now that I am on the subject, I feel impelled to set her record slightly straighter.

My going off to accompany Roland Penrose and his party to Barcelona during the first autumn of the Civil War, just when Antonia and I had begun to establish a real though not physical intimacy, made the situation more confusing for both of us than it might have been otherwise, and difficult for anyone else not to misjudge. At the end of the interpolated passage, first published in 1980 in *Journal 1936-37*, retrospectively summarizing my experiences in Barcelona and relating a visit to Oxford to address an undergraduate society there after my return, I wrote misleadingly: 'After this, nothing very noteworthy occurred before Christmas, and the next entry is for a day or two before the end of the year'. The entry is in fact dated 27.XII.36, and consists of a page of reflections inspired by current emotional disturbances; towards the end of it the name of Roland Cailleux suddenly makes its appearance, even without his first name, though we were by then already on first name terms. Three months later I was asking: 'Why can't I keep a journal? Why am I just incapable of writing it down every day?' On account of this incapacity, I can no longer date exactly the beginning of my friendship with this remarkable man, though I still clearly recall the circumstances of our first meeting. On a day that must have been early in January 1936, I received out of the blue a letter postmarked London from a Frenchman whose name was unfamiliar to me, asking me to meet him at the Café Royal one evening for drinks. The reason he gave for wanting to contact me was primarily due, he said, to his having been a friend of René Crevel. In fact I had never known the latter, but had caught sight of him once in Paris shortly before he committed suicide in the summer of 1935, aged thirty-five. Who had actually given Cailleux my address and suggested that I might be someone he would care to know was and remains a mystery to me. Possibly it was the poet Georges Hugnet, who knew my Teddington address and would also have been aware of my disappointment at never having been able to make Crevel's acquaintance, though having read some of his work I had found out a good deal about him. There had never been any secret about his homosexual inclination, so I was not slow to draw what seemed a conceivable inference. A day or two later we met for drinks at the Café Royal, where later that year English and visiting surrealists would be in the habit of meeting during the International Exhibition at the nearby New Burlington Galleries. My host turned out to be good-looking in a very French and entirely masculine way, well but informally dressed, speaking good English (he did not tell me so then, but two years earlier he had been a resident doctor at London's French hospital) and a far more than merely amusing conversationalist in French, which we spoke most of the time. I learned that he had established a practice as a specialist in gastroenterology in Chatelguyon, where he worked during the summer, spending the rest of his time travelling and writing. Apparently he had frequented Breton's circle since his medical student days twelve years earlier. He was eight years older than I, as Crevel had been eight years his senior. We soon found ourselves on cordial terms and stayed on to dine together; after the meal it seemed only natural that I should accompany him back to his suite at the Park Royal block near Marble Arch.

Park Royal was a service-apartment building which served in effect as a hotel: one could rent a furnished room or a small flat in it for a few days or indefinitely, and it had a large international clientele. The comings and goings of its clients' guests seemed unobserved and a matter of indifference to the management and staff. In view of the state of the law regarding 'consenting adults' in those days, I should no doubt have been far too anxious to spend the night comfortably with another man in an ordinary hotel, especially as I was still technically a minor. As it was, I left Roland's duplex without a qualm the following day. In the morning, he had outlined to me the ambitious plan of the novel he was then at work on, and allowed me to read a few pages of the manuscript, which duly impressed on me the certainty that its author was a doctor who would before long become known simply as a distinguished writer. The work in question must have been one of the earliest drafts of *Saint-Genès*, which was in fact published by Gallimard six years later during the Occupation. A part of Cailleux' ambition was to emulate Joyce, in so far as he intended each of the novel's sections (of which in the end there were thirteen) to be composed in the style of a different genre, as are the episodes of *Ulysses*. The subject matter, a presumably largely autobiographical study of an intensely self-analytical young intellectual's achievement of maturity, with a provincial French bourgeois family in the early part of the century as background, could hardly have resembled Joyce's less. Impressed though I was, I little realised at the time how privileged I was to have been allowed to read at such an early stage passages of a novel which, had it not appeared in Paris during the War, would have made its author an enduring name overnight. Though I was completely unaware of it at the time — my knowledge of what was happening in French literature after 1939 being limited to what I read in the Algerian-based revue *Fontaine*, which made rather a point of ignoring Gallimard's publications —

Saint-Genès ou la Vie brève received an exceptionally laudatory press. It was reviewed enthusiastically by Maurice Blanchot, Gabriel Marcel and Thierry Maulnier, among many other less well-known critics; and the poet Eugenio Montale, writing later in *Corriere della Sera*, asked: 'Poet or orator? Today, as the best representative of a previous "lost generation", Scott Fitzgerald, leaves the light of the present literary scene behind in order to enter that of legend, it becomes harder than ever to disinvolve oneself from the aura of this kind of book'. And a couple of years later, André Gide was to write to his English confidante Dorothy Bussy: 'Yesterday evening, I sent a letter to Cailleux — in which I should been happy to transcribe your opinion: "I find that he has a prodigious talent", to my mind a perfectly deserved judgement — which would no doubt have touched him more, repercussively, than a direct compliment' (*Cahiers André Gide, tome XI*).

In her life of her mother, before quoting from the entry in my Journal dated 6.IV.37, in which I referred to Antonia White's influence on me in particular, and incidentally on almost all those who knew her at that time, as dangerously unsettling, Lyndall Hopkinson writes: 'In April (David) discovered that he loved a man: "It is not a normal homosexual relationship, but it is more than friendship" ', quoting in this case from the notebook that Antonia was then keeping. The man in question was, of course, Roland Cailleux. Looking back on this whole period now, I tell myself that what may appear a palpable lack of candour, if not dishonesty, in my failure to write down exactly what was going on in my sex-life, such as it was, at this juncture, was in fact due to my inability as yet to verbalize to myself the realization then beginning to dawn on me regarding the peculiarly individual nature of my sexual capacities.

My relationship (I have come by now to detest this word and its constant repetition, but have no preferable substitute to offer) with Roland lasted initially only until he returned to resume his Spring/Summer practice at Chatelguyon (where André Gide was soon to become one of his regular patients). I can no longer recall how frequently we met again, but before he left London I had seen enough of him to have developed a strong though equivocal attachment to him. It was not long before I detected a distinctly saturnine trait in his character, linked with what may best be described as a *s'enfoutisme affiché*. He was then, it would seem, still sorting out through writing and varied erotic sallies the kind of mature persona he would eventually adopt permanently. The way he led me casually to infer that he was in the habit of entertaining in his Park Royal rooms a regular succession of guardsmen in whom he had not the slightest intellectual interest may well have been due to his enjoyment of seeming to play the role of a bisexual latter-day Valmont (*libertinage* or jacobinism seem to have provided the 'role models' of a considerable number of 20th-century French intellectuals in their formative years). He also gave me to understand that in his own country he was engaged in carrying on simultaneous intrigues with a teenaged youth less precocious than myself and a young woman journalist ensnared by his charms (only temporarily: I was later to hear her denouncing him and indeed all other men in terms as ferocious as those used by the most militant recent feminists). I could not repress my admiration for the nonchalance with which he carried off his apparent *immoralisme*; I was already too familiar with at least the reputations of a number of my compatriots of Roland's

368

generation to be shocked by the revelation of his way of life at that time.

The climactic moment of the period when I was seeing about as much of Roland Cailleux as of Antonia White, without making a more than passing reference to either one of them to the other, was reached during the 24 hours it took me that spring to pass from his bed to hers. It would be unjust of me to insinuate that any blame should be attached to Roland's example, but probably not were I to say that it inspired me to believe myself capable of achieving the rare feat of putting the bisexuality I had long since perceived in myself into actual practice. After a particularly satisfactory Park Royal encounter, I went the following evening to a rendezvous with Antonia at her Cecil Court flat off the Fulham Road convinced that my libido was sufficiently strong and versatile to enable me successfully to accomplish what I had not until then had the confidence to attempt, which was actually to go to bed with Tony, as I was not alone in calling her in those days. I do not believe I have often indulged in wilful self-delusion, but so genuine was my desire physically to satisfy this distraught and vulnerable woman in the manner customarily appropriate in such a situation that I persuaded myself that I was up to the challenge. Despite knowing that Antonia's two previous marriages had been sexually disastrous owing to her marital partners' fundamental incompatibility, and as yet unaware of what her daughter Lyndall was to describe as 'her pudeur and frigidity', I deliberately put myself in a situation that was bound to leave me faced with the admission that heterosexually I am virtually impotent.

My friendship with Roland Cailleux meant a good deal to me for a while, and may have been pivotal in my development, but was not destined to blossom for long. In mid-October, by which time I had settled into my rue de la Bûcherie attic, I wrote: 'At the end of this month I shall be seeing Kay and Roland Cailleux again. But Roland in Paris will not be the same person he is in London, and I am afraid that' followed by three dots. I had by then become aware of a certain incongruity about our association. His relationship with me would, strictly speaking, have had to be qualified as pederastic; the trouble was that even by the time I first met him I would not have thought of myself in terms of *pais/paido*. Though younger than Roland by practically a generation, my instinctive ideal of friendship was one of reciprocally recognized equality, and Roland, though he never treated me patronizingly or as though I were in some respect inferior, could hardly have been expected to regard me in such a light. Had I expressed to him the feelings I entertained about him at one time, he would probably have dismissed them as embarrassingly inappropriate. There were to be two later encounters between us, one in November 1938, when I once more found him charming and sympathetic, but finally unfathomable; and the last at the end of January 1939, when he announced with some satisfaction that he had just broken off relations with all his friends, and I finally concluded that he was an amusing *cochon*. By this time I had in any case met Bent von Müllen, my friendship with whom was closer to my ideal than that with anyone else I ever met.

It was not until more than thirty years later that I began to realize how superficial and mistaken my last judgement of Cailleux had been. I became aware that the reputation that *Saint-Genès ou la Vie brève* had earned him among the discerning had been consolidated in 1949 by the publication, again by Gallimard, of his second, even more remarkable novel: *Une Lecture*. The reading in question is that of Proust's entire *Recherche* by a not particularly literary *industriel* named Bruno, who becomes increasingly enthralled by this experience, which ends by changing his whole life. The book took Cailleux ten years to write, was received with widespread admiration and was particularly appreciated by lovers of Proust; it is bound, I believe, to be rediscovered by a future generation. Roland Cailleux died in 1980, having published two further books, the last a novel with a revealing title: *A moi-même inconnu*. In 1985, an unfinished work, *La réligion du coeur*, was published by Grasset, and the same year Mercure de France produced *Avec Roland Cailleux*, a collection of excerpts from his works and of appreciations by a number of eminent writers, among them André Gide, Marcel Aymé, Julien Gracq, Felicien Marceau and Roger Nimier, together with letters, photographs and a detailed bibliography. Cailleux had never ceased to be a dedicated medical specialist; in 1942 he married Dr Marguerite Baume, the daughter of a literary doctor who had encouraged his writing from the start, and by 1947 had become the father of three daughters of his own. I need hardly say how much I regret never having known the later Roland. Whether or not he would have welcomed an approach from me some time before 1980, I am unable to guess. However different he became in later life from the man I once thought I knew well, I cannot believe that he ever attempted completely to suppress all reminders of his ostensibly depraved youth. From his last photographs and writings it is evident that the penchant for cynicism, provocation and insolence that he shared with his friend Roger Nimier (*Le hussard bleu*) masked an unusual generosity of spirit, an esteem for *l'amitié* reminiscent of at once Montaigne and E. M. Forster, and even

371

an attachment to the fundamental virtues of the Christian tradition.

My intention at the outset of these pages was to provide a certain amount of information relevant to the writing and publication of the preceding Journals, and more particularly to certain people referred to in them more frequently than others, whose names may not mean much to readers half my age or less, though they may be well-known to some of my contemporaries. I now find that this purpose has lead me rather further than anticipated; and yet there still remain certain characters, familiar to me half a century ago but unknown even to my other acquaintances at that time, about whom I should perhaps say a word or two here. First of all there are my parents, hardly ever mentioned in my Journals, though I had certainly not turned my back on them, or revolted against them in any significant way. It has for years been one of my ambitions to devote a separate memoir to them: they deserve some more adequate allusion than the simple designations bank employee and house-wife mother of three. As seems often the case, it was not until both were dead that I fully realized how exceptional my in many ways ordinary parents were. Now I can only hope that I live longer than they did in order to rescue a few of my memories of them from permanent oblivion.

Someone connected with my earliest recollections of my mother and father was originally referred to in my Journals simply by the initials R.F.W.: these stand for Rebbie Freuer Wright. In order to explain who she was, I have to go back to 1896, when my mother began her education at a school for young ladies in Harrow, run by a Miss Florence Mole, who had studied the Froebel method in Germany. In the year when my mother reached the age of 18, Miss Mole decided it was time for her to make her retirement. She took it into her head to suggest that my mother, though still so young and devoid of all proper qualifications, should assume the direction of her school in partnership with another of her pupils whom she considered the best suited to such a position. This was my mother's contemporary and friend (by no means her only one) R. F. Wright, never known to me except by her nicknames of Ginger (her hair was unremarkably beige) or Tiny (my mother's most frequent name for her, comparatively exact). She was in fact one of the kind of people who prompt one to exclaim: Oh! I could write a book about her! I might have done so had it ever seriously occurred to me, and an odd and pathetic tale it would make; but she was so familiar a figure of my childhood that I always took her for granted until it was too late. She had a remarkable gift for dealing with children and for teaching them while keeping them continually entertained. She was as great an enthusiast for games and outdoor pursuits as for reading books of every kind. According to my mother's account, the school she ran in Harrow with this friend for a few years before 1914 was a great success with the children who attended it, but financially a precarious enterprise for two young women inexperienced in household account-keeping and afraid of offending conveniently vague parents by extracting regular end-of-term fees from them. But one day one of her pupils happened to introduce my mother to one of her older brothers, who immediately became her shy admirer and in due course her suitor. Tiny did not expect or wish for male admirers; she was already resigned to the likelihood of my mother's getting married before long. She managed to repress jealousy of my father, because he was so good-natured that she was unable to dislike him. After my mother's wedding to this young man (who worked in a bank because his father's insolvency at death had obliged all his children to get steady jobs) she had to close down the school she had succeeded in running with Ginger, as Rebbie Wright had become known to the children ('Ginger, you're barmy!': popular Edwardian cat-call). Miss Mole had retired to a sizeable house in Gaiton Road: she now offered her former pupils and my father accommodation in it at minimal rents. When I was born in her house in 1916, this benevolent landlady (to whom many other epithets are equally applicable, but I must stick to the point) became my godmother: I called her Gaga until she died fourteen years later, when she was still far from being gaga. After my father's demobilization and return from Scotland in 1918 (he had been adjudged too delicate to be sent to the Front), I found Ginger installed in a room on the same floor as ours, and she became my first and dearest friend. She had by then found an unsuitable but reliable job in a London bank, like my father: the Credito Italiano, which she tried unsuccessfully not to hate. Early every morning, before she got up to commute to the City, I would creep to her bedside, where she fed me with biscuits and read aloud to me from *The Just-so Stories* or *A Child's Garden of Verses*.

But it was not long before my father's bank sent him to work at a branch in Bournemouth, then Salisbury, where my twin brothers were born, and later Fordingbridge. Ginger/Tiny became godmother to my brother Tony (the second of the twins, eventually to die of cancer), while John's godmother was Miss Mole's one-time partner Mrs Godwin. Ginger came to stay with us as often as possible. She adored the New Forest, and when she came down in the Summer holidays we always went there on picnics with her. She adored wild ponies and dew-ponds; she had at that time a passion for Borrow and *The Romany Rye*. It was about then that it became apparent that she had developed something like an infatuation for her new landlady, whose name was Alida Klementaski and who was the wife of Harold Monro, the founder/proprietor of the Poetry Bookshop in Bloomsbury. Mrs Monro owned a house in a cul-de-sac round the corner from Mecklenburgh Square and near the Gray's Inn Road. In my early teens I used often to visit Tiny, as by now I always called her, in her rooms at the top of this house, and always found them pleasant; she seemed as happy here as she ever was anywhere, which now became decreasingly often. One such visit is transcribed almost literally in a chapter of *Opening Day*, the 'stream-of-consciousness' narrative of a day in the life of an adolescent literary aspirant that Alida Monro persuaded Cobden-Sanderson (publisher of her husband's posthumous *Collected Poems*, prefaced by Eliot) to publish in the Autumn of 1933.

The first reference to Tiny Wright in my Journals is in the entry dated 21.X.36. I had been to a party given by friends of Kay Hime's in a flat above their antique shop in Grosvenor Square. I was accompanied there by Kay, Roger Roughton and Sheila (Legge), the surrealist 'phantom' who in a wedding-dress topped by a head like a rose-bush had paraded through the New Burlington Galleries at the time of the International Surrealist Exhibition that Summer. The party went on so late that I missed the last train back to Teddington and decided to spend the rest of the night at the address in Kennington Road, near Waterloo, to which Tiny had moved after having had to leave Bloomsbury. I had occasionally slept in her rooms here during the Surrealist Exhibition three months earlier, at which time she had given me a spare latchkey in case I should ever again arrive late to be put up by her.

This was the first Autumn of the Civil War in Spain, and early that October Roland and Valentine Penrose had suggested that I accompany them with Christian Zervos and others to Barcelona to help the Republicans by working for the Catalan Propaganda Ministry. The day I decided I should take this opportunity to 'do something about Spain', I had tea with Tiny in Parton Street, in the cafe opposite Archer's now renamed Winnie's. Mussolini's declaration of war on Abyssinia and the ineffective sanctions imposed on Italy by the Western democracies had led to the Credito Italiano's London City branch getting rid of all its British staff. Tiny Wright lost the job that had supported her for fifteen years, and had then found another job so unsatisfactory that she was obliged to resign from it. She was so disconsolate that I accompanied her back to Kennington Road and had supper with her there. I doubt whether I confided in her anything about my recent involvement with Antonia White, whose *Frost in May* she had probably read.

It shames me today to recognize that the problem now continually facing Tiny concerning how she was to continue earning a livelihood seemed to me at the time of small importance compared with that of the menace of Fascism at home and abroad, or the complications of my private emotional life. From the end of 1936 till the beginning of the War, Tiny continued to undertake a series of more or less wretched jobs in order to augment the savings she had managed to accumulate while working in the City. She assured me that if ever I were to find myself in urgent need of money I should not hesitate to let her know and that she would then unfailingly send as much as she could afford. She had always believed I was born to be a writer and followed my precocious beginnings with eager interest. When I went to try and live the life of a poet in a Paris attic she probably envied my following a course she herself would ideally have followed had she had sufficient talent when young. Frustrated in every way all her life, except when collaborating with my mother in running their Harrow school, she was above all a frustrated writer, whose literary interests had to be satisfied with reading as much as she could in her spare time. The hard straits I inevitably found myself in before long in Paris reminded me of her promise of monetary aid, and more than once I was reduced to applying to her for loans I must have known I should never be able to repay. However hard-up she was by this time, I always believed she must have enough left to help me get by on the creative front.

By the time I returned from France in the early spring of the year the War broke out, to live in my family's house in Teddington, Tiny Wright had become a prematurely aged woman. As a child I had known her as a slight, boyish figure, the attractiveness of her face in no way diminished by the slight down on her upper lip. Now her once smooth face was lined and wrinkled and she was an unmistakably sour old maid. The last job she could find was as companion to a tyrannical elderly rich woman with a dog. She had for some while been feeling increasingly tired and unwell; now the doctor she could ill afford diagnosed cancer.

Tiny Wright was an orphan; her idolized only brother had vanished in the mud of Flanders the year I was born. If any other members of her old Fen-country family remained, they were indifferent to her. She could often be as difficult as she was endearing; most people nowadays would describe her as neurotic. After staying with us for over a week, she invariably began to get on my mother's nerves; even my father's patience would get noticeably tried. At the time when we knew that she could not expect to live much longer, my mother in particular found herself in a painful dilemma. Her instinct was to invite the old friend to whom she knew she meant so much to come to be looked after in our Teddington house. My father was still commuting to the City every day, as he continued to do regularly throughout the War; my brothers were going through the difficult period between leaving school and deciding which of the services they were most likely to be called-up to. I was engrossed in an intense subjective experience that must have made me seem strangely remote. The world in general was growing more strange and sombre every week. Though Tiny begged my parents to find room for her at Teddington and was obviously terrified of the death already devouring her, they could not face the prospect of sharing our home with a complete invalid. A cheap suburban nursing-home was found for her; it was not long before she was transferred to the Middlesex Hospital at Mortlake, about half-an-hour's bus-ride away. My mother went to visit her bedside whenever she could; the experience was a harrowing one for her and increasingly wore her down. The only time I could bring myself to accompany her helped me understand why. I think Tiny's death made us all feel guilty, but we were not the kind of family to talk much about such things. It was not the sort of thing I could bring myself to refer to in my Journal, though I was still keeping it at the time.

The concluding pages of the preceding Journals appear here in English for the first time. The battered exercise book in which they were written turned up again quite unexpectedly after the appearance in book form of both its predecessors. It seemed hardly worth publishing them as a pamphlet; I thought of submitting them to a review, but could not decide which one. By this time Christine Jordis had already undertaken the task of translating them into French. I sent a typed transcript of these wartime journal entries on to her and she decided to incorporate her translation of them with the book eventually published by Flammarion.

It is now August 1989, and the 50th anniversary of the outbreak of the War against Hitler approaches. I have just realized, to my surprise and dismay, that twelve years have passed since I succeeded in writing some twenty-four pages of an autobiography with the rather gimmicky title *Eyes in the Back of the Head*. It got no further than an account of my first haircut in Edinburgh. My head is still packed with a profusion of memories of every period of my life, from early childhood till today. I have never entirely succeeded in disembarrassing myself of the absurd injunction to tell the whole truth and nothing but the truth. My selective editorial capacity is deficient: adjunctive details proliferate as soon as I begin to recount a memorable episode. I shall now have to reject my unfinished first chapter of autobiography as altogether too prolix and discursive, and start again more succinctly before I am quite senile. All this by way of preluding the observation that if ever I do get on with these memoirs, it will be necessary to devote a whole section to my non-combatant wartime experiences. The foregoing journal entries of that time are intermittent, disjointed and cursory, just as my whole recollection of the War is incoherently unchronological. During those six years I stayed from time to time with friends near Bath, in South Devon, Glasgow, Oxford and East Sussex. Unfit for military service, I attempted a stage career under my mother's family name, Emery, beginning with a brief season of rep. in an adapted church hall in Welwyn Garden City, where I played 'opposite' Joan Greenwood in an arch Ivor Novello comedy. Joan had recently made her name as the Child in the London production of Claire Booth's *The Women*: it was distressing for me to see her again recently as a distraught speechless creature in the TV film about an old folk's home, *Past Caring*, made soon before her death. After Welwyn I got myself into the Coventry Repertory Company and for a year toured the country with it in a farce for ENSA. Finally I appeared for two months at the Ambassadors in *Murder from Memory*, the first play of Ronald Millar (now knighted), with a cast headed by a veteran worthy of more remembrance than he has received, Ernest Milton. In 1940, I had served for a while as a ship's cook on an H. M. Examination Vessel, a requisitioned yacht used for patrolling the Solent and hailing all craft approaching or leaving Southampton Water; this was a job I took over from my friend Desmond Ryan, who had shared with me the experience of being analysed in Paris by Dr Blanche Reverchon, the psychiatrist wife of Pierre Jean Jouve.

Towards the end of the period I have only partially recorded, negotiations were going on with Tambimuttu, whose P(oetry) L(ondon) Editions published my *Poems 1937-42*, illustrated by Graham Sutherland, in 1943. I was introduced to Sutherland by Peter Watson, the owner at that time of *Entrance to a Lane*, now in the Tate (see *Tambimuttu: Bridge between Two Worlds*, Peter Owen 1989). Throughout the War, I was collecting and reading what now seems a quite randomly heterogeneous variety of books, as certain journal entries of the time attest. Letters and journals, the works of Henry James, 19th century illustrated books both English and French, and more seriously many of the translations of Kierkegaard's writings that had then just begun to appear. In 1938 I had read the first translation of Heidegger to be published in France, Henri Corbin's version of *Was Ist Metaphysik?* and excerpts from other early works. Heidegger's 1929 lecture fascinated me from the start, though my comprehension of such texts was necessarily very limited to begin with. Under the influence of Benjamin Fondane, with whom I had many conversations in Paris after our first meeting in 1937, I was gradually grasping and developing some understanding of what Fondane and his master Léon Chestov designated Existential Philosophy, in no way to be confused with the Existentialism Sartre was to promulgate with such aplomb during the immediately post-war period. Among the many exceptional people — they included Balthus, Pierre Emmanuel and, on one occasion, Béla Bartók and his wife — whom I found myself meeting at Pierre and Blanche Jouve's Thursday rue de Tournon soirées were also two philosophers, Gabriel Marcel and Jean Wahl. The latter in particular impressed on me the special importance of Kierkegaard, about whom he was among the first in France to write about authoritatively; after the War, a survivor of Drancy, he delivered a memorable series of lectures devoted to a thorough and impartial examination of all aspects of Heidegger other than his now notorious equivocations concerning his adherence to the Nazi Party. Eventually my autodidactical effort to grapple with philosophy, its history and most recent developments, was to lead me to question whether such a pursuit is compatible with, or beneficial to, the vocation of poet, which I believed to be mine.

Before seriously confronting this question I embarked, soon after the end of the War, on the composition of a work intended to embody the fruit of my amateur philosophical speculations by outlining the possibility of formulating what I called 'dialectical supermaterialism',[*] proposing to reconcile metaphysics with revolutionary ideology by means of what I chose to nominate with the neologism 'logontology' (logos ontology). This is no place, however, to interpolate even the briefest summary of a work predestined, on account of my complete lack of the necessary training and discipline, to inevitable failure. I gave the book a title derived from an exploration of alchemy: *The Sun at Midnight*, which is indicative of a millenarian/utopian optimism in the face of the blackness of the mid-20th century human condition that was bound to make it appear un- rather than super- anything. By the time I had actually completed this opus, and the manuscript had been returned sufficiently often to make me realize that the time I had spent on it was effectively wasted, I was seriously addicted to the abuse of amphetamines.

Early in these pages I remarked that I tended to adhere to the 'warts-and-all principle'. I intended from the beginning to expose this particular wart here as I can now see that it poisoned a considerable part of my life, by reducing and nearly extinguishing my capacity to write anything at all. The topic is referred to in a sentence in the Introduction to my *Collected Poems 1988*. I refer to it again now as, though I cannot exactly date the beginning of this addiction, I am certain that it started before 1942, and I can at least explain how it came about. An American friend mentioned in the Paris part of the Journal was the first person I ever heard

---

[*] An attempt to systematize a conjugation of Marx by Kierkegaard, both of whom started by 'standing Hegel on his head' though in opposite directions, one to face the objective world, the other to encompass subjectivity. The result was intended to bring about what could only be described as a Theocracy.

refer to Benzedrine: it was than a newly discovered chemical compound, rumoured to possess remarkable stimulant properties, but I was told no more about it then than that. All my life I have been mildly afflicted by perennial catarrh, so when by 1940 the Benzedrine Catarrh Inhaler became available in all British chemists, it was doubly natural that I should want to try it out. A first trial of the inhaler, a metal tube with a hole at the rounded end (similar in appearance and function to the still obtainable and perfectly harmless plastic Vicks model), proved instantly efficacious in reducing the constant flow of redundant mucus that can make heads afflicted by it feel like stuffed blocks. Prolonged and repeated use demonstrated that the menthol-suffused fumes thus obtained soon have the equally powerful effect of counteracting the tendency to apathy that assails those prone to fits of dejection. Briefly, amphetamines in the short run are obviously among the most potent of anti-depressants. Resort to them results in a restored and increased interest in whatever is to hand, and in the acceleration of trains of thought and associations of ideas that has led to their having long been popularly known as 'speed'.

Catarrh inhalers came packed in small oblong cardboard boxes containing leaflets in small print of instruction for use and no doubt some caution against possible side-effects, to which one was no more obliged to pay attention than a smoker is to Government health warnings. The two most noticeable side-effects ensuing from longer, more frequent inhalations of Benzedrine than are strictly necessary to dry up the sinus are insomnia and loss of appetite. On account of the first, Benzedrine in tablet form was in constant use by innumerable members of the armed forces, particularly the RAF, throughout the War; the second accounts for its use at one time in almost all forms of slimming treatment, though in the days of iron rationing there can hardly have been so many keen slimmers as there are now. A poem of mine called 'A Wartime Dawn', dated April 1940, would probably never have been written had I not by then already become an inveterate Benzedrine user. If ever I suffered from insomnia in Paris, it was due to raging toothache caused by the shocking state of teeth that no dentist had examined since I left school. The leaflets accompanying inhalers never gave a hint of warning against removing their contents, little rolls of wadding saturated in amphetamine and menthol, from their tightly sealed metal containers. Such a prohibition would have amounted to suggesting that the contents might be susceptible to other forms of application. It did not take me long, however, to discover how easy a matter it was to break open the thin tin-like sheath in order to take out the redolent wad of stuffing and soak it in water prior to swallowing the resultant liquid drug at a gulp. The taste was nauseating, but I always had strong peppermints handy to suck after a dose. The result of this kind of misuse was immediate, intense and long-lasting.

I have claimed inability exactly to recall when my Benzedrine addiction began. But having turned back to glance at my Journal entry for August 16th 1939 — a half-century ago — I find the words '*White Nights*' (underlined). This is to me sufficient indication that I was already staying awake for nights on end during the feverish end of summer that preceded the final declaration of war against Hitler's Germany on September 3rd; and I cannot doubt that this was as much on account of having consumed strong doses of Benzedrine as of being consumed with anxiety on account of the imminence of the chaos of war. I now recall filling at just about this time an entire foolscap-sized red-covered Straker's blank-paged exercise-book with a feverishly scribbled pencil manuscript to which I gave the title: 'The Shadow of the Rock'. My intention was by means of this essay to objectify to myself by verbalizing them all the negative factors — failings, weaknesses, 'complexes' — that seemed ordained, because of being inseparable from my individual temperament, to frustrate me from ever fulfilling myself satisfactorily by means of writing. It was meant to be an exploration of my limits, but the undertaking revealed its own futility by resulting in a labyrinthine series of interminably rambling sentences, packed with bracketed sub-clauses and hatched with corrections, alterations and additions that finally rendered it virtually illegible. What I was trying to enunciate came rushing to my head and hand with such urgent rapidity that I could never at any moment catch up with myself. The attempt to wrest coherence out of a confused multiplicity of insights and realizations ended in an even more desperate incoherence. The irony I could not then appreciate about this failure is that I was then quite unaware that the most solid feature of the rock whose shadow I believed to be hanging over my future as a writer was a habit I was becoming increasingly dependent on while not yet even admitting that it was a habit.

About half-way through the War a rival to Benzedrine as a catarrh inhaler appeared on the market: it was called Methadrine. Similarly priced (less than half the cost of a packet of cigarettes today), it came cased in plastic rather than tin. I could not give a *Which* report on it today, but remember finding it pleasanter and productive of quite as powerful an effect. From my point of view — and I have often since wondered from how many other people's — it had a patent advantage over the first-established brand: its flat end unscrewed so that the contents could be removed when used up and replaced by a refill purchasable even more cheaply from any chemist. I still have a distinct recollection (and it is of the kind that it is natural in such cases to repress) of finding myself confronted, in one of the theatrical lodging bedrooms allotted weekly to members of the company I toured with for ENSA, with the problem of how to dispose inconspicuously of half the contents of a small suitcase: an accumulation of dozens of ripped open Benzedrine inhaler cases. The problem now became one of having to avoid purchasing refills too often from the same chemist so as not to arouse suspicion. An element of inadmissible furtiveness became part of everyday life. And before the end of the War I was often finding myself obliged to find a late-night chemist such as the one at the corner of Wigmore and Marylebone High Streets once well-known to registered drug-addicts, in order to obtain the still quite unprohibited refill I needed as a 'fix'. By now I had begun to experience riding on the relentless switchback from high to low to high to which drug addicts all over the world have committed themselves.

I have become sufficiently detached of late from my earlier years to feel able freely to admit and discuss the period during which I suffered from amphetamine dependence and its results. Were I an efficient journalist I would have been quite capable of producing what might well have proved a sensational series of articles, of the 'I Was a Middle-aged Speed Addict' type, but somehow this is not quite the kind of thing the readers I like to imagine I have expect of me. In these days of 'crack-explosion' panic and hard drug-baron warfare, amphetamines, though they now constitute an illegal and often seized substance, appear a comparatively trivial subject of concern. I would like to point out that my addiction came about in the first place not because of my desire to escape from depressing realities (or succumb to a despairing fundamental death-wish, as Pasolini maintained in his discussion of the drug problem in Italy), but rather in the hope of apprehending and understanding them more intensely, while entertaining the deluded belief that my ability to come to grips with them as a writer would be enhanced by a wonder stimulant. To conclude the topic, I will outline some of the most drastic consequences for me of the persistent assault on the central nervous system that amphetamine abuse represented.

After my brief appearance as David Emery on the West End stage, I was alone one morning with my mother in our Teddington home when she came upstairs to find me lying face downwards on the landing, paralysed by sudden weakness and unable to get up. The local GP when summoned diagnosed internal haemorrhage resulting in uninterrupted loss of blood. I was rushed to the same Middlesex Hospital near Kew in which our much-loved friend Tiny Wright had died in agony a few years earlier. I was suffering the effect of a ruptured stomach ulcer. If the emergency had not been dealt with by a complete blood-transfusion, I might well have died. There could be little doubt that the ulcer had resulted from the abrasion of the intestinal lining by the powerfully amphetamized and mentholated fluid I had been consuming regularly for months on end. I remained in that hospital for six weeks, and the best consolation the stay there brought me was a visit from the actress Catherine Lacey, whose portrayal of Aunt Agatha in the original production of Eliot's *The Family Reunion* at the Westminster Theatre I had greatly admired before the

War. I had once met her briefly simply because her husband was like myself playing a small part in *Murder from Memory*; my only explanation of how she knew I had been seriously ill is that Michael Redgrave, with whom I had been friendly for a while, had somehow informed her of my condition. She must have extracted from me a fairly accurate account of how I had contracted my ulcer in the first place, because I can still remember her pleading with me to make the effort completely to break off the habit that had caused it. Later I was told that one mid-day at this time Brian Howard left the group he was consorting with in Soho's so-called French Pub with the explanation that he felt obliged to visit the hospital in which a young English poet he had known in Paris lay dying. Needless to say, he never succeeded in finding his way to Mortlake, but the story, if true, is especially touching to me in retrospect (Brian courageously put an end to his own life in the South of France in 1958).

My resolution after the burst gastric ulcer incident never to use Methadrine again was sincere enough at the time, but deplorably short-lived. I cannot embark here on an account of the sequel to my relapse, but should nevertheless relate that in succeeding years I began to suffer increasingly from aural hallucinations, continual inner voices murmuring utterances that were never quite comprehensible. This in turn led to a kind of paranoia that only momentarily persuaded my simultaneously lucid sane self that I was being watched disapprovingly by shadowy vigilante groups. (The poem 'Beware Beelzebub' in *A Vagrant* resulted from this experience, but is not therefore necessarily a specimen of paranoid poetry.) When in Paris for a week this Summer, I bought as I usually do there the latest issue of the *Nouvelle Revue Française* (No. 436) and was casually scanning the contents when I was suddenly arrested by finding halfway through an article on the Pre-Socratics by Philippe Barthelet (whom I cannot recollect ever having met) my own name, in a sentence in which it was preceded by five other names of writers whom I have always regarded with veneration, and completed by the following words:

> incapable d'écrire durant vingt ans, interné quatre fois: 'Des voix intérieures me chuchotaient sans cesse des phrases inachevées et inintelligibles où je pouvais toujours distinguer ces mots: "les dieux, les dieux. . ." '

This is a perfectly exact description of what I experienced daily over a period of many years after having ceased to be able to write anything at all in the mid-50s. It is true that more recently I have on occasion told friends and one or two interviewers about my 'voices', but I had no idea how M. Barthelet came to hear about them until I remembered that Professor Michèle Duclos of the Université de Bordeaux had interviewed me in London in June 1984, and that I had talked to her frankly but not at length about amphetamine addiction and being haunted by voices always referring to 'the gods' (plural). Later that year the interview was printed in a special number of the *Cahiers sur la poésie* of Bordeaux University's English studies department, devoted to me and my work on account of the fact that my poetry had been chosen in 1984 as an optional subject for students of English preparing that year for the *agrégation* exam. It hardly occurred to me then that five years later I should find my experience quoted in what has for the last three quarters of a century been the most widely read literary review in France, in wording not dissimilar to that used in my interview with Mme. Duclos.

Though I thought I had always been inclined to be reticent about the experience that finally led me to three 'nervous breakdowns' and subsequent incarcerations, I now find that it appears to be common knowledge at least among a small but representative segment of the French intelligentsia.

The context in which Philippe Barthelet refers to me and to five other far more illustrious (and dead) poets is his contention that those writers who find themselves called upon to quit the illusory tranquillity of 'everyday life', in order to face the unknown and ask the kind of questions that logical positivists dismiss as perniciously meaningless, have most often to pay for their defiance by ending up on the wrong side of the barrier set up by the secular authorities to divide sanity and normality from their supposed opposites, — or, as a quaint vernacularism used to have it, in Queer Street. A French expression commonly used to designate such figures is *poètes maudits*. Being still alive and reinstalled at last on the safer shore of recovered mental balance, I am inclined to shun the histrionic glamour associated with the tag *maudit*. It is one that might well be applied to such a poet as Dylan Thomas, when one thinks of his last years, but how he would have mocked it as a young man![*] It would be fatuous of me to regard my poetic output as seriously rivalling that of Dylan Thomas, and I am as much alarmed as gratified to find myself being placed by a serious French critic in a sort of pantheon devoted to doomed visionaries. This being so, I am

---

[*] Dylan would no doubt have continued to do so to the end, — though the last time I saw him, a year before his death, alone in Manhattan's White Horse Tavern, he unmistakably had a 'little black dog sitting on his shoulder', to use the expression with which he referred to the fits of depression that beset him from time to time.

prompted to bring this Afterword to a close by attempting to answer the question as to whether the path I chose to follow as a poet at the time when I was writing the preceding Journals can be considered to have been (drugs and visions apart) an intrinsically dangerous, possibly fatal one.

At an early age, before I had been attempting to write poetry for long, I became distracted from the commonly accepted English tradition of what is meant by the term poetry by a preliminary exploration, before I knew more of the French language than I'd acquired at school, of the work of such poets as Baudelaire, Rimbaud and Mallarmé, which led me to adopt without at first realizing it a conception of poetry fundamentally different from that of most of my countrymen. The *New Country* poets of the generation before mine were exciting because of their awareness of society's urgent need of drastic change, their expression of a longing for 'new styles of architecture, a change of heart'. In the post-Hugo tradition of French poetry culminating in the surrealist movement, I found an implicit belief in poetry's ability to induce a transformation of consciousness and overcome the contradiction between waking reality and dream, in conformity with Rimbaud's injunction: '*Changer la vie*'. In the Thirties it was still possible to believe that the surrealist movement could be seen as allied to the revolutionary aims formulated by Marx and his followers, and suppose that a revolution of consciousness must be concomitant with social and economic revolution. As a participant in the surrealist movement I felt obliged to make myself familiar with the basic principles of dialectical materialism, the philosophy still dutifully believed by countless millions throughout the world to be the necessary foundation of any practical achievement of socialist society 'on earth'. When studying the required texts, I came repeatedly on the expression 'mere subjectivity'. I could not repress for long my instinctive revolt against what I saw as a cavalier dismissal as 'mere' of the *sine qua non* of personality, of respect for the individual as a person as much as a unit, and of spirit as opposed to conditioned reflexes. It began to dawn on me that the Communism regarded by so many poets and intellectuals of those days as providing the best hope for the future of mankind is based on a materialism that however dialectical is bald, reductionist and, paradoxically, because its morality has no transcendental sanction, puritanically intolerant. It is also essentially the same as that which forms the effective ideological basis of our Western consumer society, for which religion, metaphysical speculation and/or, for that matter, 'transcendental meditation', are no more than leisure activities to be either indulged in or ignored because we are free, as are the market forces determining this society's vicissitudes.

At this point I must restrain myself from launching into a polemical digression. In the Introduction I wrote for the 1988 edition of my *Collected Poems*, I referred to the autumn of 1937 when, having returned to Paris 'I had become not so much disillusioned with Surrealism as begun to wish to explore other territories than the sub- or unconscious, the oneiric and the aleatory'. I also referred to a poem written a year or two later as 'an unmitigated overstatement of a theme that has remained constant in almost everything I have written since then: the intolerable nature of human reality when devoid of all spiritual, metaphysical dimension.' The official line regarding materialism of the surrealists faithful to Breton was that any alternative to it must be spurned as 'fideism', a vitiating submission to self-delusion and superstition as represented by the Christianity of Churches committed to satisfying the Capitalist Establishment's need to keep the masses duped into conformity with a judgmental morality. When after writing a poem containing the thrice repeated line 'Christ of Revolution and of Poetry' I returned to revisit the surrealist group's Montmartre meeting-place, I found myself facing a severe Breton at the head of the communal café table: 'I am told that you have become not only a Communist' (meaning Stalinist rather than Trotskyite) 'but a Catholic', he announced to me in his iciest manner. This should not have taken me altogether by surprise: I was aware of stirrings of similar disapproval among the younger, more recent recruits to the movement in London; but I was dumbfounded by Breton's demeanour of implacable intransigence on this occasion. Yes, I had been briefly an active member of Harry Pollitt's CP, believing it to be the most unequivocal opponent of Oswald Mosley's Blackshirts; yes, I had received a (Protestant) religious education, but could never for a moment have been attracted by conversion to Roman Catholicism. I left the Café de la Place Blanche without having uttered a word of explanation or self-defence and never, to my later deep regret, became reconciled with Breton, whose suspicion of my loyalty to him had already been aroused in 1936 when he found I was reading Benjamin Fondane's *Rimbaud le voyou*. Never have I resorted, however, to describing Breton as the Pope of his sect; his authoritarian propensity was only one element of a complex character that few critics have attempted to analyse sympathetically. Nevertheless, Breton the promulgator of edicts and indictments is the figure most likely to strike present-day students of the movement he founded. In retrospect I see that my experience was in many ways similar to that of Cecil Collins, a contributor at Herbert Read's invitation to the International Surrealist Exhibition of 1936, whom I did not get to know at all well until the post-war years when he and his wife had settled in Chelsea. In his recent book on Collins[*], William Anderson quotes Julian Trevelyan's reminiscence: 'Collins, whom I knew well, had far too much of a personal religious mysticism to make a good surrealist. He had always been a cat that walks by himself, prophetic, poetic, visionary', and adds 'André Breton issued a general anathema condemning tendencies such as those shown by Collins, and henceforth any paintings sent by Collins to Surrealist exhibitions were rejected.'

In the summer of 1989, the surrealist group of Chicago produced another volume of their occasional publication *Arsenal*, a compilation of over 200 pages among the items of which is the first English translation of a text by Breton that I had never seen before: 'Whither Surrealism Now? — A Message Read Over Radio Canada (1953)', from which I extract the following:

> If surrealism has often been the expression of intolerance, disgust and even hatred, it must be fully understood that it has been so in the name of love; I mean, what surrealism continues to struggle against today is all that combines to make man lose his ability to love. Perhaps it will be discovered some day that the power of love is all that surrealism has been seeking, sometimes desperately, to restore! It is not only a question of exalting the love of man and woman, but of recovering a kind of lost innocence — of the redirection of all that makes life worth living.

---

[*] *Cecil Collins -- The Quest for the Great Happiness*. Barrie & Jenkins, 1988.

> During these last years surrealism has often had the opportunity
> of turning to account everything that could link the poetry of this last
> century to initiatory tradition.

It is plain to me from these words that individuals such as Cecil Collins and myself were bound sooner or later to find ourselves at odds with official surrealism, on account of a prolonged misunderstanding due to the refusal of Breton and his followers to realize that a recognition of the all-important power of love, combining Eros and Agape, is inseparable from the discovery of the philosopher's stone, the corner-stone of a truly human society, compounded by a refusal to admit that all initiatory traditions are of a fundamentally religious nature, notwithstanding the inability to recognize them as such on the part of those who mistake religiosity for the religion whose place has historically been usurped by it.

Looking back to the years of my youth as recorded in my Journals as well as to those that have succeeded them, my principal desire now is to make sense of them, to perceive in my recollections some overall and unifying meaning. Materialist scientific rationalism has left us with an irredeemably meaningless universe, in which the history of humanity is but a tale told by an idiot, signifying nothing. The call to challenge the implicit nihilism of the world-view that has dominated the century now drawing to a close leads whoever hears it onto a path finally indistinguishable from that of initiation.

In order to bring these pages to their necessary conclusion, I must return as briefly as possible from ostensibly portentous generalisation to the factually particular. There remain a few elegiac footnotes to be added to references in my Journals to certain people of special consequence to me during the years between 1936 and 1942. Rereading the scant entries made before the outbreak of war and after returning from Paris in 1939, I was disappointed to find no mention of the last time I saw Roger Roughton, an occasion I still nevertheless remember clearly enough. Late one afternoon in the early summer of that year Roger made an unexpected appearance in Teddington in the company of Sheila Legge, the surrealist 'phantom' to whom I had introduced him three years earlier; they called in on their way back from a day at Kempton Park races. I was never to see either of them again. Two years later, stepping onto the escalator at Piccadilly Circus Underground station, I found myself next to an acquaintance who had been a friend of Roger's. As we descended to the platforms he broke the news to me of Roger's suicide in Dublin. In the issue of *Horizon* for the following July Cyril Connolly published 'The Human House', a text of eight pages that represents Roger Roughton's last testament and farewell to his friends. In it he freely expressed the side of himself he most often preferred to keep carefully concealed. Its poignancy cannot be summarized, but I am prompted to quote a couple of passages from it, as they may help to explain why I regard his early death as an unforgettable loss:

'For a long time I have distrusted those among us whose outlook is wholly emotional; I distrust them still. But never let your distrust of false emotion stifle true emotion. Lack of emotion, though, is not a vice, it is a terrible disease. Look with infinite pity on those who are cursed by it, help them if you can.

'My own and dearest friends, always aim at the impossible — though you are saints and I have nothing to teach you — never be satisfied: that is love, and the secret of life.' The young man stopped;

then he turned away, to run for ever from the room. And the ecstatic human house went spinning on its wheel.

These valedictory pages were passed on to Connolly by our mutual friend John Davenport: I am at a loss now to explain how it was that I hardly ever referred to him in my Journal — he was a link between the Bedales generation of Kay Hime, and Antonia White and many other literary contemporaries we both knew.

It was not until the War was over that I learnt of the fate of Bent von Müllen, whom I had been longing to see again as soon as peace made it possible. One day when I was in the editorial office of Tambimuttu's PL Editions in Nicholson and Watson's Manchester Square building I was handed a letter I had written to Bent that for some reason had been returned to that address from Copenhagen. It was accompanied by a letter from Bent's mother, in which she simply communicated to me the fact that, not long after the Nazi occupation of Denmark, following an incident involving the shooting of a German officer by supposed members of the local Resistance, both Bent and his father and four of their neighbours had been arrested by the Gestapo and summarily hanged as hostages. This news affected me as a bereavement from which I recovered only very slowly. It reached me at the time when the reality of the death camps as revealed by such photos and films as those taken by the Allies at Belsen and Auschwitz had just begun to beset the consciousness of post-war society, and for a long while I found it almost as difficult to assimilate.

Not long after this I first heard what had befallen Benjamin Fondane, whose name I had given to a poem inspired by his influence that first appeared in my *Poems 1937-42*. A

Rumanian Jew of German descent born in 1898, who adopted French nationality forty years later, author in his youth of several works of poetry and criticism in his native language, of nine later works in French, three of them published posthumously, Fondane lived in semi-clandestinity in Paris under the Nazi occupation, was betrayed by a concierge to the Gestapo in March 1944, then after being first sent to the camp for French Jews at Drancy he passed through Auschwitz to die in a gas-chamber at Birkenau on the 3rd of the following October. The Marseilles revue *Cahiers du Sud*, for which Fondane had written a regular feature on philosophy, published a memorial issue of tributes to him in 1947. It was not until 1978 that the revue *Non-Lieu*, under the direction of Michel Carassou, brought out a similar, more comprehensive special issue devoted to Fondane, which contained contributions by Victoria Ocampo, E. M. Cioran and Stephane Lupasco, the great logician, among many others. Not long after, the Centre Pompidou staged an evening of *Homage à Benjamin Fondane*, consisting of a number of speeches and a reading by Roger Blin (head of the cast of the original *En Attendant Godot*) of some of Fondane's poems. A similar occasion at the Sorbonne was organized a year or two later. A series of reprints of Fondane's complete works in French was published by Editions Plasma, under Michel Carassou's direction, between 1979 and 1984; it included *Le Mal des fantômes*, a volume containing the whole of Fondane's *oeuvre poétique*, to which I was honoured to be asked to contribute a preface, which I ended by quoting six words from Dante's *Purgatorio*: '*e il pensamento in sogno transmutai*'. In 1984, Michel Carassou wrote to tell me that two letters I had written to Fondane in July and August 1937 had been discovered among the papers preserved by his widow, and that he intended publishing them in a small edition together with extracts from the speech I had delivered at the Centre Pompidou's commemorative programme; the little book, *Rencontres avec Benjamin Fondane*, came out the following autumn (*Arcane 17/Le temps qu'il fait: octobre 1984*). Three years later a translation of these pages by Robin Waterfield appeared in no. 17/18 of Eddie Linden's review *Aquarius*.

I have previously remarked on the number of missed opportunities of later interest in the keeping of my Journal. The omission of almost all reference to my relations with Fondane between July 1937 and the end of 1938 now strikes me as especially inexplicable. Among the writers I was lucky enough to have frequented in Paris before the War, Pierre Jean Jouve and Benjamin Fondane both had a decisive and lasting influence on me. During about eighteen months I went as frequently as possible to talk with and listen to Fondane at his apartment near the mysterious Arènes de Lutèce, 6 rue Rollin, not far from the rue de la Bûcherie. All too late now to regret having kept no record of those precious evenings: at least recollection of this rare man's passionate dissatisfaction with both the tyranny of scientific imperialism and the submission of surrealism to the dictates of Marxist dialectic has provided me with a constant paradigm.

Glancing back at these last few pages of more or less necrological notes, I detect something cold-blooded about my apparent detachment. Yet it would be surprising if I had not yet learnt to regard mortality with at least simulated indifference. Intending to finish at this point, I was reminded that among those who meant most to me all those years ago there is one who still haunts me from time to time as the embodiment of an old unfulfillable ideal, and that is Kay Hime. She eventually married the admirable Freddie Devenish who had rescued her from a marriage that would have been disastrous. He then took her away as he had long promised he would on the yacht that was the principal other interest of his life for a prolonged honeymoon in the South Seas. An early poem of Lawrence Durrell, the magically burlesque mini-epic entitled 'The Death of General Uncebunk — A Biography in Little' (1938), is retrospectively dedicated *To Kay in Tahiti: now dead*. Durrell and his first wife Nancy fell for a while under Kay's youthful spell, as I had. At some time early in the War, I remember a weekend spent with Kay and Freddie at the house they had let near Haslemere. I was depressed to recognize that an unmistakable disenchantment had set in between them. The marriage was not to last. Before long, Kay found a second husband, with whom she had the children she needed to live for, and brought them up with the girl she was already looking after, Natalie Davenport, daughter of her school-friend Clement Forbes-Robertson, by then married to William Glock. In the Fifties, at the time when Douglas Cleverdon was preparing the *Night Thoughts* he had commissioned from me for production by the BBC, I went to a lunch-party at his house at which Julian Trevelyan was a fellow-guest. Julian, who had first introduced me to Kay many years previously, said he was sorry to have to tell me that she had just died of cancer. The shock this announcement caused me made me realize that the feelings I had entertained about her in the Thirties must have been rather more than ephemeral adolescent romanticizing, otherwise recollection of them would not have survived the many years when I had ceased to see her or even think of her at all. Since then I have gradually come to be aware that for me mourning is a slow and difficult process: though not unemotional by nature, I tend to repress my deepest feelings and feel incapable of giving them adequate expression.

Three months ago, Lucien Jenkins, the editor of Skoob Books Publishing, wrote to me: 'You have spoken to me about your feeling that your output of poetry has been disappointing and in the Afterword' (what had been written of it then) 'you write about that sense of "the discrepancy between precocious promise and minimal published work". I think that's a very important subject and well worth your writing about, if you choose to and if you can.' I have in fact chosen to write about this subject, and as a result have been led to continue longer than I at first intended. When the preceding Journals were first published, I had only just begun to recover from the blight of a deep-rooted sense of waste and failure, involving loss of confidence and self-esteem. Having attempted to disclose the chief factors responsible for my inability during more than a decade to make any use of the gift I believed I had when young, years during which I was without any other gainful or practically useful occupation, I have begun to feel more optimistic about the possibility of producing further chapters of reminiscence, though I remain wary of giving way to the enticement of discursivity. Periods of frustration and idleness have been alleviated by good fortune in friendship and by experiences of people and places that still seem worth recording before they are altogether forgotten.

Leafing through an old commonplace book in which I have occasionally copied out excerpts from books I've been reading that expressed my current preoccupations better than I could hope to myself, I have just come across a passage from one of Samuel Beckett's *Texts for Nothing* that seems to provide exactly the sort of conclusion I need to enable me to leave off — for the time being:

> There's my life, why not, it is one, if you like, if you must, I don't say no, this evening. There has to be one, it seems, once there is speech, no need of a story, a story is not compulsory, just a life, that's the mistake I made, one of the mistakes, to have wanted a story for myself, where life alone is enough.

David Gascoyne
19 November 1989

69 Narcissism

40 J.V. Foix
55 Empson
299-300 Cocteau,
"Opium", aesthetics of
failure

Forthcoming titles from
SKOOB BOOKS PUBLISHING

RAINER MARIA RILKE, *The Sonnets to Orpheus,*
translated by Leslie Norris and Alan Keele
The fifty-five sonnets were written in early 1922, in a fury of
creative activity perhaps unequalled in literature: they arrived with
such power that Rilke completed them in less than three weeks.
The Sonnets to Orpheus use the myth of Orpheus' love for
Euridice, her death, his search for her and his own violent end to
explore the meaning of death and the value of art.

"Between one language and another there exists for poetry a kind of
creative limbo which can be inhabited by anyone. The real translator
operates there at his peril, but with resourcefulness and daring. Norris and
Keele give us not only accurate translations, but work that contains that
'x-quality', without which poetry would not be poetry."   *James Dickey*

ISBN 1 871 438 60 8 paperback

GÜNTER EICH, *Pigeons and Moles: Selected Writings,*
translated by Michael Hamburger
Sceptical, witty, anarchic, Eich wrote a poetry of unease in
which the search for meaning combines with a suspicion of the
old humanist certainties. Chosen and translated by Michael
Hamburger, *Pigeons and Moles* offers a substantial selection
from Eich's bitter and graceful poems, his acclaimed radio plays
and the controversial late prose poems.

ISBN 1 871 438 81 0 paperback

MICHAEL HAMBURGER,
String of Beginnings, Intermittent Memoirs 1924–1954
Opening with an account of his childhood in Weimar Germany,
Michael Hamburger's witty and thoughtful autobiography tells
of his family's move to Britain following the Nazis' rise to power,
his first encounters with the British, his years at Oxford, and
his service in the post-war army of occupation in Austria. *String of
Beginnings* is the frank and entertaining story of the early life of
one of the most powerful poets and translators working today.

ISBN 1 871 438 66 7 paperback